GENERAL
Matthew B. Ridgway

GENERAL
Matthew B. Ridgway

From Progressivism
to Reaganism,
1895–1993

Jonathan M. Soffer

Westport, Connecticut
London

Library of Congress Cataloging-in-Publication Data

Soffer, Jonathan M., 1956–
  General Matthew B. Ridgway : from progressivism to Reaganism,
1895–1993 / Jonathan M. Soffer.
    p. cm.
  Includes bibliographical references and index.
  ISBN 0–275–95074–3 (alk. paper)
    1. Ridgway, Matthew B. (Matthew Bunker), 1895– . 2. Generals—
United States—Biography.   3. United States.   Army—Biography.
I. Title.
E745.R53S64   1998
355'.0092—dc21
  [B]   97–44895

British Library Cataloguing in Publication Data is available.

Library of Congress Catalog Card Number: 97–44895
ISBN: 0–275–95074–3

First published in 1998

Praeger Publishers, 88 Post Road West, Westport, CT 06881
An imprint of Greenwood Publishing Group, Inc.

Printed in the United States of America

♾

The paper used in this book complies with the
Permanent Paper Standard issued by the National
Information Standards Organization (Z39.48–1984).

10 9 8 7 6 5 4 3 2 1

Copyright Acknowledgments

The author and the publisher gratefully acknowledge the use of the following:

Excerpts as submitted from *Soldier: The Memoirs of Matthew B. Ridgway* by General Matthew
B. Ridgway and as told to Harold H. Martin. Copyright © 1956 by Matthew B. Ridgway and
Harold H. Martin. Copyright © 1956 by Curtis Publishing Company. Copyright renewed in
1984. Reprinted by permission of HarperCollins Publishers, Inc.

Excerpts from "All for One or One for One: The U.N. Military Staff Committee and the
Contradictions of American Internationalism" by Jonathan Soffer, *Diplomatic History* 21 (Winter
1997). Copyright © 1997 by the Society for Historians of American Foreign Relations. Reprinted by permission of Blackwell Publishers.

"I remember [my father] less as a soldier, though, than as a man of infinite kindliness and patience—though with that iron in the soul that a soldier must have."
—Matthew B. Ridgway
(*Soldier*, 19)

Contents

Photo essay follows page 108

Acknowledgments

It is impossible to thank everyone who has helped me with this manuscript. I would like to thank the Eisenhower World Affairs Council for supporting me with an Eisenhower/Clifford Roberts Fellowship in 1989–1990, as did the National Historic Publications and Records Commission, which awarded me a postdoctoral fellowship at the Eisenhower Papers Project at Johns Hopkins. I would also like to thank Polytechnic University in Brooklyn, NY and Bilkent University of Ankara, Turkey and its rector, Ali Doğramacı. Both institutions provided generous research support. Dr. Daun Van Ee, the editor of the Eisenhower Papers, and Dr. John English, of Queens University in Ontario, read the entire manuscript and made valuable suggestions. Dr. Ronald Grele, of Columbia University, has been with this project from the beginning and stayed with it to read portions of the final manuscript. Professors Alan Brinkley, of Columbia, and Robert Buzzanco, of the University of Houston, also helped with their comments on parts of the manuscript. Of course, the responsibility for any errors lies with me and not with anyone else.

I would also like to acknowledge my dissertation advisor, Professor James P. Shenton, and Professor Anders Stephanson who helped me through some difficult stages of the project, Professors Eric Foner and Elizabeth Blackmar, of Columbia University, and Professor Louis Galambos, at Johns Hopkins,

who were always ready with good advice about academia in general. Profes-
sor Joshua Freeman of Queens College helped me choose to write about
Ridgway. The late Forrest Pogue also met with me at an early stage of the
project and encouraged me to take it on. David Keogh, along with Dr.
Richard Sommers, as well as Pamela Cheney of the U.S. Military History
Institute in Carlisle, Pennsylvania, worked with me during many months of
research on the Ridgway and other military papers. Will Mahoney and Rick
Peuser of the Modern Military Branch of the National Archives were a big
help, as was Kathy Nicasio at the Civil Branch. Thomas E. Camden, Larry
Bland, and the staff of the George C. Marshall Foundation also helped me,
particularly with some previously untranscribed oral history interviews between Forrest Pogue and Matthew Ridgway.

I would like to thank my parents, Sanford and Miriam Soffer, for their
unwavering support. Most of all, I would like to thank Pamela Brown.

CHAPTER 1

Introduction: Ridgway and the Corporate Order

To understand the history of a city, one must first look at its newest buildings, as historian Henri Pirenne once observed. In a city, new construction provides a clue to the patterns of historical change. Similarly, a man's most recent actions may reveal the historical contradictions of his life. Such was the case on May 5, 1985, when Matthew Ridgway stood at attention next to President Ronald Reagan as they joined Chancellor Helmut Kohl in a memorial service to German soldiers in a cemetery at Bitburg, Germany. Ridgway's posture was remarkable for a man who had just turned ninety; his extraordinary military bearing had been commented on by almost all the journalists who had written about him since World War II. The presence of the old warrior did not mollify critics of Reagan's commemoration of soldiers who died defending Nazism.[1]

Ridgway's decision to travel to Bitburg cannot be dismissed as the acquiescence of old age. His mind was sharp, and his action was entirely consistent with his long-term political agenda. Though some of the German troops buried at Bitberg might have actually shot at him in the Battle of the Bulge, Ridgway attended as a favor to the president who had finally implemented the levels of military spending the general had advocated for more than three decades. Since his days at the North Atlantic Treaty Organization (NATO), the general had always advocated a conciliatory policy toward the German right and toward conservative elements in other countries in the name of anticommunist unity. For Ridgway, rearmament was necessary to maintain such unity. This study attempts to explain the social vision that underlay Ridgway's stance.

Ridgway took a significantly different approach to the construction of a Cold War society from other members of the policy-making élite, such as Dwight David Eisenhower. Cold Warriors all shared a nebulous commitment to what they called "freedom." While Ike tended to equate freedom with private enterprise, Ridgway, and those who shared his point of view were much less committed to *laissez faire*. Ridgway's background, having grown up in the "Old Army," his ideological predilections, and his high bureaucratic position overdetermined his campaign to shape America and its allies into nations that made military security their first priority.

Ridgway envisioned a nominally pluralist society with corporatist elements mobilized and coordinated to win the Cold War (as it seemed to have won World War II). Only relative harmony between social classes, even if it required state intervention, could bring America victory.[2] Though this study reflects my empirical findings that Ridgway expressed a corporatist ideology, I have not attempted here an "organizational synthesis" or "corporatist" approach to twentieth-century military history. My argument that Ridgway, one of the dominating figures of the postwar army, held corporatist ideals, however, attests to the importance of such approaches. Only such organizational studies can determine the degree to which postwar society really operated in accord with Ridgway's ideology. Ridgway's failure to spur rearmament at the rate he would have liked in the 1950s also attests to the limits of the political popularity of corporatism, particularly in America and Europe.

In his ambivalence about the free market, Ridgway foreshadowed a particular group within the Reagan coalition, and later became one of its elder statesmen. This tendency among Reagan's supporters argued for the buildup of a state-controlled military-industrial economy through deficit spending. Ridgway's life story has much to do with the historical development of this particular brand of military Keynesian ideology.[3]

At this point, some readers who associate *ideology* with systematized dogmas may have bridled. As Terry Eagleton has pointed out, the term *ideology* is highly contested. The term is used here to mean the language in which Ridgway and others revealed their beliefs, their sense of history, and their vision of social relations as they experienced them, combined with their prejudices, hopes, ambitions, and desires. Used to convince others to accept the ideologist's ideal view of such power relations, ideological statements in this sense are not merely an idea or an ideal. Such statements are intended to mobilize others for action, to gather support for particular systems of social relations, or to effect social change.[4] Nevertheless, these articulations often contain fissures of contradiction. The definition of ideology as language explicitly rejects characterizations of ideology as a totalizing worldview, such as Stalinism or fascism, and it requires the analysis of the inconsistencies of someone's thought on the grounds that these may reveal more about his motives and options than any seamless coherence would.[5]

Critics of this approach might argue that my analysis depends too much on close and symptomatic readings of texts that were group efforts and not designed to bear such scrutiny. One of Ridgway's speechwriters reports, however, that the general participated fully in the writing of his speeches. Archival evidence confirms his extensive labor over many policy papers and important memoranda. As Ridgway took his own thinking on matters of state seriously, so should we. A more difficult problem is that of Ridgway's many silences. Although he has donated tens, perhaps hundreds, of thousands of documents to the archives, he held back much material on his personal life. There are no copies of letters to and from his three wives. He himself destroyed much of the material on his secret dealings in Latin America as he hastily departed for duty with the 82d Division in 1942. In addition, the Ridgway papers themselves reveal certain conceptual gaps. Ridgway was not an intellectual; he often did not define his terms specifically. For example, when he refers time and time again to "spiritual values," as the foundation of American civilization, he provides only a sketchy definition. He did not construct elaborate models of utopia; often they must be gleaned from careful study of his texts.[6]

Despite the simplicity and frequent vagueness of his rhetoric, Ridgway knew how to move and motivate people, particularly in a battlefield situation. Indeed, the greatest importance of this study may be to document the varying power and popularity of military corporatist ideology among both common soldiers and political elites. The general liked to ask for seemingly impossible sacrifices—a fine trait for a warrior speaking to warriors, but not for a diplomat speaking to diplomats. Ridgway and his political allies initially failed to persuade the people of what was then called the "free world" that continuing heavy economic sacrifices to build a military machine should be their first priority. Many people in the West wanted a Cold War, but few supported a slowing of economic development to wage it to the extent to which he did.

There is a danger, of course, of emphasizing ideology to the diminution of material factors, which has been one of the principal criticisms of Melvin Leffler's work on "the American conception of national security." To understand the material consequences of language, one must always remember that the purpose of rhetoric is to overcome resistance. Americans, despite the militarization of American society cited by Michael Sherry, have a peculiar sense of obligation to the military, because they see themselves as members of a society in which the main purpose of the state is to protect their private interests. As Michael Walzer and Robert Westbrook have pointed out, Americans fight for the security of their families and property, not out of deference to an overlord. In Korea, for example, soldiers and officers were retreat-minded at the time Ridgway took command, in part because their sense of obligation had broken down in the face of the Chinese intervention. With a combination of rhetoric about obligation and reorganization, Ridgway successfully stemmed the pressure for withdrawal from Korea.[7]

Ridgway made his reputation primarily on the battlefield in World War II and Korea. General Maxwell Taylor has described Ridgway's direct command of Eighth Army in Korea, which lasted approximately four months, as "the finest example of military leadership in this century."[8] Battlefield acumen, while it cemented Ridgway's reputation, composed a relatively small part of his career. Though I have included limited narratives of some of Ridgway's most important battles, I have not attempted a definitive biography. My focus is on politics and ideology and does not seek to duplicate the work of those numerous historians who have chronicled Ridgway's famous battles in detail.[9]

In many ways, Ridgway was a unique, rather than a representative, figure, even when compared to his airborne protégés James M. Gavin and Taylor, with whom he had the most in common. Ridgway became a Republican when he left the service, while Gavin and Taylor served in high appointed positions under President John F. Kennedy—a Democrat. The three did share some corporatist tendencies, however, particularly a lack of concern about using state power to make national security the preeminent concern of American society. They also shared a suspicion of purely technological solutions to military problems.

Taylor in the 1950s was close to Ridgway's position on the substantive issues, but was more pragmatic, sophisticated, and connected politically.[10] By the 1970s, both Ridgway, who opposed the American commitment to Vietnam, and Taylor, who was an architect of the policy, expressed dissatisfaction with the social disunity that followed the Indochina war. Both believed that fighting the Cold War should be the priority of American society. Unlike Taylor, Ridgway generally avoided crude descriptions of Cold War opponents as "conspirators." Journalists have praised Taylor for his polish, intellect, and analytical sophistication, which made him the military darling of the New Frontier. The intelligent, but unintellectual, Ridgway, however, often had the better grasp of history.[11]

Ridgway's corporatism stands out from that of senior officers active in the early Cold War. Other than Eisenhower, the outstanding antistatist in the Army was Ike's erstwhile rival for the 1952 Republican presidential nomination, General Douglas MacArthur. Writing in his *Reminiscences* in 1964, MacArthur recapitulated a nonstatist view of American society, often a much-simplified version of the social thought of Herbert Hoover.[12] He claimed that the obligation of the individual soldier arose from a mystic tie to the nation. Americans, he asserted, do not fight because they believe in freedom, liberalism, or any other ideology but merely because "their country called." This concept of direct obligation to the state significantly contrasted with Ridgway's oft-repeated concept that the American soldier fought to preserve the integrity of individual human rights. MacArthur must have realized that the problem of obligation was not so simple as he claimed, despite his charges that what he would call "simple patriotism" was under attack by liberal internationalists.[13]

Liberals, according to MacArthur, not only destroyed patriotism but undermined the basis of American military power—industry built by free enterprise. MacArthur claimed that the "Marxism-inspired device of confiscatory taxation" (by which he meant the income tax) had undermined American thrift and individual initiative—and, thereby, American military power. In addition, free enterprise seemed besieged by "centralized planning."[14] Such a minimal state could not possibly support the type of coordination between the state, corporations, and American society that men like Ridgway and Taylor saw as indispensable to maintaining American military power. Ridgway and Taylor lived in the real world of defense budgets and industrial mobilization bases; the degree of state interference in the private sector of the economy did not much concern them. To them, a modern military establishment without close coordination and regulation of private defense contractors was inconceivable.

While Ridgway differed from MacArthur and Eisenhower over the degree to which the size and activities of the state should be a primary concern, he differed from other military leaders, such as Air Force generals Curtis E. LeMay and Nathan F. Twining, over the limitations of military technology, especially on the efficacy of a nuclear deterrent in waging Cold War. For Twining, the limited war approach provided "Neither Liberty Nor Safety," the title of his blistering attack on such theories, and implicitly on Taylor and Ridgway. Twining expressed qualified sympathy for advocates of a preemptive atomic strike against the Soviet Union in the 1940s. These extremists, he says, were "never given a fair hearing" by the State Department or the military establishment."[15] To Ridgway, "nothing could more tragically demonstrate our complete and utter moral bankruptcy than for us deliberately to initiate a 'preventive war'," a step which he says would doom American civilization by transforming it into an empire based on conquest instead of consent—an empire like that of Rome, likely to crumble from "inner decay."[16]

Ridgway's position is more than superficial moralism. He evokes a fear of degeneration into tyranny as old as the Republic. Moreover, as a serious reader of Clausewitz, he understood moral superiority as the underpinning of *morale* superiority, an absolutely necessary ingredient for overcoming the friction of war. This reading of Clausewitz through republican traditions also betrayed some of his more interesting historical/strategic ideas:

America, so long as it maintained its moral superiority, would be an exception to the cyclical forces that he believed had caused the decay of earlier empires.

In contrast, Nate Twining's understanding of military strategy was vastly simpler. He described the Strategic Air Command as "the umbrella of stark, naked power without which containment and collective security would not have survived." For Twining, power came out of the belly of a bomber, and was not, as Ridgway believed, in a dialectical relationship with politics and the moral qualities of the individual. As this study shows, Ridgway was one of the first generation of senior officers whose career developed in part from political and diplomatic assignments. Perhaps his considerable politico-military experience saved him from reducing grand strategy to a matter of buying the right military technology, even if it did not make him much of a diplomat. Diplomacy is, in part, the art of reaching international agreements of mutual interest. But Ridgway's diplomacy was often no diplomacy at all. He consistently opposed strategies of compromise at the United Nations disarmament negotiations in the late 1940s, in the Korean truce talks, and even with NATO allies.[17]

Decisiveness, self-confidence, and single-mindedness of purpose are important qualities in a battle leader, and Ridgway possessed these in abundance. Even as a young officer, Ridgway was an overly serious and perhaps somewhat humorless workaholic. He was never good at telling jokes, and, after he attained prominence, avoided them in his public speeches. He himself understood that he was no diplomat. Though he turned down President Truman's offer of an ambassadorship, later assignments forced him into greater diplomatic responsibilities.

Though Ridgway lacked the subtlety and warm smile of a Dwight D. Eisenhower, his arrogance did not cross over the line to the supreme self-absorption of a Douglas MacArthur or to the mysticism and histrionics of a George S. Patton. He drove his subordinates relentlessly but praised and rewarded those who met his standards. He was rumored to have a terrible temper, but he rarely showed it in public.

To understand the lineage of Ridgway's ideology, it is necessary to examine his predecessors as well as his contemporaries. Ridgway rose through the ranks in part because of his connections to two powerful patrons who represented two different traditions within the Army. One tradition emphasized nationalism, expansion, and reform. The other focused on professionalism and managerial competence. His "mentor," as he described him, was Major General Frank McCoy, a close friend of Theodore Roosevelt, Henry Stimson, and Leonard Wood—all nationalists and pillars of rugged individualism. T. R. and his circle were famous for their advocacy of a strong government, military preparedness, masculinism, and the assertion of American power around the world. Like McCoy, Ridgway preferred the strenuous outdoor life to any other. The younger man felt a bond with McCoy and the tradition he represented. While Roosevelt and his set were sometimes considered foreign policy "realists," whose primary objective was to maximize American power, they also had a strong sense of calling to reform the world around them and believed in the use of state power to accomplish their reforming goals. As military governor of Cuba in 1899, for example, General Leonard Wood, accompanied by Frank McCoy, then a young officer, embarked on a mission to establish, as he put it, "a republic modeled closely upon the lines of our own great Anglo-Saxon republic." With a missionary zeal, the Harvard-trained General Wood embarked on a series of widespread political, administrative, and sanitary reforms of Cuba and its society.[18] Bacevich suggests the existence of such a tradition of "Emory Upton, Leonard Wood, Billy Mitchell, and others, including a generation later, Matthew B. Ridgway and James M. Gavin," who attempted to influence the formulation of national policy.[19] McCoy, who later married Wood's niece, carried on this tradition. He was known as one of the army's greatest soldier-diplomats of his time, and he made Ridgway his apprentice. When he was sent as a special presidential envoy to Nicaragua in 1928, McCoy took Ridgway with him to reform the Nicaraguan electoral system and establish a government committed to democracy (so long as it was pro–North American) in Nicaragua, whether the Nicaraguans wanted it or not.

General of the Army George C. Marshall, Ridgway's other patron, represented a somewhat different, though not necessarily opposing, tradition. Marshall has been called the "organizer of victory" in World War II, a term originally applied to an earlier defender of democratic forces, Lazare Carnot, who helped put together the novel mass armies that saved revolutionary France from invasion in 1793. Just as Carnot pioneered the organization of new citizen armies, Marshall was skilled in the new managerial techniques that had become prevalent in the first two decades of the twentieth century. Though imbued with an older Southern military tradition, he was a master administrator in contrast to some of his more flamboyant subordinates, such as Patton or MacArthur.[20]

Ideology invokes a vision of the future and a belief that a particular social group can carry it out. One tenet of Ridgway's social vision, which also derived from the Theodore Roosevelt Progressives, was the idea of a public interest that transcended any interest group or social class. Ridgway believed that the public interest could be determined by fair-minded, disinterested, but charismatic public servants like himself. This élite would use the state apparatus to mediate between social classes and assure their cooperation with the Cold War buildup. Perhaps the best example of such cooperation in Ridgway's personal experience occurred in 1936, when, on quite short notice, Ridgway persuaded General Motors to let the military use General Motors trucks for war games without compensation. That instance of state–private sector cooperation was emblematic of Ridgway's later postwar social vision. Ridgway tended to cite the public interest in security as a justification for many actions that advanced the bureaucratic interests of the Army. At first, Ridgway's original social vision, which required a broad social consensus, did not gain political support, though he learned this slowly and painfully. If the Cold War confirmed the belief that the Soviets were a serious threat, there was a continuing controversy over the degree to which the American economy should be turned to warlike pursuits. Ridgway's experience with trying to promote defense buildups, or to prevent cuts in NATO and in the military itself, led him to recognize that there was not sufficient political will to match Soviet military capabilities.

It was this recognition that gave him an appreciation of the limits of American military power and made him hesitant about intervention in Quemoy and in Indochina. He believed such interventions would require an enormous effort for success, more than was prudent given America's worldwide commitments. Ridgway consistently refused to underestimate the cost of utilizing military power, whether discussing the budget or intervention abroad. Instead, by 1953, he supported an alternate strategy based on the concept of an army geared up to fight limited wars for limited objectives. A form of this strategy did gain acceptance under the Kennedy administration, which also increased the military budget. During the presidency of Jimmy Carter, Ridgway participated in organizations that campaigned for increased defense spending, such as the Committee on the Present Danger. Only the Reagan administration, however, seems to have raised defense spending for both personnel and hardware to levels that Ridgway found satisfactory.

Ridgway took a Janus-like position toward technological change. He understood that technology, especially the atomic bomb, had fundamentally changed warfare and even the nature of the American state. As Army Chief of Staff, he supported new research and development for equipment such as missiles and helicopters that he believed would bring the Army into the new era. At the same time, he remained skeptical of the claims of airpower enthusiasts like Admiral Arthur Radford and General Curtis E. LeMay that airpower and atomic bombs were a push-button panacea for America's military problems. Though he himself was an excellent logistician, he deplored the tendency to replace heroism with management. "I certainly have the impression that management is overemphasized," he told an interviewer. "The human element is the vital thing. You can have the best logistical manager in the world, and your troops will fail in battle."[21]

To some extent his ambivalence about technology was a result of a typical bureaucratic quest for larger budgets and institutional expansion. He recognized the power of technology, but it offended his sense of what a professional soldier should be. Ridgway believed in charismatic leadership by men who were deserving because of their strength and spiritual power as well as their technical expertise. As many Americans increasingly devoted themselves to comfort and consumerism, Ridgway appealed to the rugged individualism of an earlier time. The disjunction between those earlier values and the postwar world led him on his crusade for rearmament.

NOTES

1. *New York Times*, May 6, 1985.

2. Michael J. Hogan, "Corporatism," *Journal of American History* 77 (June 1990): 153–168, 154. See also Ellis W. Hawley, "The Discovery and Study of a 'Corporate Liberalism,'" *Business History Review* 52 (Autumn 1978): 309–320; Thomas J. McCormick, "Drift or Mastery? A Corporatist Synthesis for American Diplomatic History," *Reviews in American History* 10 (December 1982): 318–330. On the partial, rather than total, nature of corporatist "mechanisms," see Leo Panitch, "Recent Theorizations of Corporatism: Reflections on a Growth Industry," *British Journal of Sociology* 31 (June 1980): 159–186, 181. Other works that have heavily influenced my approach to biography and the history of military ideology are Michael Sherry, *Preparing for the Next War* (New Haven: Yale University Press, 1977), viii–x; Anders Stephanson, *Kennan and the Art of Foreign Policy* (Cambridge: Harvard University Press, 1989), 266–273; Frederic Jameson, *Fables of Aggression: Wyndham Lewis, The Modernist as Fascist* (Berkeley: University of California Press, 1979); and Robert Griffith, "Dwight D. Eisenhower and the Corporate Commonwealth," *American Historical Review* 87 (February 1982): 87–122.

3. See Iwan W. Morgan, *Deficit Government: Taxing and Spending in Modern America* (Chicago: Ivan R. Dee, 1995), 159–173.

4. Terry Eagleton, *Ideology: An Introduction* (New York: Verso, 1991), 1–2.

5. Michael Hunt, *Ideology in American Foreign Policy* (New Haven: Yale University Press, 1987), 12, 15–18.

6. Author interview with Col. John Trussell, March 14, 1990. On symptomatic reading, see Louis Althusser, *For Marx*, translated by B. R. Brewster (London: Verso, 1977), 63–71. For examples of the application of this method in contemporary American history, see Ronald J. Grele, *Envelopes of Sound: The Art of Oral History* (Chicago: Precedent, 1985), 138; Jonathan Soffer, "Oral History and the History of American Foreign Relations," *Journal of American History* 82 (September 1995): 607–616.

7. See Bruce Cumings, " 'Revising Postrevisionism,' or The Poverty of Theory in American Diplomatic History," *Diplomatic History* 17 (Fall 1993): 539–569. Michael Walzer, *Obligations* (Cambridge: Harvard University Press, 1970), 82, 97–98; Robert Westbrook, " 'I Want a Girl, Just Like the Girl, That Married Harry James': American Women and the Problem of Political Obligation in World War II," *American Quarterly* 42 (December 1990): 587–603; and "Fighting for the American Family: Private Interests and Political Obligations in World War II," in Richard Wightman Fox and T. J. Jackson Lears, eds., *The Power of Culture: Critical Essays in American History* (Chicago: University of Chicago Press), 195–222.

8. *Virginia Pilot and Ledger-Star*, February 12, 1984, Ridgway MSS, Box 34G.

9. I am, of course, greatly indebted to the work of Clay and Joan Blair, in their two battlefield biographies of Ridgway entitled *Ridgway's Paratroopers* (New York: Times Books, 1985) and *The Forgotten War* (New York: Times Books, 1987). Roy Appleman provides a close narrative of Ridgway's Korea battles in *Ridgway Duels for Korea* (College Station: Texas A & M University Press, 1990).

10. Maxwell D. Taylor, *The Uncertain Trumpet* (New York: Harper, 1960), 68–70. For a good sample of Taylor's management style and ideology at the time, see "The Parable of the Unhappy Mess Sergeant," 124–127, in *Uncertain Trumpet*.

11. Maxwell D. Taylor, *Swords and Plowshares* (New York: Norton, 1972), 16–17, 411–412, a book otherwise notable for its sour predictions of the decline of U.S. power.

12. General of the Army Douglas MacArthur, *Reminiscences* (New York: McGraw-Hill, 1964), 414–418. While his clearest published statement of his ideology was written relatively late, he had probably held such views for many years. See D. Clayton James, *The Years of MacArthur* (Boston: Houghton Mifflin, 1985), 3:15.

13. MacArthur, *Reminiscences*, 414–418.

14. Ibid.

15. Nathan Farragut Twining, *Neither Liberty nor Safety* (New York: Holt, Rinehart & Winston, 1966), 19, 23.

16. Matthew B. Ridgway, *Soldier* (New York: Harper, 1956), 280.

17. Twining, *Neither Liberty nor Safety*, 31, 88.

18. A. J. Bacevich, *Diplomat in Khaki: Major General Frank Ross McCoy and American Foreign Policy, 1898–1949* (Lawrence: University Press of Kansas, 1989), 12.

19. Bacevich, *Diplomat*, 176.

20. See Forrest C. Pogue, *Organizer of Victory 1943–1945* Vol. 3, *George C. Marshall* (New York: Viking, 1973).

21. John Blair (hereafter JB), Interviews with Matthew B. Ridgway, November 24, 1971 and March 24, 1972, U.S. Army Military History Institute, Carlisle Barracks, Pa., 1:1:32.

CHAPTER 2

Early Life

Matthew Bunker Ridgway was born on March 3, 1895, in Fort Monroe, Virginia. Matt and his sister Ruth, four years his senior, were "military brats" whose home shifted all over the country. Ridgway's family consisted of mostly affluent Episcopalian New York City professionals, and Ridgway has been described as almost "Edwardian" in manner. His father, Thomas Ridgway (West Point, 1883) was a native of Staten Island, New York. Matthew's grandfather, James Ridgway, had been a judge in Brooklyn. Thomas Ridgway was an efficient officer, who had commanded the American artillery battery in Beijing during the 1900 Boxer Rebellion. Ridgway described his mother, Ruth Starbuck Bunker Ridgway, originally of Garden City, Long Island, as a "good disciplinarian and a very cultured woman." She was "practically a concert pianist" who filled the home with "beautiful music."[1]

Ridgway remembered a brief period at his mother's parents in Long Island, while his father served in China, as his only real stint in civilian life until his retirement. When his father returned in 1901, the family moved to Fort Walla Walla, Washington. The old post still retained something of the atmosphere of the frontier. The six-year-old Matt saw Indians in traditional clothes knocking on the front door to call on his father. It was at this tender age that Matt got his first gun, an air rifle. He substituted hard grains of winter wheat for ammunition because his father would not give him BBs.

When the boy shot a local farmer in the rump, "it was the last time I ever pointed a weapon at man or beast without fully intending to kill, a principle that my father pounded into my head through the seat of my pants when he came home that night."[2]

After Walla Walla, the family spent 1902–1907 at another ancient frontier post, Fort Snelling, Minnesota, high atop a hill that dominates the Minnesota and Mississippi Rivers below. Now part of a museum, the Ridgways' quarters are today restored to a rather nicer state than in Thomas Ridgway's day. The Ridgways arrived in a harsh Minnesota December and huddled around the only fireplace, their singing along with his mother's piano music the only competition for the howling winter wind.[3]

Though he did not realize it at the time, Matthew's father gave him much of his soldier's education in those years. Matthew grew up around horses, which still pulled the artillery. Most of all, his father taught him the skills of hunting and camping so he was able to sleep anywhere. Matthew later wrote: "One of the hardships that besets a soldier, therefore—the living outdoors in rain and snow—never greatly bothered me, even in the gray gloom of the Ardennes, the wet and biting cold of Holland or the often bitter temperatures of Korea."[4]

From Fort Snelling, the family moved to a series of eastern posts. Thomas was transferred to the coast artillery in January 1912, when an injury caused by an explosion in a laboratory he was visiting cost him sight in one eye. Although the senior Ridgway remained in the Army until 1919, when he retired as a full colonel, the injury kept him from further promotion during World War I.[5]

Meanwhile, Matthew shifted schools, going from North Carolina to Virginia to Boston. The teenaged Ridgway considered several possible careers. He briefly considered entering Annapolis after seeing the Great White Fleet assemble at Hampton Roads. A visit to his uncle Robert Ridgway, one of the principal designers of New York's IRT subway, turned his thoughts toward engineering. Nonetheless, he settled on West Point, spending a brief time at Swavely's, a Washington, D.C., school that specialized in preparation for the West Point exams. On his first try, he failed geometry, so he returned to Swavely's. The second time he took the West Point exam, he passed, with a score of 96 in geometry, evidence of the dedication that he would later show as an officer. On the strength of his performance, he received a Presidential Appointment to the U.S. Military Academy at West Point.[6]

Ridgway entered West Point on June 14, 1913, eventually becoming a cadet lieutenant. In a class with such notables as J. Lawton Collins, Mark Clark, Joseph Swing, and H. Norman Schwarzkopf Sr., Ridgway was a leader among cadets. *Howitzer*, the West Point yearbook, described him as "the busiest man in the place, handling well the jobs of several men." Though he never succeeded in making a varsity athletic team, he became manager of the football squad—"the best football manager I've seen at West Point in the last ten years," according to the coach. Some of his activities indicate the importance of Christianity to the young cadet. He served as superintendent of the Sunday school and sat on the YMCA advisory committee.[7]

"As chairman of the V.C. his steadfast personal record has been a worthy standard for others to emulate," wrote the *Howitzer*. The "V.C.," or vigilance committee, was supposed to report to the Commandant on breaches of discipline among the cadets. Officially, the committee members had no power to administer disciplinary action, but in practice their unilateral action could make or break a cadet, sometimes in kangaroo court fashion.[8]

Ridgway's action in one such disciplinary matter led superior officers to question his judgment. As a young man, he was hardworking and dashing but could also be harsh and arrogant. According to an investigation of the Inspector General's office, Ridgway was one of the leaders of the ostracism of L. E. Gray. Gray, a cadet, had complained to the duty officer when a first classman named Cameron struck him. The Academy subsequently court-martialed and dismissed Cameron.[9]

The day after Cameron's court martial, Ridgway and other members of the vigilance committee allegedly approached Cadet Gray and suggested that he resign because of his allegedly dishonorable report on Cadet Cameron. Gray then tendered his resignation to the Commandant, who refused to accept it. Then Ridgway and one other cadet, "the leading spirits in the affair," according to the investigator from the Inspector General's office, organized the ostracism. No cadet spoke to Gray for months. The report claimed that Ridgway and the rest of the vigilance committee ignored the warnings of an instructor and the Commandant that they were absolutely wrong to censure Gray. The investigating officer, a Major A. E. Ahrends, alleged that Ridgway, among others, bordered on mutiny in his conduct and should have been arrested and punished. Ridgway had graduated by the time of the report and seems to have suffered no disciplinary action as a result.[10]

Ridgway's classmates, commenting on the tall handsome cadet's attractiveness to women, called him "the Black Knight of the Hudson." Ridgway first married Julia Caroline Blount, a twenty-one-year-old woman from the town of Florida, New York, just before his graduation at West Point. The couple had two daughters, Constance, born in Texas in 1918, and Shirley, born in 1920. In 1930, Matthew divorced Julia; and a few days after the divorce was final, he married Margaret (Peggy) Howard Wilson Dabney, who was the widow of a 1915 West Pointer Henry Dabney. Peggy and Matt had no children, but in 1936 Ridgway adopted Peggy's daughter, Virginia.[11]

Upon Ridgway's return to the United States in 1946, after four years as a commander in Africa and Europe, he realized that his life had diverged from his wife's. He wanted a divorce, and seems also to have cut his ties with young Virginia. In December 1947 he married Mary Princess (Penny) Anthony, twenty years his junior, whom he met when she was working as a secretary to an admiral who served with Ridgway in Washington on the

Inter-American Defense Board. Penny, a descendant of Susan B. Anthony, was a glamorous and strong woman who matched Ridgway's love for outdoor sports and the strenuous life. Their marriage lasted forty-six years. Ridgway had one son with Penny, Matthew Jr., who was killed in 1971 in a tragic accident during a canoe portage.[12]

After graduation from West Point, Ridgway began a long, slow climb through the Army hierarchy. As a green second lieutenant, Ridgway was sent to the Third Infantry Regiment in Eagle Pass, Texas, on the Mexican border. It was 1917, and owing to the shortage of officers, young Lieutenant Ridgway was given command of an entire company, rather than just a platoon. Ridgway later wrote that at Eagle Pass he had learned the basic lessons necessary to any young officer, namely, "to take any job that was handed to him, whether he knew anything about it or not; to issue orders as if he meant them and expected to be obeyed; to temper justice with judgment in all matters of discipline; to be firm, but fair in dealing with his men." Many years later, a member of the company wrote him, remembering the solicitude that Ridgway had for each of its members. Ridgway patiently took one new soldier aside and taught him how to tell left from right so that he could learn to march.[13]

In September 1918, orders came from Washington that quashed Ridgway's last hopes of combat service in World War I. Ridgway was sent back to West Point as an instructor. To increase his consternation, he was ordered to teach French, even though Spanish had been his best language. Ridgway protested that he "didn't know enough French to order a scrambled egg in a French restaurant." He desperately crammed and barely managed to teach the class. His cramming did him little good—he still could not speak French in 1952 when he became NATO commander. Fortunately, after three months, the war ended, and the Academy reinstituted Spanish instruction. Ridgway, who had learned his lessons well from his Spanish teacher, Joseph Stillwell, threw himself into the study of the language until he was completely fluent. His language skills helped make his career. Ridgway would become the Army's leading expert on Latin American affairs.[14]

To keep up his contact with the infantry, Ridgway volunteered as an instructor in tactics and drew the notice of General Douglas MacArthur, who was appointed Superintendent of West Point in 1919. MacArthur, who made drastic and controversial reforms, recognized Ridgway's leadership ability and made him faculty director of athletics—a signal honor for such a young officer. It was in this position that he first met George C. Marshall, then Chief of Staff to General Pershing. As athletic director, Ridgway went to Washington to get General Pershing's permission for the Army to play away games with other teams than the Navy. His work with West Point athletics led to an offer from the New York Giants to handle college football relations with their stadium, the Polo Grounds, but Ridgway did not want to live in New York and turned down the job.[15]

Ridgway's appointment as athletic director may have rescued him from obscurity; it was probably also the reason that the Adjutant General, Major General Robert C. Davis, took the unusual step of writing Ridgway to ask where he wanted his next assignment. Ridgway got his wish: to attend the infantry school at Fort Benning to take the company officer's course. Moreover, after graduation in 1925, Davis promised to send Ridgway to the Fifteenth Infantry Regiment in Tientsin, China. This was considered the "cream" of foreign assignments, and Ridgway would have the phenomenal luck to serve under then–Lieutenant Colonel George Catlett Marshall, who proved crucial to Ridgway's future. Marshall, the executive officer in temporary command of a regiment that had been allowed to deteriorate under a sloppy, alcoholic colonel, assigned Ridgway to command the headquarters company. Ridgway later recalled that the outfit suffered as a military unit because of the comforts of an urban garrison life, including a high venereal disease rate, and because of a lack of space for training. Ridgway and others helped Marshall greatly improve the morale and military readiness of the unit.[16]

From China, Ridgway did a hitch as commander of Company E of the Ninth Infantry Regiment, in Fort Sam Houston in San Antonio, Texas, and later became regimental adjutant. The Ninth was part of the Third Brigade, commanded by General Frank McCoy. Impressed with the young captain, McCoy invited Ridgway to accompany him on a military-diplomatic mission to Nicaragua that departed at the beginning of 1928.[17]

RIDGWAY AND SANDINO

In 1927, Major General Frank R. McCoy invited Ridgway to accompany him to Nicaragua. Their mission was "to supervise a free election in that strife-torn little republic." Ridgway quickly ditched plans to try out for the Olympic pentathlon team and agreed to join the man who became his mentor.[18]

Frank Ross McCoy qualified, if anyone did, as a member of the inner circles of Bull Moose Progressivism. He served as President Theodore Roosevelt's military aide and was the protegé of General Leonard Wood, whose niece, Frances Judson, McCoy married in 1924. In 1927, Secretary of State Frank Kellogg dispatched McCoy's close friend and confidant, Henry L. Stimson, to Nicaragua to negotiate an end to fighting between Nicaraguan Liberals, under General José M. Moncada, and the Conservative, U.S.-supported government of Adolfo Diaz.[19]

The strife between the two parties began after U.S. Marines pulled out of Nicaragua in August 1925 and Conservative Emiliano Chamorro overthrew an elected Liberal Party government in the coup of January 1926. A Liberal insurgency followed, supported by arms from Mexico. This prompted President Calvin Coolidge to return the Marines to Nicaragua. A small detachment landed on Christmas Eve 1926, followed by a larger landing in January 1927.[20]

According to Stimson, the United States considered its vital interests at stake in Nicaragua because Nicaragua's geography offered one of the most promising routes for an additional canal across the Central American isthmus. Under the Tipitapa Agreement of 1927, which Stimson negotiated, General Moncada agreed to disarm and to participate in a U.S.-supervised election. Both Stimson and leaders of the two main Nicaraguan political parties believed that such an election was the only way to break what Stimson termed the "revolutionary habit."[21]

A faction of the Liberals, led by César Augusto Sandino, refused to accede to the agreement. Sandino continued the Nicaraguan civil war from the hills. Fearing that Nicaragua would become infected with what he perceived as the radical contagion of the Mexican Revolution, President Coolidge ordered the Marines to fight a counterinsurgency against Sandino and appointed McCoy, a veteran of the Philippine Insurrection, to supervise the elections and salvage the Tipitapa Agreement. Felix Frankfurter, who was close to both Stimson and McCoy, wrote the latter: "There was gladness when I read that you were put in charge of America's honor and good sense in Nicaragua . . . it seemed like an old family party that you should succeed Stimson in the task."[22]

McCoy made an initial trip to Nicaragua in 1927, where he determined that only complete control over the election process could insure both its surface fairness and a result in accord with North American policy. Harold W. Dodds, a political science professor who later became president of Princeton, drafted a measure known in Nicaragua as "la ley McCoy" that gave McCoy virtual dictatorial powers over the election process. "Armed with such authority, he could block the candidacy of any Nicaraguan unacceptable to the United States and to discredit political elements inclined to question the election's legitimacy," concluded McCoy's biographer. Then he returned to the United States to gather his staff, which included the thirty-two-year-old Captain Ridgway, and took them to meet with Stimson and President Coolidge.[23]

The officers, together with Dodds and other advisors, left by steamer for Managua in the beginning of January 1928, stopping in the Canal Zone. Meanwhile, the pliant Nicaraguan president Adolfo Diaz threatened to resign owing to domestic opposition to "la ley McCoy." Upon hearing this news, McCoy and his party departed immediately for Managua on a Navy ammunition ship and cabled Dana Munro, the North American chargé, to do anything possible to forestall the Diaz resignation. Ridgway recalls departing so suddenly that there was no time for the officer diplomats to collect the laundry that they had sent out for washing. They proceeded uncomfortably to Managua, clad in wool suits.[24]

McCoy was successful in keeping Diaz in office. However, McCoy never persuaded Conservative Party leader Emiliano Chamorro to consent to the electoral law, which allowed the United States to disqualify him from running for president. The United States wanted to keep Chamorro out of power because of his history of upsetting elections by force. Chamorrista deputies blocked approval of McCoy's law in the lower house of the Nicaraguan legislature. Undeterred, the U.S. general instructed President Diaz to impose the election law by executive order. Diaz complied because he feared that the United States was prepared to seize control of the entire country by military force if he did not do so. The decree also gave McCoy complete control over the Nicaraguan Nacional Guard.[25]

Ridgway became secretary of the Nicaraguan Election Commission at a salary of $232 per month from the Nicaraguan government, which paid the sum out of a U.S. bank loan. In this job, Ridgway gained considerable expertise in the delicate diplomatic task of carrying out the election, partly because McCoy took the young officer into his confidence. Ridgway helped rewrite, translate, and distribute the election laws. He probably also helped make the military arrangements for the supervision of the elections by U.S. troops. Ridgway worked hard on the elections and considered the effort a success, though in his memoirs he never mentions the unilateral imposition of the election law. "There was no rioting, no disorder, and I am positive," he wrote, "that no election was ever held in any land that was fairer or more impartial," even though he must have known that McCoy used his power on the election board to insure that only two candidates for president were on the ballot and that both were amenable to U.S. interests.[26]

Though McCoy had successfully limited the voters' choices, the U.S. Marines fairly enforced the regulations on election day. Of course, the presence of U.S. troops at each polling place probably discouraged the participation of voters who opposed U.S. intervention. The Marines were assisted by the Guardia Nacional, a new police force officered by U.S. Marines, which Stimson hoped would be an impartial force for democracy. His hope was vain. Six years later, the U.S.-trained Guardia became the core of power around the Somoza dictatorship. Both Liberal and Conservative participants in the electoral process agreed, however, that the 1927 results were honest and abided by them.

The Nicaraguan elections gave Ridgway a taste of the possibilities and limitations of direct interference in the affairs of another nation, justified by the Progressive idea that Americans had a special mission to civilize the world. Elections alone, however, were not enough. Though Ridgway and McCoy both believed the elections to be an unqualified success, the McCoy mission did not manage either to secure complete American control of Nicaragua or to extricate U.S. forces from an intervention that most observers considered to have been a mistake. Nor did McCoy ever interest U.S. policy makers in financing the vast economic and sanitary reforms he believed necessary to bring Nicaragua lasting democracy.[27]

McCoy himself realized that Nicaragua's real problems remained unsolved. During a brief trip to Washington before the election, he unsuccessfully urged a reform program to alleviate Nicaraguan poverty. The other major problem he faced, with Ridgway's assistance, was the counterinsurgency war fought by the Marines and the U.S.-trained Nicaraguan National Guard against the original Sandinistas. McCoy, who had extensive experience in counterinsurgency warfare in the Philippines, criticized the Navy and Marine Corps commanders in charge of the war, particularly for their failure to capture Sandino, as he had captured the Moro "chieftain" Datto Ali. As the president's personal representative, McCoy considered himself in a position to object to Navy and Marine operations though he was outside the chain of command, allegedly telling General Logan Feland, the Marine commander, "If you haven't got Sandino in a month, I will feel you have failed and I shall so report to the State Department." He sent Ridgway into the field to investigate the conduct of the war.[28]

Throughout his life, Ridgway disapproved of revolutionary upheaval, which is evident from the compilation of intelligence information on Augusto César Sandino that he sent to General McCoy in the fall of 1928. Ridgway's description of Sandino contains a good deal of ideological tension, which might be expected from a discourse about banditry borrowed from the brutal put-down of the Philippine Insurrection. The report seeks to marginalize and discredit Sandino as a "bandit," denying the Nicaraguan leader's very ability to hold clear or valuable political ideas. Ridgway's redefinition of Sandino's opposition to what the U.S. officer saw as McCoy's benevolent and civilizing reforms as outlawry served to provide ideological closure for a program of capitalist modernization imposed from above. Observing that Sandino was "fired by the idea of rule by the laboring classes, the bolshevism that aims at the brotherhood of all men and control by the present laborers," Ridgway dismisses Sandino's politics as a "childish lack of control of passion and inconsideration for other's rights" that Ridgway considered "typical" of the Indo-Spanish. Disdaining Sandino's ability to make political calculations, Ridgway claimed that Sandino originally supported the Nicaraguan Liberal Party only because he mistakenly believed that Juan Batista Sacasa and other well-known Liberals shared Sandino's politics. According to Ridgway, Sandino split off from the Liberals only when he realized his mistake and began attacking Americans only because "his imagination produced the concept that the *départemento* of Segovia needed protection from the 'invader.' "[29]

Ridgway saw Sandino's nationalism as imaginary; only Sandino's "crimes," which Ridgway cataloged in detail, were real. Citing, but dismissing, Sandino's not unreasonable argument that "no government imposed by a foreign power can help but become a tool, out of gratitude to that foreign power," he trumpeted the success of U.S. efforts to defeat a man who was "broken, discouraged, and had no place to turn," and had therefore become more moderate.[30]

Ridgway's dismissal of Sandino was authorized by his clear belief in his own ability to discern a neutral, technically ascertainable Truth, as when declaring that "of all the writers praising Sandino and denouncing American Foreign policy, not one has been based on plain, solid fact." According to Ridgway, Indo-Spanish people like Sandino did not, and could not, share in this Truth because of their supposed childishness and naiveté.[31]

The U.S. government's official description of Sandino as a bandit contrasted with his reception as a nationalist hero by many Latin Americans, and even many people in the United States contested it. Senator Burton K. Wheeler (R-Mont.), declared, for example, that "if the business of the Marines was to fight bandits, they could be put to better use in Chicago." As liberal journalists like Carlton Beals of *The Nation* began to lionize Sandino, the banditry discourse was seriously strained. After General Feland told a congressional committee that the Marines "use the word 'bandit' in a technical sense, meaning a member of a band," "Beals wondered how the Marines would classify John Philip Souza."[32]

Concerned with perfecting the techniques of counterinsurgency warfare against the Sandinistas, Ridgway also examined minutely the technology of counterinsurgency, devising complete estimates of the U.S. force's logistical needs. Though he believed the guerrillas' lack of training and poor shooting would prevent them from taking heavy Marine casualties, Ridgway observed that the Sandinistas fought "coolly and courageously," and were "capable of prolonged physical hardships and operations on reduced rations." Despite his attempt to ignore the political dimension of the war, Ridgway did notice that the early Sandinistas held certain of the advantages available to a guerrilla army supported by elements of the local populace. With experience, the Sandinistas learned to make better use of cover, he observed. In addition, he found that Sandino's army was "thoroughly familiar with all trails, water holes and important terrain features." Sandino's mobility was much greater than that of the Marines, and his intelligence service superior. Sandino therefore could outmaneuver and dodge, prepare ambuscades, and escape with little probability of being seriously punished or destroyed. Though Ridgway understood the military advantages that kept the Sandinistas going, he failed to comprehend that their superior intelligence and ability to ambush successfully might be due to a base of political support among the campesinos.[33]

Against the Sandinista's hometown advantages, the United States sent Marines armed with the finest military technology available at the time. This colonial war supplied the emerging technological élite of the U.S. military with battlefield tests of new equipment designed to improve the American counterinsurgency effort. Ridgway evaluated the efficiency of machine guns, small arms, and the use of radio in combat. He examined the many uses of aviation—supply of troops in the jungle from the air and transport of troops by plane, tactical air support of ground forces, reconnaissance—and he described a system for airplanes to pick up messages and packages off the tops of trees. He also reported on the climate, local sicknesses, venereal disease, and troop morale. The deployment of scientific technique in a counterinsurgency was relatively new, and it foreshadowed the post–World War II dependence of the U.S. military on technology. It is frequently said that the Spanish Civil War gave the Axis the opportunity to test its new weapons. The war against Sandino provided the United States with a similar opportunity, if on a much smaller scale.[34]

In his travels as a military observer, Ridgway examined the wild border area around Puerto Cabezas, on the Northern Caribbean coast, as a possible landing site for U.S. armed forces. More than fifty years later, he sent a copy of that study to the Pentagon, supposing that it might be useful for any Reagan administration plan to invade Nicaragua.[35]

Ridgway was a keen observer of nature, a hunter and conservationist in the tradition of Theodore Roosevelt. When not engaged in his election commission duties, or scouting Marine operations against the Sandinistas, Ridgway indulged his passion for hunting. "Some of the hunts we had in Nicaragua were potentially about as hazardous as the jungle flights I took with the Marines," he observed later. Though he shows a love of natural beauty, the hunt is a story of risk and loss—it is a metaphor for battle. The "monster crocodiles" are the enemy of the man with a civilizing mission. "I hunted them by creeping up on them, crawling on my belly through the slime. I would shoot them just between those little knobs in which their eyes are set, which is all you can see sticking up when they are in the water. It was a fine test of marksmanship, for it was all offhand shooting at unknown ranges, at a very small target, and you had to get a brain shot to kill," the General later reminisced. "Some of the places I crawled through, wearing nothing but shorts and shoes, I wouldn't wade through now wearing armor plate and hip boots, for a thousand dollars."[36]

At the end of the Nicaragua assignment, Ridgway and a young Lieutenant named Irwin Alexander traveled home overland through El Salvador, Guatemala, and Mexico, mostly by horse or bull cart. They lived with a Mexican family for a month to perfect their Spanish. From their experience with their hosts, "Ridgway gained a profound respect for the simplicity, the gentleness, the graciousness, the basic goodness and humanity of the Latin American of the poorer class—the little man who lives out his life in hardship and believes implicitly that the Good Lord will give him ease and happiness in the hereafter." Despite his sympathy for the poor, Ridgway still attached great importance to race. As the officers bathed in their rooms, in flame-heated pottery jars, the "owl-eyed children peeped in the doorways at these strange gringos whose faces and hands were brown as theirs, but whose bodies were so strangely white."[37]

McCoy had been very pleased with Ridgway's services in Nicaragua and wrote Ridgway a letter of commendation for his "extraordinary initiative, tact, and personal and professional attainments" as well as his "thorough knowledge of the Spanish language." When Ridgway and Alexander reached Mexico City, the American embassy informed the young Captain that Mc-Coy desired his services again in Washington to serve on a commission that was attempting to settle the Chaco War between Bolivia and Paraguay. Ridgway returned to Latin America often. In 1930 he again assisted the Electoral Commission in Nicaragua, which, relying on the precedents of 1928, he found "child's play" in comparison with the earlier election. The election, from Ridgway's perspective, was a success, though "there are some things that should not be allowed to reoccur [sic] in 1932." The "bandit situation," however, was still quite serious. The application of military force had broken up the large groups; now there were many smaller groups operating in a larger area. Consequently, Ridgway protested plans to reduce the size of the Nicaraguan Guardia Nacional. Ridgway saw little prospect for democracy in Nicaragua as a result of his and McCoy's efforts, absent a long-term intervention. "Improvement will only come, in my opinion, when the present generation has passed into senility and turned over control of affairs to the succeeding generation which will have grown up with American standards before its eyes." Significantly, the young officer quoted Kipling's poem *The Proconsuls*—"Little honor does he reap of his generation"—on the lack of appreciation at home for imperial officials who act for the long-term interests of the empire. Nearly twenty years later, he sent the same verses to another revered superior, George C. Marshall, then embarked on his mission to reconcile Mao Zedong and Jiang Jieshi.[38]

After several months with the commission, Ridgway left to take the advanced course at the Fort Benning infantry school, then directed by George Marshall. Marshall had completely changed the curriculum of the school, stressing individual initiative for the unexpected things that happen on a battlefield. Ridgway later recalled one Benning exercise in particular, in which he was a brigade commander. There had been hints, mostly ignored, in the intelligence, of an unspecified number of tanks of undetermined types, which most of the officers, except Ridgway, paid little attention to. When the hostile tanks emerged unexpectedly from behind a smoke screen, probably on Marshall's explicit orders, the infantrymen in the exercise bolted as fast as they could, even though it was just a peacetime maneuver.[39]

Ridgway graduated first in his class at Benning in June 1930. Marshall asked him to stay on as an instructor, but he was excused from graduation exercises to return to Nicaragua to help organize the 1930 elections. After an apparently uneventful fifteen months on troop duty in Panama, Ridgway then left for the Philippines as a military advisor to the Governor-General,

Theodore Roosevelt Jr. Roosevelt and Ridgway became close friends and frequently traveled through the islands together. Once, Ridgway got to chase and capture Japanese raiders at sea. On another occasion, he took Governor Roosevelt's mother, the former First Lady, Edith Roosevelt, on a tour of the Malinta Tunnel, which was then under construction.[40]

Ridgway called McCoy his "mentor" and Roosevelt his friend. The young officer's love of the "strenuous life," his nationalism, his belief in a strong and technically proficient executive power that could harmonize class differences, and his belief in preparedness all tied him in spirit to the Bull Moose Progressivism of President Theodore Roosevelt—a spirit and ideology of which McCoy and Roosevelt Jr. were important heirs.[41]

Ridgway returned to the United States in 1933 via Manila, Hong Kong, and Hamburg (though there is no recorded account of his first trip to Europe in that momentous year). Through the influence of Roosevelt Jr. and McCoy, he obtained a coveted two-year appointment to the Command and General Staff School at Fort Leavenworth, Kansas. Training at Leavenworth was a prerequisite to becoming a general. In the summer between the two years, Ridgway was on leave, camping out in Colorado. After graduating, Ridgway became G-3 (operations and training) officer for the VI Corps of McCoy's Second Army, based in Chicago, and later as the Second Army chief of staff. At that time, Marshall was on duty with the Illinois National Guard, and Ridgway, who lived near him, often sought out his advice. By 1935, war seemed likely. Ridgway began planning maneuvers in rural areas near Chicago for the summer of 1936. Up to this point, Ridgway worked intensely, believing his career was on the line.[42]

Ridgway distinguished himself brilliantly in the war games. General Marshall, in command of one of the two opposing armies, had conceived a plan for a rapid flanking envelopment but discovered that he lacked the trucks to accomplish the maneuver. Using McCoy's prestige, Ridgway contacted top officials of General Motors, who lent the Army two hundred trucks, which Marshall deployed to win the war game before the other side even realized he had them. This kind of close corporate-military cooperation would become a model for Ridgway.[43]

At the end of the maneuver, Ridgway collapsed in the bathroom from exhaustion and gashed his head. The next day friends found him lying in a coma with blood around his head and immediately took him to the hospital. After the incident, Marshall congratulated Ridgway but gave him a fatherly warning about overwork: "There is no need for you to demonstrate any further you are an energetic, able workman," counseling Ridgway to use the time before his next assignment to "cultivate the art of playing and loafing" and "to establish the reputation of being something of a dilettante."[44]

Ridgway entered the War College in August 1936 and graduated in June 1937. One of his biggest assignments was a report, prepared with a group of other young officers, to study the war-making potential of Mexico. Ridgway chaired the group and wrote the geographic, population, and social sections. His main concern in those sections was to classify and describe the people of Mexico by race and class and to discuss how such divisions affected Mexico's war-making potential. He concluded that the masses of Mexicans were insufficiently committed to their nation-state and that their concerns were too localized to make Mexico a strong military power.[45]

Some of Ridgway's observations about Mexican social classes and the labor movement were adroit and intelligent. Nonetheless, Ridgway relied heavily at that time on racial categorization, a schema that appears only sporadically in his statements during and after World War II, though they were fairly typical for a man of his time and profession. Ridgway divided Mexicans into three "races": "pure white," "Indians," and "mestizos." He is hardly complimentary about the 3 percent of Mexicans who were of Spanish "stock." Their "dominating traits are a certain instability of character and emotionalism, aversion to manual labor, love of high sounding phrases and ease of being swayed by oratory, procrastination, pride, and an underlying streak of cruelty. They lead in wealth, industry, the professions and in the government." His description of the Spanish echoes an ancient Anglo-American cant about Spanish cruelty dating back to the time of the first Queen Elizabeth, and frequently repeated even by such phlegmatic observers as Henry Stimson.[46]

The Mexican Indians, who composed about 45 percent of the population, won more of Ridgway's sympathy. They "ask principally to be left alone on their own land and in their own villages," he wrote, adding that Indians "have more patience and endurance to pain and fatigue than white men." His most serious objection to Indians was that they contributed very little to the building of a nation-state. They were, he said, "ignorant, indolent, without initiative or imagination, will follow a successful leader, but have little or no patriotic or national sympathies."[47]

According to Ridgway, the vast majority of the Mexican population were "mestizos" or of "Indian blood crossed with white in every degree." While admitting the difficulty of generalizing about the mestizo whose characteristics "vary from those of the creoles to those of the Indian," Ridgway overcame his reluctance and chose "to characterize the mestizo as unreliable in business and battle, superstitious, cruel, secretive, ignorant, pervaded with a distinct sense of inferiority to the white man and with a concomitant recognition of strength and force." Like the Indians, Ridgway faults the mestizos for the priority they accord to local concerns instead of to the overall health of the nation-state.[48]

After World War II, Ridgway became a proponent of racial integration. The relatively methodical scientific racism he employed in the War College report is exceptional. The War College report also contains a section on class, about which Ridgway observed that "to this day parallels of class and race go deep into the fabric of Mexican life." While some of his classifica-

tions seem crude, his description of Mexican working-class life and radicalism is free of the sort of crude antirevolutionary rhetoric contained in his
earlier report on Sandino. He observed, for example, that "the Mexican peon
is naturally a laborer and his relations to the employer are basically patri-
archal." Unions were organized factory by factory, with the idea that it was
up to the employees of a factory alone to bring pressure on an employer, "a
sort of primal communism which is far more Indian than any of the modern
phases of socialism which are found in more completely developed industrial
nations."[49]

In his War College paper, Ridgway is finally able to distinguish between
indigenous Mexican radicalism and Bolshevik manipulation, a distinction often lost in the campaign against Sandino and in most other U.S. counterinsurgency campaigns of the twentieth century. His brief moment of
recognition of independent action by Latin American workers dissolved
when the start of World War II raised his fears of fascist or communist
influence in labor movements.

The academic problems of war with Mexico would recede rapidly in the
next few months, as the question of war in Europe and in the Pacific became
more and more of a possibility. Ridgway drew a choice staff assignment as
assistant chief of staff, G-3, Fourth Army, at the Presidio of San Francisco,
one of the most beautiful posts in the Army. From the eucalyptus-shaded
hills, he conducted a series of command post exercises. One of the most
controversial of these exercises postulated the neutralization of the Pacific
Fleet, a scenario dismissed at the time as completely unrealistic. Later, Ridgway thought that the most important maneuvers, like the earlier ones with
General Motors, required cooperation with private enterprise—in this case,
the American Railway Association, which plotted every train to the West
Coast from the Atlantic, an indispensible preparation for rail transport during the war.[50]

One of Ridgway's houseguests at the Presidio was George C. Marshall.
While Marshall was staying there, he got official notification that he had
been selected as the next Army Chief of Staff. Marshall asked the younger
officer to accompany him on a trip to Brazil, which aimed at keeping the
Brazilians in the American fold. The trip would be Ridgway's first real contact with the forces then dividing the world by war.[51]

NOTES

1. Blair, *Ridgway's Paratroopers* (hereafter CBRP), 4; Ridgway résumé, August
1972, Mellon Institute Papers, Pittsburgh, Pa.; JB, 1:1:27.

2. Matthew B. Ridgway, *Soldier* (New York: Harper Brothers, 1956), 19–20; JB
1:1:1–2.

3. Ridgway, *Soldier*, 20.

4. Ridgway, *Soldier*, 20; JB, 1:1:3.

5. JB, 1:1:6.

6. Ridgway, *Soldier*, 23.

7. *Howitzer: The 1917 Yearbook of the United States Corps of Cadets* (West Point, 1917), 149.

8. Ibid.

9. Major A. E. Ahrends Memo to the Inspector General, U.S. Army, n.d., based on Ahrends investigation probably conducted October 13–16, 1917, based on the contents of the document. Ahrends certified this document as a true copy in 1922, but the discussion of the events indicates that the document was originally written in 1917, when those concerned were studying at West Point (Clay Blair Collection, U.S. Army Military History Institute, Carlisle Barracks, Pa.).

10. Ibid.

11. CBRP, 530 n. 13. Ridgway has kept details of his first two marriages obscure. His papers include no correspondence with his former wives or their children, nor are there any letters to his third wife, Penny.

12. Ridgway, *Soldier*, 184.

13. Ibid., 32; Bill Irwin to Ridgway, April 19, 1951, Ridgway MSS, Box 18.

14. Ridgway, *Soldier*, 32–34.

15. Ibid., 34; Matthew Ridgway, Oral History Interview with Forrest Pogue, February 26, 1959, Marshall MSS, George C. Marshall Foundation, Lexington, Va., 1; JB, 1:2:4–5.

16. JB, 1:2:5; CBRP, 8–9.

17. Mellon Institute résumé in possession of author; Ridgway, *Soldier*, 36, 37.

18. Ridgway, *Soldier*, 37.

19. Bacevich, *Diplomat*: on Wood, passim and 115; on Theodore Roosevelt 44; on Stimson, 56; Nicaragua, 120. Ridgway describes McCoy as his "mentor" (see Ridgway, *Soldier*, 44).

20. Neil Macaulay, *The Sandino Affair* (Durham: Duke University Press, 1985), 24–30.

21. Henry Lewis Stimson, *American Policy in Nicaragua* (New York: Scribners, 1927), 11, 37, 78, 106. On the intervention from the Nicaraguan point of view, see Gregorio Selser, *Sandino*, trans. Fredric Belfrage (New York: Monthly Review Press, 1981), 52–62.

22. Bacevich, *Diplomat*, 121; Macaulay, *Sandino Affair*, 60. Frankfurter quoted in Bacevich, *Diplomat*, 130. Frankfurter was a protegé of Stimson, who gave the future justice his first job as an assistant United States attorney in New York City.

23. Bacevich, *Diplomat*, 123; JB, 1:2:13; Macaulay, *Sandino Affair*, 126. According to Ridgway, Stimson's book on Nicaragua "was our bible down there" (see Stimson, *American Policy in Nicaragua*).

24. Bacevich, *Diplomat*, 124; wool suits, JB, 1:2:13.

25. Bacevich, *Diplomat*, 126.

26. Gregorio Selser, 73, says that the Commission's expenses were paid for by the Nicaraguan government out of an American bank loan; Ridgway quoted in *Soldier*, 38; Bacevich, *Diplomat*, 132, 133; Ridgway to McCoy, November 13, 1928, "Memo on Sandino," n.d., RG 43, National Archives, Records of the U.S. Electoral Mission in Nicaragua, file B-1, "Bandits."

27. Bacevich, *Diplomat*, 137.

28. Ibid., 126; Macaulay, *Sandino Affair*, 127.

29. "Memo on Sandino," n.d., probably November 13, 1928, RG 43, National Archives, Records of the U.S. Electoral Mission in Nicaragua, file B-1, "Bandits."

30. M. B. Ridgway, Captain 9th Infantry, "Notes on Military Operations of United States Naval Forces in Nicaragua," Report to Chief of Infantry, Washington, D.C., July 1927–October 1928, Ridgway MSS, Box 2.

31. Ibid.

32. Macaulay, *Sandino Affair*, 81, 112.

33. Ibid.

34. Ibid. The U.S. Marines also used airplanes to bomb and strafe people more than ten years before Spanish Generalissimo Francisco Franco bombed Guernica. On July 16, 1927, Sandino's small force, augmented by hundreds of unarmed campesinos assaulted a U.S. Marine detachment in the town of Ocotal. Sandino's army withdrew, but many of the campesinos remained and began to loot the town, whereupon the Marines began to open fire and called in seven airplanes by telegraph. The airplanes bombed and then strafed concentrations of Sandinistas, pursuant to orders from Marine General Feland to "gun the bandits down mercilessly wherever they are encountered." One U.S. soldier and 300 Nicaraguans, including women and children, were killed. An additional 100 Nicaraguans were wounded (see Selzer, *Sandino*, 80, 81). According to Macaulay, *Sandino Affair*, 76–81, the incident, which lasted about forty-five minutes, was "the first organized dive-bombing attack in history." Ridgway, describing another bombing incident at Ciudad Antigua on December 6, 1927, which he says was exaggerated in the American press, noted that "aviators did drop several bombs in this bandit retreat but anyone at all familar with 17 lb. fragmentary bombs knows that they will not demolish. A careful inspection of the entire town after the event showed no evidence whatever of damage except for three or four small steel fragments. The Church to this day bears not a mark. The aviators were exceedingly careful, their object being to clear the town, not destruction of life or property" (see "Memo on Sandino," n.d., probably November 13, 1928, RG 43, National Archives, Records of the U.S. Electoral Mission in Nicaragua, file B-1, "Bandits," 7).

35. Ridgway interview with Harold Hitchens, March 5, 1982, Columbia University Oral History Research Office, 32.

36. *Ridgway, Soldier*, 39.

37. Ibid.

38. McCoy to Ridgway, December 13, 1928, "Proconsuls," typescript, with attached handwritten note, Ridgway to McCoy, August 6, 1928, McCoy MSS, Box 22. Ridgway to McCoy, September 23, 1930 and November 6, 1930; Ridgway to General Francis LeJau Parker, September 20, 1930, Francis LeJau Parker MSS, Box 9, Library of Congress. Ridgway to Marshall, October 28, 1946, China Mission 1945–47, General Correspondence, George C. Marshall Papers, Box 123, Marshall Foundation.

39. Ridgway, interview with Forrest Pogue, February 26, 1959, 4.

40. Ibid. Ridgway, *Soldier*, 42; JB 1:2:20–23.

41. Ibid.

42. Ridgway, *Soldier*, 45; JB 1:2:25, 26.

43. CBRP, 8, 9; JB, 1:2:27–29.

44. JB, 1:2:31; CBRP, 9; Colonel George C. Marshall to Major M. B. Ridgway, August 24, 1936, Ridgway MSS, Box 34D.

45. Army War College Document 2–1937–1 B, U.S. Army Military History Institute, Carlisle, Pa.; Ridgway, *Soldier*, 44–45; JB, 1:2:32–35.

46. Army War College Document 2–1937–1 B, 5, U.S. Military History Institute, Carlisle, Pa.; Stimson, *American Policy in Nicaragua*, 5.

47. Army War College Document 2–1937–1 B, 5, U.S. Military History Institute, Carlisle, Pa.

48. Ibid.

49. Ibid., 6.

50. Ridgway, interview with Forrest Pogue, February 26, 1959, 15.

51. Ibid.

CHAPTER 3

Military Diplomacy and Hemisphere Defense on the Eve of World War II

General Marshall's trip to Brazil underlined U.S. concerns about the increasing political and commercial influence of the Axis. Germany had expanded its Latin American trade through the thirties by purchasing raw materials in return for blocked "aksi" marks that could only be exchanged for finished German goods, including armaments. The United States held aloof from the Latin American arms trade through the decade. As a result, many Latin American armies, such as those of Bolivia, Chile, and to some extent Argentina, were German trained, and many officers, some of them of German and Italian extraction, sympathized with fascism.[1]

In May 1939, General George C. Marshall, the U.S. Army chief of staff-designate, visited Brazil in response to an invitation from the (pro–United States) foreign minister Oswaldo Aranha. Aranha hoped to forestall a trip to Germany by the Brazilian chief of staff, General Pedro Aurelio Goes Monteiro. A few months before, the German high command had invited General Goes Monteiro to attend 1939 maneuvers in Silesia and to command a Wehrmacht division in the war games.[2]

Although the Brazilian President Getulio Vargas had established himself as dictator with the support of the fascist Integralistas (also called "green-shirts") in 1937, he quickly repudiated them. His government, already sympathetic to U.S. policy, became even more pronouncedly anti-fascist when an anti-Nazi decree prompted an Integralista coup attempt on May 18, 1938.[3]

When Marshall went to Brazil, he took Major Matthew B. Ridgway with him. Ridgway eventually became the army's top planner for hemispheric defense. On the trip, Marshall's primary missions were to establish rapport with the Brazilian officers and secure a line of communication between Natal, Brazil, and Dakar (Senegal), the shortest air route between the New World and the Old. Another was to curb the extensive operations of SCADTA and other German-run airlines in South America. Army planners feared that the Germans would use the airline for bombing the Panama Canal, or at the least for spying.[4]

When Marshall and Ridgway arrived in Brazil aboard the cruiser *Nashville* on May 25, 1939, they received an unexpectedly warm welcome. They attended numerous parades and receptions. Perhaps the most interesting was a party with Marshall, Goes Monteiro, and Countess Edda Ciano, the daughter of Duce Benito Mussolini. She treated Marshall coldly and Goes Monteiro with the greatest attention. One historian commented "It was as if two jealous suitors were meeting in the presence of the desired one."[5]

While Marshall attended ceremonies, Ridgway and Colonel Lehman W. Miller met the officers of the Brazilian Army and gathered detailed information from them on Brazil's capabilities and strategy. The defense interests of the United States and Brazil, however, did not completely coincide. While the Yankees worried most about the threat from across the Atlantic to Brazil's "bulge," the Brazilians still looked south to their German emigré colonies and to their traditional Argentine enemies. Ridgway explained that the United States wanted to construct and staff airbases in northeastern Brazil, using U.S. personnel to defend Brazil and the Panama Canal. The Brazilians agreed, so long as U.S. personnel wore civilian clothes.[6]

The Brazil visit was a success. General Goes Monteiro returned with Marshall to the United States, where he was given full honors. Monteiro wrote President Vargas, however, that he was annoyed at the insinuations of the press that he was pro-Nazi. The general claimed he was working for an "approximation" with the United States, fearing that if Brazil did not ally itself with the United States, Argentina would.[7]

At this stage, American planners remained focused on the Natal "bulge" and the German threat. The balance of power within South America concerned them less. Despite the difference in perspective, the George C. Marshall–Goes Monteiro exchange was a success. Soon after Goes Monteiro's U.S. visit, war broke out in Europe, preventing his trip to Germany. Eventually, Brazil became the closest ally of the United States in the region, the only one to send troops to the European Theater. Ridgway made two more trips to Brazil as Marshall's emissary before the entrance of the United States into the war. In November 1939, Ridgway joined Army Air Force General Delos C. Emmons in a demonstration of U.S. airpower. They flew to Brazil in the new Flying Fortress long range bombers for the 50th anniversary of Brazilian independence. On the way, Ridgway made an aerial survey of the routes to the bulge. When he got to Brazil, he offered some limited surplus artillery and other arms to the Brazilians and brought a list of raw materials that the United States needed from Brazil. Ridgway managed to close a deal in which both the United States and Brazil would make simultaneous purchases for equivalent amounts of cash—despite State Department squeamishness about what was in essence the same kind of goods-for-goods deal for which it frequently denounced the Germans.[8]

Ridgway's final prewar trip to Brazil occurred just after the Vichy French Admiral Darlan reached an agreement with Hitler that seemed to make Nazi occupation of Dakar imminent. Marshall dispatched Ridgway to Rio to negotiate bases for U.S. ground troops in the bulge. Foreign Minister Aranha hinted that only a personal appeal from President Franklin Delano Roosevelt might persuade Vargas. By this means, Vargas did agree to allow an American army planning group into Brazil. However, President Roosevelt apparently wanted more information before speaking directly to Vargas about the deployment of U.S. troops. The Navy and the State Department had little interest in the deployment of the troops in the bulge, and stalled the matter. Fear of an attack from Dakar also declined after Germany attacked the Soviet Union on June 22, 1941. Not until April 1942, after Ridgway had left the War Plans Division for troop duty, did Brazil agree to a complete joint defense agreement that allowed U.S. troops to operate from Brazilian soil.[9]

RIDGWAY AT THE WAR PLANS DIVISION

After the May 1939 trip to Brazil with General Marshall, Ridgway returned briefly to the West Coast, where he organized a huge Command Post exercise. This exercise, which later proved invaluable in the Pacific War, aimed at deploying as much force as possible on the West Coast. Ridgway was criticized at the time for his prescient assumption that the U.S. Pacific Fleet could be neutralized.[10]

Soon after the maneuvers, Ridgway was ordered to report to the War Plans Division, where he would join the nucleus of officers who would lead the U.S. Army in World War II. Ridgway hated the desk job. In his memoirs, he wrote that "there was nothing of great significance about my service with the War Plans Division." In contrast, one scholar found that Ridgway was "the single most influential person" in the War Department who was concerned with Latin American relations, an area Roosevelt and Marshall considered vital.[11]

At first, Ridgway worked mostly on the familiar "color plans," which unrealistically posited bilateral belligerence between a variety of nations, then on the "rainbow plans," which plotted the defeat of a coalition of enemies.

In addition, he was the point man for relations with Latin America. Much of this work remains murky because he destroyed many of his papers from this period for security reasons in his haste to leave for duty with the 82d division.

The War Plans Division work had highly political overtones, and Ridgway's work often blurred politics with military technique. For example, Ridgway's concern with possible Soviet capacity for sabotage, and the role of the American state in combating it, arose in the period of the Nazi-Soviet Alliance. In a memo for the chief of plans, Ridgway claimed that "sabotage of munitions and other plants, propaganda and subversive political activity, labor disturbances, etc. would undoubtedly be increased and have a material effect in hampering our preparations for and conduct of war." Ridgway hoped the War, Navy, and Justice Departments would "intensify the effort to uncover and to uproot the political activities in the United States and her possessions of Russian agents and sympathizers," and "organize and direct a press campaign to assist in this task."[12]

The beginning of the war in Europe also changed the role of the United States in the hemisphere. For the duration of the war, military considerations replaced commercial ones, though sometimes the two went hand in hand. The United States now wished to become the sole arms supplier to Latin American armies, in order to insulate the hemisphere from Axis influence, subversion, or possible invasion. In general, the State and War Departments viewed Axis internal subversion as the primary threat. Axis subversive activity included organization for espionage, sabotage, and propaganda, including the wooing of Latin officers with Fascist sympathies, and commercial penetration of strategic industries. U.S. war planners most feared the network of German-run airlines that, at worst, might prepare welcoming bases for the Luftwaffe.[13]

According to Forrest Pogue, General Marshall and President Roosevelt heavily stressed the threat of Nazi attacks on South America to garner public and congressional support for rearmament. The threat of attacks on the "bulge" of Brazil included submarine marauding in the South Atlantic and the possiblity that Nazi airpower might gain a logement near Natal, putting Rio de Janeiro and the Panama Canal within range. Bombing could easily put the canal out of commission by sinking ships in the narrow channel and wrecking the canal's complex machinery.[14]

In July 1940, just after the fall of France, Ridgway, as the Army's Latin American desk officer, first reported the arms needs of each country and recommended to General Marshall a policy for supplying arms to the region on a country-by-country basis. "Brazil was to receive capability to defend against a major attack from overseas, and against internal disorder until the U.S. army could come to the rescue. Mexico was placed in a similar category. Ecuador, Colombia and Venezuela should be given arms to protect against minor attacks to ensure internal stability."[15]

Internal stability was not the only concern for Central American governments. Presumably any attack threatening the region would be parried by U.S. forces stationed in the Panama Canal Zone. The most pro-Axis nations, those in the Southern Cone, would receive arms only after the requirements of the other republics had been decided upon.

It was imperative, according to Ridgway's proposal, to make financial arrangements with the Latin nations so they could afford the arms. It was also necessary to ensure United States–Latin political cooperation to subsize these arms shipments. Arms aid also became a method of ensuring political cooperation. President Roosevelt approved the policy on August 1, 1940, and it was implemented by February 1941, when $400 million in arms aid for Latin America was included in the Lend Lease aid bill. Of this sum, $324 million or 71 percent went to Brazil, mostly to equip the division that was eventually sent to fight in Italy under the Allied Command.[16]

An important step in the implementation of this arms program was the creation, with the War Plans Division, in December 1940, of the Joint Advisory Board on Latin American Republics. Colonel Ridgway "was the chief architect and moving spirit" of this board until his departure in 1942. The job of this board was to process all Latin American munitions requests, to draft a detailed program for arms aid to Latin America, and to strike a careful political balance in allocating arms among the republics.[17]

Ridgway had his fingers in many pies of Latin-American military relations. He made at least one clandestine trip to Colombia to negotiate arms deals. As a member of the Joint United States–Mexican Defense Commission, an organization which was first organized secretly, he gathered intelligence from one of the few sympathetic Mexican officers and concluded difficult negotiations for the placement of early warning aircraft detectors on Mexican territory. Early in 1942, General Eisenhower reported a conversation with Hull and Ridgway, who "wanted a bribe to give Chile in the way of defense materials, so as to get favorable vote on breaking off with Axis."[18]

Trading arms for politico-military concessions was the thrust of the U.S. arms policy that Ridgway coordinated. Though hampered by State Department and congressional opposition, Ridgway and the military continued to pursue the policy through the postwar period. In the course of the war, they hoped to eliminate all European influences from the armies of Latin America.

NOTES

1. Ridgway, *Soldier*, 48; Stetson Conn and Byron Fairchild, *The Framework of Hemispheric Defense* (Washington, D.C.: Office of the Chief of Military History, 1960), 5–7, 32–34, 207–208. Frank McCann, *The Brazilian-American Alliance* (Princeton: Princeton University Press, 1973), 133–135.

2. McCann, *Brazilian-American Alliance*, 133–135.

3. Ibid., 28–30, 58, 89, 96.

4. Roderick A. Stamey Jr., "The Origin of the U.S. Military Assistance Program," Ph.D. diss., University of North Carolina, Chapel Hill, 1972, 36–40, 135; Ridgway, *Soldier*, 48 (Ridgway mistakenly refers to the airline as Avianca); McCann, *Brazilian-American Alliance*, 136–137.

5. McCann, *Brazilian-American Alliance*, 136–137.

6. Ibid., 138; Ridgway, *Soldier*, 48.

7. McCann, *Brazilian-American Alliance*, 139–140.

8. Ibid., 145–146.

9. Ibid., 146, 242; Conn and Fairchild, *Hemispheric Defense*, 284–288.

10. Ridgway, *Soldier*, 46, 47.

11. Ibid., 48; Stamey, "Origin," 135.

12. Ridgway to Chief of Plans Section, December 12, 1939, Ridgway MSS, Box 2.

13. Stamey, "Origin," 139, 140.

14. Forrest C. Pogue, *George C. Marshall* (New York: Viking, 1963), Vol. no.1 336–337; Conn and Fairchild, *Hemispheric Defense*, 212.

15. Ibid., 213.

16. Ibid., 213–224.

17. Ibid., 215, 216.

18. Robert Ferrell, ed., *Eisenhower Diaries*, (New York: Norton 1981) January 22, 1942, 44.

CHAPTER 4

Training the All-American

On December 7, 1941, Ridgway had just escaped his desk for temporary duty at the Fort Benning infantry school. He relished the refresher course and its mostly outdoor exercises, along with its promise to bring him what he craved most—command of an infantry regiment. He must have felt a heady mixture of dismay and excitement at the news of the attack on Hawaii, which sent him scurrying back to a wartime Washington flushed with the administrative demands of modern war.

Every day Ridgway would go to work in the "shabby" Munitions Building in downtown Washington. At six A.M., he would start extra duty, assigned by General Marshall, summarizing the day's operation reports, with little maps and sketches. It was Washington's most up-to-date source on the state of the war, and it had to be on the desks of President Roosevelt, Secretary Stimson, and General Marshall by 8 A.M. He would continue with his regular duties until ten or eleven at night. Ridgway was famous for driving himself to the limit, but even he admitted the routine "left him a bit hollow-eyed." As General Marshall would write to Admiral Harold R. Stark, "Now-a-days, Sundays are like Mondays and every other day of the week."[1]

Though he desperately wanted to escape Washington, Colonel Ridgway had strong opinions on the basic "action needed at the top." With the Civil War in mind, Ridgway hoped General Marshall would be able to "crush political intermeddling" and "interference," reflecting the value Ridgway placed on "neutral" professional judgment and corporatist control of the war effort.[2]

Every day he would perch on Marshall's doorstep, where his old friend Walter Bedell Smith sat as Marshall's gatekeeper, hoping for some crumb of news that he was destined for regimental command, until the acid-tongued Smith, tired of Ridgway's impatience, finally told him to get lost. It took until the end of January, but Marshall gave him a better command than he had dared to hope for—an assignment as Assistant Division Commander to Brigadier General Omar N. Bradley, who would be reactivating the 82d Division. Bradley, head of the Fort Benning infantry school, was an old friend from West Point; and in all probability it was Bradley who had sent for him. The appointment brought Ridgway his first star—unofficially making him a division commander-in-training. In a brief year and a half, he had advanced in grade from major to brigadier general. Marshall's orders, he later wrote, "meant everything I had ever dreamed of."[3]

Ridgway could not get out of Washington fast enough. Within two hours after his meeting with the Chief of Staff, he burned his papers at the War Plans Division, left the packing to Peggy, jumped in his car, and sped south to Fort Benning, where he planned to return to the infantry refresher course he had missed on Pearl Harbor day. Ridgway knew that Bradley, the first general selected by Marshall to command a division, would insist on making the 82d one of the best divisions in the Army. Each man considered himself "lucky" to have the other. Peggy, however, felt less than lucky. Stuck in Louisiana with a husband devoting all his attention to the 82d Division, she soon fell ill and returned to Washington. Ridgway's friends would sometimes look in on her; Matthew and Peggy still corresponded, though the letters are not part of Ridgway's papers. The couple would never live together for the rest of the war; Matthew made the transition from obscure colonel to famous general in Peggy's absence.[4]

The 82d was an "experiment in mobilization." Instead of sending draftees as replacements to a regular division, the unit would be created from scratch by Bradley, Ridgway, and a cadre of eighteen hundred officers and enlisted men from Major General Jacob L. Devers's 9th division. About sixteen thousand draftees descended on the 82d for training. Faced with the task of creating a division out of a group of individualistic young draftees, Bradley and Ridgway employed a combination of strict discipline, a nurturing concern for morale, the establishment of heroic traditions of leadership, physical conditioning, and education in the tactical and technical skills.

They were well aware that they faced a difficult task in initiating American draftees reared with an individualistic political ideology and in a culture of consumption, into a military society that placed a premium on values such as deference to rank and self-sacrifice for the good of the Army. Bradley and

Ridgway's response was to make morale their first priority. As Bradley put it: "I conceived the notion—radical at the time—that we would do everything within our ability to make the draftees feel they were coming to a 'home' where people really cared about their welfare. This is not to say we intended to coddle the recruits. In fact, we intended to be tough as hell on them, but in an intelligent, humane, understanding way." In a liberal society where the roots of obligation lay in the defense of the family, rather than the defense of the state, Bradley and Ridgway understood that an effective unit had to be like a family, with officers as stand-ins for both wise patriarchs and nurturing mothers.[5]

Both Bradley and Ridgway recognized their good luck in reactivating a division with a glorious past in World War I. By playing up the deeds of the past—even though the "All-American" division had ceased to exist between the wars—they believed they could "plant in each man's mind the idea that valor endured from generation to generation; that the great deeds their fathers had performed could be repeated by the sons." They wanted their troopers to believe they could handle any situation they encountered— a self-contained rugged individualism that framed Ridgway's construction of manhood itself.[6]

Bradley and Ridgway brought the 82d's most famous World War I soldier, Sergeant Alvin York, to address the division at a time so early in the training that recruits did not yet know how to march. Amidst bands and a full division parade, York told the 82d and a nationwide radio audience how he single-handedly destroyed 35 machine guns, killed 25 German soldiers, and captured 132 men, disabling an entire enemy battalion.[7]

Sergeant York was a major media figure who had been portrayed the year before by Gary Cooper in Howard Hawks's classic film. Ridgway later credited York's visit and other division rituals, such as the revival of military bands, with the early establishment of the 82d's famous esprit de corps.[8]

Bradley recalled later that York had told him that he would not get very far in the world because he was "too nice," a remark that perhaps indicates one of the principal differences between the World War I and World War II armies. The leadership of the 82d emphasized concern for soldiers's psychological well-being. Ridgway called this approach "intelligent supervision." Because the American soldier was so individualistic, he required an explanation of the reasons behind the orders he was given if he were to develop trust in leadership and if he were to accept the regime of "constant and effective" surveillance that the Army placed him under.[9]

In one of his early talks with officers, Ridgway made it clear that he expected them to coax soldiers to "exceed their best efforts through the desire to do better than before, not through fear." "*BUT*," he added, "there must be unfailing compliance with orders." This was in keeping with the best traditions of the American army as Colonel Stuart Cutler pointed out when he distributed the advice of Major General John M. Schofield, a great nineteenth-century superintendent of West Point, to the officers of the 326th Glider Regiment:

> The discipline which makes the soldiers of a free country reliable in battle is not to be gained by harsh or tyrannical treatment. On the contrary such treatment is far more likely to destroy than to make an army. It is possible to impart instruction and give commands in such a manner and in such a tone of voice as to inspire in the soldier no feeling but an intense desire to obey.[10]

Ridgway believed the legitimation of officers' authority was integrally related to morale, which he defined as almost congruent with officers' authority, that is, "the *will* to do cheerfully and the *courage* to carry out unfalteringly any task assigned." While this seems fairly true of any army, Ridgway and Bradley innovated by incorporating therapeutic elements in training designed to instill self-confidence and confidence in leaders. Ridgway gave a surprising amount of personal attention to the division's chaplains whose job was redefined to include therapy. Ridgway admonished them to learn as much as they could about the men in order to provide effective counseling services. "How can you talk to these men if you don't learn their problems?" he asked them rhetorically.[11]

From the time new recruits arrived, Bradley and Ridgway were determined to make sure that their soldiers knew they were in a well-run outfit whose officers cared about their welfare and their problems. Most of the draftees coming into the 82d were from the South, so their reception centers were relatively close at hand. Bradley's G-1 (Personnel), Ralph P. (Doc) Eaton, who would later become Ridgway's chief of staff, sent advance men to the centers to greet and interview each soldier.[12]

When the trains full of draftees arrived, greeted by a brass band, the division already had a preassigned unit, equipment, and bedding waiting for them. Laundry service was available for their uniforms, and the division mess cooked them a hot meal.[13]

Even in classes, Ridgway wrote in his notes that the "enthusiasm and imagination of the instructor must preclude all boredom." On the first weekends, officers were instructed to provide "plenty of supervised activities" to help the draftees adjust to their new situation.[14]

The division also received many new officers from the three-month training program that qualified them as "ninety-day wonders." Ridgway hoped to imbue them with the rugged individualism and self-control characteristic of the masculine models of the Progressive Era. He told the officer candidates to "eliminate everything from your make-up and appearance that in

any way impedes your progress" through a period of "more constant surveillance than you have ever been [under] before."[15]

Some of his advice to the officers sounded like self-critique: "Don't jeopardize your health by cutting down on your sleep, ruining your eyes, etc.
Fellow candidates have more respect for men who can get their work done
in the designated time rather than having to rely on extra time." Could these
be the words of Matthew Ridgway the workaholic?[16]

Just as the officer candidates were instructed to mold their psyches under
the strict surveillance of the Officer Candidate School, the bodies of rank
and file soldiers had to be disciplined. Bradley, and Ridgway, who ran the
training program, were appalled at the physical condition of the draftees. As
Bradley put it, they were "soft as marshmallows."[17] (As the 82d was not yet
an airborne division, the recruits lacked the physicial abilities of carefully
screened paratrooper volunteers.) The generals inaugurated a strenuous
physical conditioning program designed to prepare the troops for the physical demands of battle. Officers and non-commissioned officers had to be
warned not to watch for men who could not handle the training and to make
sure the men were not pushed too hard.[18]

The training of many of the newly created divisions would be set back by
unexpected changes in personnel and policy. By May, it seemed that Ridgway
might depart soon for a new division command, by September 1942, and
would soon get his second star.[19]

General Marshall had other plans, however, and transferred Bradley, much
to his disappointment, to the 28th Division, a Pennsylvania National Guard
unit that needed a troubleshooter. Ridgway, on the other hand, would take
command of his beloved 82d on June 26, 1942. He was promoted to the
rank of temporary major general on August 6. "The name Ridgway is an
electric current to my soul," his old mess sergeant from his first command
in Eagle Pass, Texas, wrote him, after reading about his new command in
the papers.[20]

Shortly after Ridgway took command, the division began to motorize. But
something more stunning than trucks and jeeps was in the offing. In an age
when most people still looked up at the sky in wonder when an airplane
passed over, Major General Floyd Parks informed Ridgway in a whisper that
the 82d was to become an airborne division. "I told him I didn't know what
an airborne division was," Ridgway later wrote.[21]

The change remained a closely guarded secret for the first few weeks,
along with plans to split the division to provide a cadre for the new 101st
Airborne. Ridgway's senior staff was hardly enthusiastic about gliders or par-
achutes. Officers feared they would be given suicide missions, that gliders
would be death traps, and that an elite parachute battalion would be difficult
to integrate into a draftee infantry division, especially if the unwilling infantry gliderists were not receiving the same hazardous duty pay of the para-

troops. Ridgway shared these concerns to some extent, but his can-do attitude led him to perceive new opportunities from the new technology, and he worked hard to persuade his officers that their fears were unfounded.[22]

Ridgway, who characteristically did not want to ask his men to do anything he had not done himself, immediately snuck off to Fort Benning for his first jump. His quick ground school training did not quite take, and Ridgway landed bruised but uninjured. He later told his officers about the "feeling of serenity and peace you feel while going down" without mentioning the impact that was "like jumping off the top of a freight car, travelling at thirty-five miles an hour, onto a hard clay roadbed."[23]

Ridgway started working with airborne pioneer Bill Lee to set up basic airborne training for the 82d and 101st. The two men were old friends and wanted to make sure that the 101st got off to a good start. Each general kept his principal subordinates and flipped coins to divide the rest of the outfit. Besides, there were plenty of men to spare, as Army Ground Forces Commander General Leslie J. McNair, overwhelmingly concerned with mobility, had decided that airborne divisions should be about half the size of a normal infantry division in order to enhance their mobility, but with a corresponding reduction in firepower.[24]

Ironically, the intense family spirit of the 82d almost proved to be Ridgway's undoing when he officially announced the partition of the division into two on August 15, 1942. His men identified so thoroughly with the 82d that forty-five hundred men went AWOL the next day, according to Clay Blair, who cited an anonymous source. The source told Blair that Ridgway "was baffled." The unnamed officer told him, "You scared the pants off 'em," observing that Ridgway had expected the troops "to be as fired up as he was." Ridgway did not understand why his men would not want to go to the 101st and why they would not want to be gliderists, according to the officer. Most of the men soon returned, but the split of the division, the prospective conversion of the division into two glider regiments, the integration of a new paratroop regiment, and the logistics of moving the division slowed training until the final move of the division to Fort Bragg. Frequent personnel changes at all levels during the initial weeks at Bragg slowed down training still further.[25]

That fall, Ridgway took a test ride in an experimental glider. The glider was supposed to jettison its wheels and land on skids; but when Ridgway and his pilot tried to land, the wheels would not drop. They almost smacked into a bomber on the runway. Then the pilot yelled "jump," and Ridgway skidded onto the pavement, leaving part of the skin from his behind at Wright Field. When he got back to his staff, he praised the glider to the skies; his staff remained skeptical.[26]

Ridgway had hoped to have the division largely trained by January 30; it took far longer. Personnel shifts caused a major portion of the delay. Hundreds of officers and men left to supply a full cadre to the 98th infantry division. The 82d had to integrate a whole regiment of paratroops—the 504th under Colonel Theodore L. Dunn. Dissatisfied with Dunn's perform-ance in training his regiment (and perhaps because of Dunn's drinking prob-lem), Ridgway replaced Dunn with Lieutenant Colonel Reuben H. Tucker III, thirty-one years old, who would soon become one of the youngest and most highly decorated full colonels in the army. Artillery Commander Brig-adier General Joseph M. Swing went out to command the 11th Airborne division, and Ridgway moved his chief of staff, Brigadier General Maxwell D. Taylor, into Swing's slot. Taylor, who was more interested in artillery than administration, was a happy man. To replace him, Ridgway made a surprise choice, Ralph P. Eaton, who at first told Ridgway that he did not want the job. Eaton told Ridgway that he was "too stupid—not smart enough to be your chief of staff." Ridgway, thinking of Taylor, told Eaton, "I don't want anymore *smart* chiefs of staff."[27]

During the transition period, Ridgway once more emphasized the impor-tance of "molding" units. He showed his understanding of the disciplinary power of symbols of unit pride. "Little things can help greatly," he told the officers of the reunified division, "guidons, signs in your areas, letterheads on your official papers, particularly those on the bulletin boards." In the reorganization, again, there was a strong effort to make certain that the men understood "the reasons why." Ridgway suggested putting organiza-tional diagrams of each unit and the next higher unit on the bulletin board so that every enlisted man would understand how his unit fit into the division structure. More important, he enjoined officers, "Tell your men all you can of their new unit, its probable missions, the reasons for the organization and equipment it has been given. Tell them of your training problems ahead, stimulate their thoughts, invite their suggestions to improve our technique and tactics."[28]

All the shifts in personnel—really the creation of an entirely new organ-ization—and a shortage of gliders and pilots meant that training of the re-organized division would just be starting, rather than ending, by January 1943. Even then, it would go more slowly than planned because of a shortage of gliders, pilots, and airlift capacity—a problem that would plague the air-borne throughout the war. But the war would not wait. By February, General Marshall had decided to commit the 82d to battle in Operation HUSKY, the invasion of Sicily.[29]

Ridgway had three months to finish training the division and get it to North Africa. Moreover, the glider shortage was so acute that there was little hope of training both of the regiments in time. One of the glider regiments would have to be rotated out of the division and replaced with trained paratroops. Fortunately, Ridgway got one of the most spirited units in the Army—the 505th Parachute Infantry Regiment, commanded by Colo-nel James Maurice Gavin.

The overworked division commander got a welcome break from the training routine in mid-March 1943, when General Marshall ordered him to North Africa to confer with the planners for Operation HUSKY.[30] When Ridgway arrived, General Sir Harold Alexander was trying to trap Rommel's Afrika Corps between his own Anglo-American First Army coming from the east and General Bernard Montgomery's Eighth Army pushing from the west. In Tunisia, Ridgway saw his first battlefield. In a week, he learned about such practical matters as the ineffectiveness of American antitank weapons. When a group of trucks ahead of him were strafed by a Messerschmidt, he vowed never to let vehicles bunch up on the road.[31]

Ridgway was less than happy with the proposed plans for the airborne invasion of Sicily. The British 1st Airborne division commander, F. A. M. "Boy" Browning, shared the general skepticism of British officers toward U.S. forces. He planned to drop only a U.S.-reinforced regiment as an adjunct to the British airborne operation. Browning, who doubled as Eisenhower's airborne advisor, had considerable political influence. Ridgway, who knew his way around a planning staff, politicked with friendly commanders on the scene, like Omar Bradley and Mark Wayne Clark, to expand his division's role. Technically, the 82d would still be in training when it arrived in North Africa and therefore under Clark's command. In addition, Ridgway sent Maxwell Taylor to North Africa to counter Browning's plans.[32]

Ridgway returned to the 82d during an inspection by Generals Marshall and Arnold and by British Foreign Secretary Sir Anthony Eden. Arnold strongly criticized Ridgway for a glider demonstration. The Air Corps commander thought the demonstration was unrealistic. Ridgway conceded the problem, but insisted that such care was necessary owing to the shortage of gliders. The division could hardly afford smashups that might put its training out of commission altogether. Arnold was not entirely satisfied with this explanation; but after the inspection, the 82d did get more gliders and gained considerably more confidence with them.[33]

Gavin, who had literally written the book on airborne warfare[34] (*Trials and Techniques of Airborne Troops*, U.S. Army field manual FM-31-30, [Washington, 1942]), had evolved tough, unorthodox, training methods. He conceived of the paratrooper as a self-contained individual trained for combat in any situation that he might encounter on landing. He took his men on tough overnight marches through the swamps, simulating combat conditions. Gavin designed these marches to develop physical toughness. With their jump boots, baggy pants, and tough training, Gavin's men had an extraordinary degree of pride in themselves and in their unit. Sometimes this toughness and unit pride caused considerable problems for integration with the 82d. At one point, a young lieutenant, it is said, walked up to Ridgway and told him, "Sir, Colonel Gavin sends his compliments and told us he wants us to cooperate to the utmost with the 82nd Division." A shocked Ridgway replied that he expected more than cooperation—the 505 was *part* of the 82d division. While physical training was tough, Gavin was tolerant of the paratroopers' behavior off-duty, which was often rowdy and confrontational, especially when they encountered the "straight-leg" army. Troopers often fought in bars, and Gavin remembers that even the officers were so rowdy that "they'd have to send the MPs to the officer's club to keep the peace."[35]

Ridgway must have been worried about integrating a new unit into his division on such short notice, but he was proud of the division's fighting spirit. "Peg darling," he wrote his wife, "it would have thrilled you to have seen 9500 of the finest men in mass today." He realized, as he told his men, that the division's role as the first employing the new technology into battle "will turn the spotlight on us."[36]

The division embarked for North Africa on April 29. While politicking for a greater U.S. role in the Sicily invasion, Ridgway worried about the lack of preparation caused by the constant organizational changes. Shortage of aircraft and pilots had made the airborne training and technique spotty, especially for night operations. Ridgway would have to make up the deficit while his men were camped in a gritty, dusty, fly-infested camp in Oudja, French Morocco. Ridgway had picked the site because of its proximity to Clark's Fifth Army headquarters—a case of Army politics winning out over comfort. Despite the discomforts of Oudja, General Dwight D. Eisenhower inspected the division at the end of June 1943 and pronounced the 82d "in splendid shape."[37]

NOTES

1. Ridgway, *Soldier*, 49–50; CBRP, 11, 14; Marshall to Stark, May 20, 1942, in Larry I. Bland, ed., *The Papers of George C. Marshall* (Baltimore: Johns Hopkins University Press, 1991), 3:206–207.

2. Ridgway "Notes on Action Needed at the Top," January 21, 1942, Personal Files, Ridgway MSS Box 3.

3. Ridgway, *Soldier*, 50.

4. CBRP, 15; Omar N. Bradley and Clay Blair, *A General's Life* (New York, Simon & Schuster, 1983) (hereafter CBGL), 104; Ridgway, *Soldier*, 50.

5. CBGL, 106; Michael Walzer, *Obligations* (Cambridge: Harvard University Press, 1970) 82, 97–98; "American Women," 587–603.

6. Ridgway, *Soldier*, 51, 52.

7. Ibid., 52; CBRP, 532 n. 23; CBGL, 107.

8. CBGL, 107; Ridgway to Clark, May 9, 1942, Personal File. PF January 1942–November 1943, Ridgway MSS, Box 3.

9. "Notes on Army Commander's Training Comments," Matthew B. Ridgway (MBR) Training Notebook, April–May 1942, Ridgway MSS, Box 4.

10. "Early Officer Talks," Ridgway Training Notebook; Ridgway to Bradley, June 6, 1942, Ridgway MSS, Box 4.

11. "Morale, Discipline, Leadership—Outline of a 30-Minute Talk for Chaplains," Speeches to Troops, 1942–44, Ridgway MSS, Box 4.

12. CBGL, 106.

13. Ibid.

14. "Notes of Conversation with Army Commander, April–May 1942," in Training Notebook, Ridgway MSS, Box 4.

15. Training Notebook, Ridgway MSS, Box 4.

16. Ibid.

17. CBGL, 106.

18. Training Notebook, Ridgway MSS, Box 4.

19. Clark to Ridgway, May 9, 1942, Personal File, January 1942–November 1943, Ridgway MSS, Box 3.

20. Kerr to Ridgway, August 6, 1942, PF January 1942–November 1943, Ridgway MSS, Box 3.

21. Ridgway, *Soldier*, 54.

22. CBRP, 33.

23. Ridgway, *Soldier*, 56.

24. CBRP, 33, 34.

25. CBRP, 38; Ridgway, "To the Officers and Enlisted Men of the 82d," August 14, 1942, Ridgway MSS, Box 4.

26. Ridgway, *Soldier*, 57.

27. CBRP, 40 (e.o.), 36, 42.

28. Ridgway, "Outline," n.d. but after August 14, 1942, Ridgway MSS, Box 4.

29. CBRP, 43.

30. Ridgway, *Soldier*, 58, 59.

31. Ibid., 58, 59, 62.

32. CBRP, 65.

33. Ridgway, *Soldier*, 60.

34. James M. Gavin, *Trials and Techniques of Airborne Troops*, U.S. Army field manual FM-31-30 (Washington, D.C., 1942).

35. James M. Gavin, *Airborne Warfare*, 17; James M. Gavin, *On to Berlin: Battles of an Airborne Commander, 1943–1946* (New York: Viking, 1978) (hereafter OTB), 2, 3; CBRP 51, 52.

36. Matthew Ridgway to Margaret Ridgway, Easter, 1943, Speeches to troops, Ridgway MSS, Box 3.

37. Ridgway, *Soldier*, 62, 63; T. B. Ketterson, "The 82d Airborne Division: Sicily and Italy," unpublished unit history, 2 Ridgway MSS, Box 5; Eisenhower to Marshall, June 26, 1943, Alfred D. Chandler Jr. et al., eds., *The Papers of Dwight D. Eisenhower* (Baltimore: Johns Hopkins University Press, 1970), 2:1212 (hereafter DDE Papers).

CHAPTER 5

The Lessons of Sicily

General James Gavin optimistically called the 82d Airborne's initial operations in the Sicily invasion a "SAFU"—a self-adjusting fuckup. Ridgway wholeheartedly endorsed his description. General Maxwell D. Taylor, the 82d's artillery commander, referred to the parachute operations as "ill-starred," though they accomplish their mission of absorbing part of the enemy counterattack against the Sicily beaches.[1]

The difficulties of the Sicily operation raised considerable doubts about the efficacy of large-scale airborne operations in the minds of Generals McNair and Eisenhower, among others. Despite the high casualties and the demonstrated inadequacy of the technology, the Allies continued to wage airborne warfare. Ridgway and Gavin contended that the valor of their troops overcame the technological problems and achieved their objectives—albeit with high casualties.

Training problems encountered back in the United States, shortages of airplanes and pilots, and interallied politics complicated invasion planning for Operation HUSKY.[2] Ridgway pressed from the outset for the employment of his full division, though uncertain about the ability of his troops and troop carriers to conduct night operations. Stung by the superior attitude of the British, who doubted the combat readiness of U.S. troops, Ridgway insisted on the ability of his men to fight. He wanted to prove them in combat. Seventh Army commander George S. Patton shared these views. Patton supported Ridgway's efforts to hold onto enough air transport for the whole 82d, which the grasping Major General F. A. M. Browning, the senior British airborne officer, tried to spirit away. Ridgway's tiff with Browning earned him a stiff chewing out by Eisenhower's dyspeptic chief of staff, Major General Walter Bedell Smith, especially after Ridgway refused, with Patton's blessing, to give the British officer copies of his plans. It may be that only General Patton's support (and Smith's friendship) kept Ridgway in North Africa.[3]

The main plan for the invasion of Sicily called for amphibious landings by General Bernard Montgomery's Eighth Army near Syracuse on the southeast coast and General Patton's Seventh Army near Gela on the south coast to Montgomery's left. The armies would then launch a two-pronged drive on Messina. The plan was largely Montgomery's, and, as was his wont, designed cautiously to ensure maximum concentration of Allied forces. Montgomery also believed his plan would also get him to Messina first, so he could reap the public relations rewards of conquest.[4]

The 82d Airborne planned to land the 505th Parachute Infantry Regimental Combat Team, commanded by Colonel James M. Gavin. Gavin's men would land on high ground in the area northeast of Gela and try to protect the amphibious landing on the Gela beaches from counterattack by Axis forces. The paratroopers would also disrupt enemy communications and movement of their reserves during the night. After these missions were accomplished, the 82d was to join up with the 1st Division as soon as possible and assist that division in capturing a nearby airfield. A second airborne regiment, Colonel Reuben Tucker's 504th, planned to follow on D-day+1. General Ridgway would land by sea on the beaches with the 1st Division shortly after the invasion began, though some of his staff would jump in a third lift on D-day+1.[5]

As the day for the operation approached, General Eisenhower, deep in a subterranean bunker in Malta, weighed the effects of the unseasonable gale force winds on the invasion. As in the more famous D-day operation, he made a last minute decision to go ahead, though Eisenhower considered the air drop a relatively minor part of the operation.[6] Indeed, one must wonder at the quality of Eisenhower's information, as he wrote Marshall on July 10 that the airborne landings had proceeded "fairly satisfactorily."[7]

General Ridgway was far from satisfied, as he landed on the beach on D-day morning. Major General Terry De la Mesa Allen told Ridgway that his men had had no contact with the paratroopers. Actually, the 82d had been scattered by the high winds for sixty miles over central and southern Sicily. Accompanied only by his aide, Don Faith, and a bodyguard, Ridgway set out on "as lonely a walk" as he ever hoped to take forward from the beachhead in search of his troopers. As the three walked down a road, a Messerschmidt buzzed the pair but did not fire at them. Then a vehicle approached from far down the road. The general and his small party ducked into the cactus. Soon it became apparent that it was U.S. jeep carrying none other than Ridgway's old friend Brigadier General Theodore Roosevelt Jr., the assistant division commander of the 1st Division, out far ahead of his own patrols. He had not seen any paratroopers either. Ridgway and Faith forged on until they found Captain Willard Follmer, who had broken his ankle in the jump. Soon after, Ridgway found other small groups of his men, from company I of the 505th. He learned that company A of the 1st Battalion was in contact with the 16th Regiment of the 1st Division. Then Ridgway returned to the 1st Division command post to report the presence of elements of the 82d and make contact with the 504th Regiment before it took off from Tunisia.[8]

Reassembling the division would be a long and painful process. As late as 7:55 P.M. on the 12th, Ridgway had to report to the Seventh Army that "no formed element of Combat Team 505 [is] under my control. Expect some today based on 1st Division Reports. Elements of Combat Team 504 dribbling in." Gavin did not reach the division command post until the morning of July 13, confirming the 1200 troops under his command. By midnight on July 14, the division still had only 3790 men of 5733 that it was supposed to have under its control. Most of the rest were prisoners or casualties.[9]

Even with reduced numbers, the 505th Regimental Combat Team accomplished its tasks. The 1st battalion under Colonel Arthur P. Gorham was able to marshal about 200 soldiers. The other 400 were dropped fifty miles away. With that fraction of his strength, Gorham fought off part of the Hermann Goering Division and went on to hold his objective—the important road junction and the high ground at Piano Lupo. Lieutenant Colonel's Mark J. Alexander's 2d Battalion landed together, but twenty-five miles from its designated drop zone. The battalion destroyed pillboxes and captured the town of Santa Croce Cammarina.[10]

Gavin, with a small band of staffers, also landed about twenty-five miles from his drop zone. He and his staff traveled to the northwest. By the next day he had found about 250 men from Colonel Edward C. Krause's 3d Battalion and ordered them to advance to their preassigned objectives. Gavin and his men moved toward the sound of the fighting and on the morning of the 11th occupied the high ground at Biazza Ridge on the highway from Vittoria to Gela. As an armored column from the Hermann Goering Division moved down the road. Gavin fought off several attacks from this superior German force—with the help of newly arrived parachute artillery, a battalion from the 45th Infantry Division, and naval gunfire. He then counterattacked, forcing the Germans to flee from the battlefield. Both Gorham, who was killed in action, and Gavin received Distinguished Service Crosses for their actions.[11]

Combat Team 504, commanded by Colonel Reuben Tucker, was supposed to have had a relatively routine air landing at the Allied-held Farello

Aerodrome on the morning of D-day+1. Instead, the drop would turn into one of the worst friendly fire disasters of the war. Of 144 planes, 23 failed to return. Most were destroyed by fire from Allied ships and ground batteries, though there is evidence that some were destroyed by hostile fire.[12]

Though Ridgway had repeatedly requested clearance for the planes from Allied and naval headquarters, one machine gunner opened fire when the planes passed overhead. A chain reaction of fire from both ship and shore ensued. Naval authorities, little interested in the airborne action, had at first represented through Browning that they could control only fire from men-of-war and not from the miscellaneous merchant vessels and small craft. Only after the intervention of General Patton, did they agree to guarantee the convoy's safety—but only if it followed a designated route. Ground forces also failed to control their fire.[13]

In addition to these coordination problems, Ridgway had not anticipated the possibility that friendly fire would so disperse the transport planes that they would be forced out of the designated safe course and that the parachutists would be dispersed over the zones of actions of three infantry divisions whose sign and countersign might be changed without notice to the 82d. Some troopers were shot as they landed because they did not have the proper code answer when challenged. More stunningly, Ridgway reported, they had not realized that the formation might coincide with enemy air attacks on shipping. The Luftwaffe had attacked the Anglo-American naval forces at 10:10 P.M.—just one-half hour before the overflight of the unlucky troop carrier wing, which contributed to the trigger happiness of naval and shore gunners.[14]

After the friendly fire incident, Eisenhower sent Patton, Air Chief Marshal Sir Arthur W. Tedder, and General Carl A. Spaatz an angry memo ordering an investigation. Patton complained about Eisenhower's tone: "It is most upsetting to get only piddling criticism when one has done a good job," he wrote in his diary the next day. Patton was outraged at Eisenhower's memo, believing that his headquarters had taken "every possible precaution," and feared that Eisenhower was "looking for an excuse to relieve me." He declined to court-martial anyone for the disaster, exclaiming that "if they want a goat, I am it." The cause, in his estimate, was simple: "Men who have been bombed all day get itchy fingers."[15]

A few days later, Eisenhower seems to have come to the conclusion that the problem was systemic, informing General Marshall a few days later that he believed the drop had gone awry despite "a very carefully coordinated plan." Eisenhower wrote the chief of staff that "even in the daytime we have great trouble in preventing our own naval and land forces from firing on friendly planes." "This seems particularly odd," he continued, "where we have such great air superiority that the presumption is that any plane flying on a straight and level course is friendly," and he called for additional training to make troops more aware of the danger of friendly fire.[16]

Ridgway also saw the problems as systemic and not emanating from his

division or the Air Corps. He tended to blame higher command and especially the navy for not understanding the critical nature of fire control.
Finger-pointing or disciplinary action was of doubtful value, the general
believed, because it would only increase interservice acrimony without solv-
ing the problem.[17]

The 82d Airborne had achieved many of its objectives, but only at great
cost. The head of Army Ground Forces, General Leslie J. McNair, was
skeptical about elite units from the beginning—he thought they drained off
too many of the best men from ordinary units. He and General Eisenhower
questioned the continued existence of the airborne division. Eisenhower had
already concluded that "when we land airborne troops in hostile territory
we should *not* do so in successive waves, but should do so all at once in order
to maintain the advantage of surprise." Despite Ridgway's urgings to the
contrary, Eisenhower wrote Marshall, "I do not believe in the airborne *division*" (emphasis original). He thought that airborne troops should be limited to units that were the size of a regimental combat team because of
limited air transport and the difficulty of gaining control over a whole division once it was dropped.[18]

Ridgway, quite naturally, was more enthusiastic about the prospects for
the airborne division, whose primary role, he believed, should be "to pursue
and exploit where high stakes justify great hazards." He believed that the
division, once landed, should fight on as light infantry; he wanted to keep
the division (and himself) in the war in Sicily. Indeed, throughout the war
the airborne troops would be more effective as elite light infantry than in
parachute drops. Nor was Ridgway the only airborne proponent. Patton had
been "well pleased" with the 82d, which, in part because of its dispersion,
had interfered with German communications and still obtained many of its
objectives. The division needed better training for night operations, better
navigation techniques for its transport planes, more planes so that the entire
division could be dropped at once, and better antitank weapons.[19]

Ridgway proved the 82d's usefulness as light infantry in a six-day advance
west against nominal opposition toward the Sicilian cities of Trapani and
Palermo. The infantry moved so fast that it astounded even General Patton.
Though there had been heavy fighting in other parts of Sicily, for the 82d
it had been "more like a maneuver than a shooting war." At Trapani, Ridgway had been "brave under fire to the point of being exhibitionistic," according to Lieutenant Colonel Harrison B. Harden Jr., an admittedly
unfriendly artilleryman whom Ridgway relieved of command after the battle.[20]

A friendlier source, James Gavin, told a story years later about Ridgway's
very personal approach to battle with the Germans:

> It was always Ridgway versus the Wehrmacht in my mind. He'd
> come up to the front and go around the road bend and stand and
> urinate in the middle of the road. I'd say, 'Matt, get the hell out

of there, you'll get shot.' No, he was defiant. Even with his penis
he was defiant.[21]

The Sicily operations showed that American paratroops still had a long
way to go before their successful tactical employment. Planners at higher
headquarters still lacked clear notions of what a proper mission for the airborne troops would be, suggesting a plethora of possible missions for the
division in the forthcoming invasion of Italy.[22]

The most famous of these missions was known as "the Rome job," or
Operation Giant II, the proposed airdrop on Rome that coincided with the
surrender of Marshal Pietro Badoglio's government. This operation derived
from Eisenhower's attempts to enter Italy as he had entered North Africa:
with as little opposition as possible from the locals. Eisenhower had been
negotiating with Badoglio, a former Fascist, who had overthrown dictator
Benito Mussolini and sent representatives to Sicily and Lisbon for secret
negotiations with the Allies. Badoglio's government requested an Allied drop
on Rome to protect the government from the Germans. The unit selected
for this mission was the 82d Airborne. Eisenhower's skepticism about the
airborne division contrasted with his possible overestimate of its capabilities
for the very chancy Rome mission.[23]

When Ridgway heard about the plans for the Rome job, he hit the roof.
The division commander scarcely credited Italian claims that they would be
able to help secure the division once it arrived. He doubted that his men
could be resupplied once dropped. In meetings with the Italian representatives, he could see their fear of the Germans, which made him wonder
whether they would deliver on their promises to supply the 82d if it dropped
on Rome. He also wondered about the ability of his light infantry division
to hold on against six German divisions rumored to be near Rome. The 82d,
a unit without heavy artillery or strong antitank capabilities, would have to
resist without any air support, as they would be beyond the range of Allied
fighters. Ridgway protested, first to his old friend Walter Bedell Smith, who
was Eisenhower's chief of staff. Smith was sympathetic enough to arrange a
meeting with General Sir Harold R. L. G. Alexander, the Allied supreme
commander for the Mediterranean Theater. Alexander brushed Ridgway off.
Consequently, Ridgway began the intensive preparations for an operation
that he believed might squander his division for no perceptible military advantage. He revived a suggestion to send Maxwell Taylor secretly into Rome
to talk to Marshal Badoglio personally and assess the situation, but Alexander
initially rejected the plan as too dangerous. Ridgway's concept of courage
was to calmly prepare for calculated risks; he did not believe in asking men
to take risks that were incalculable. He took one more calculated risk with
his career by returning to his old friend Smith to persuade him to support
the idea of the Taylor trip. Smith agreed, and changed Alexander and Eisenhower's mind.[24]

Eisenhower later wrote that Taylor's trip, accompanied by Colonel William T. Gardner, a former governor of Maine, who was the intelligence officer for the 51st troop carrier wing, was one of the bravest acts of the war. Taylor quickly sent back the coded message "situation innocuous," which meant that he believed the Italians did not have the strength or resolve to support the airdrop. General Alfred M. Gruenther personally carried Eisenhower's subsequent message canceling the operation to Ridgway, who had already loaded his division on airplanes for takeoff. Some historians have charged that picking Taylor, a "Ridgway man," to assess the situation in Italy predetermined the outcome of the mission. Smith supposedly later regretted the choice of Taylor. Both Smith and Badoglio's representative, General Giuseppe Castellano, continued to believe after the war that the Rome job could have succeeded.[25]

Ridgway's campaign against the "Rome job" distinguished him both as a soldier and as a bureaucratic infighter. It also tells us something about his fervent belief in his own professional and technical judgment and about the lengths to which he was prepared to go when he saw a serious error at higher levels, reading his own judgment as more dispassionate, neutral, and scientifically accurate than that of the generals with greater political responsibilities who had been negotiating with Badoglio. Ridgway, while willing to accept high casualties for victory, rejected the concept that the model soldier should accept suicidal orders without protest, which had been prevalent in the British and French armies in World War I. He deserves credit for his refusal to perpetuate the traditions that allowed slaughters such as the Nivelle offensive or the battle of the Somme—thoughtless sacrifices of men for minor gain—which he characterized in his memoirs as "the peak of stupidity in military operations." Ridgway strongly believed in aggressive offensive action as the basis of a winning strategy. "I don't want to give the impression," he later wrote, "that I, as a senior U.S. Army commander, was thinking solely in terms of saving the lives of my men," but aggressiveness had to be limited by a commitment to "the dignity which attaches to the individual," which Ridgway believed was "the basis of Western Civilization." The synthesis Ridgway reached was that commanders should sacrifice lives only when there is a reasonable possibility of significant military success. More often than not he would disapprove of operations, such as the Rome operations, that would confer primarily political rather than military advantages.[26]

It is not clear, however, that his opposition to the Rome job was entirely disinterested. It is true that he risked his career in challenging the job, but his career was at risk anyway. Even if he survived, what would have been the future for airborne generals if the 82d had been lost? If generals are risk managers, as Ridgway's formulations would seem to imply, then he was performing his job brilliantly. Soon, circumstances would hand him the opportunity to demonstrate conclusively the worth of an airborne division for rapid reinforcement during a battle—a role somewhat different from that origi-nally planned, the classic drop behind enemy lines to seize objectives there. Meanwhile, the keyed-up troopers, having de-planed at the last minute, faced continuing debate over their employment. They did not have to wait long.

The Germans launched a devastating counterattack against the Allied beachhead at Salerno on September 12 and 13, nearly splitting the U.S. forces from the British. General Alexander placed the 82d under Fifth Army General Mark Clark's command as a reserve force. Clark then wrote Ridg-way, entrusting the message to an Air Corps pilot, Jacob Hamilton, who flew to Sicily about an hour after Ridgway had taken off to go see Clark on the battlefield. Ridgway's staff realized the importance of the message and re-called Ridgway's plane. They did not know that in the letter Clark asked Ridgway to provide immediate reinforcements to the beachhead that night along with a famous plan to mark the drop zone with cans of gasoline in the shape of a huge letter T. Ridgway sent Hamilton back with the message "can do"—a message delivered only after German aircraft fire wounded Hamilton as he was jumping out of a jeep.[27]

The division staff completed all plans and loaded the troops within eight hours of the initial message. On that first night, the 504th Parachute Infantry Regiment landed on the battlefield in what was one of the most successful American airborne operations in World War II. The regimental com-mander, Colonel Reuben H.Tucker III, assembled most of his troops within an hour and reported to a surprised General Clark that his men were ready for battle. Clark sent them on a tough drive inland toward Altavilla, for which Tucker was awarded a Distinguished Service Cross. The advance, as the division history notes, was particularly difficult because the area had been a firing range for a German artillery school, so virtually every target was registered.[28]

Buoyed by this success, Clark redirected the 505th Parachute Infantry Regiment, scheduled to drop the next night from Capua (behind the German lines) to Paestum on the coast, where it could be used to reinforce the beachhead. In addition to the flaming Ts, the new Eureka-Rebecca radar sets significantly aided these operations, allowing them to home in on DZs. According to the after-action report, Paestum was the 505th's "most suc-cessful jump" to that time, "largely due to the radar."[29]

The same night the 505th dropped into Paestum, the 509th Airborne battalion demonstrated that the art of dropping soldiers at night behind enemy lines had not yet been perfected. For unknown reasons, General Clark let stand the plan to drop the 509th on the town of Avellino. Une-quipped with the new radars, and landing in territory unmarked by friendly forces, the regiment scattered over a wide territory, its power dissipated. Many were killed or taken prisoner, though fragments of the division were able to disrupt German communications. By September 18, Ridgway had landed elements of the division staff and set up a forward command post at

Paestum. The division was fragmented at this point, its elements plugged into various gaps in the front. Clark, worried that General Ernest J. "Mike" Dawley was faltering as corps commander, took the unprecedented step of appointing Ridgway as the temporary assistant corps commander. On September 17, at Clark's behest (seconded by Ridgway's private recommendation to Clark), General Eisenhower relieved Dawley and busted him back to colonel, after observing him at a briefing, on the grounds that "he can not repeat nor exercise high battle command effectively when the going is rough." Gavin, who had worked closely with Dawley during the invasion of Italy, later wrote that he thought the general had done "all a man could do under the circumstances."[30]

By all accounts, Ridgway handled the corps level job so well that Clark requested that he be given the corps command. Instead, however, the job went to the more senior John P. Lucas.[31]

On September 18, the Germans, having taken a significant toll of the invading force, began to withdraw, and the Allied forces consolidated their position at Salerno, with more strength arriving daily by sea. The 82d was reunited and placed in reserve for a couple of days and on September 27th joined several other units under Ridgway's command in a breakout maneuver aimed at Naples. After hard fighting, the 3d Battalion of the 505th reached the city on October 1. The 82d had proved its worth once again as an elite unit of light infantry. Once the 82d got into the valley, the biggest obstacle to its progress were the throngs of villagers on the outskirts shouting and celebrating the Americans' arrival.[32]

Just as the 505th was set to enter the city, General Clark ordered Gavin to organize a triumphal march into Garibaldi Square. Gavin did so, but the order to clear the streets was so effective, it seemed that the place was entirely deserted, as Clark rode through the streets in the turret of a tank. Ridgway rode with him, with his Springfield rifle in his hands, gazing at the rooftops to pick off any potential snipers. Later, it turned out the crowds were waiting for the generals at the Piazza del Plebescito, where conquerors had traditionally been received.[33]

As Clark and Ridgway neared the center of the city, they heard shooting as Neapolitians settled old scores with one another. Ridgway quickly stopped the shooting. He ordered that any civilian in proximity of a gun would be summarily shot. As the official division history put it, "The city was a scene of ruin, starvation, and general wretchedness." The Germans had done their best to make the city a burden rather than an asset to its new landlords, systematically destroying the water, gas, and electrical systems and the rail system. The Germans booby-trapped many buildings, with the bombs set to go off forty-eight to seventy-two hours after the Germans had quit the town. The quarters of an engineer battalion blew up, killing and injuring many inside. German air action continued, and Ridgway had a close call out on his balcony when a blast from a German bomb wrecked his room but left him untouched. After a few days, however, businesses began to open up again, and the troops settled down to more or less pleasant occupation duty. As in Sicily, the division established its own official brothels. Eventually inflation hit, and soldiers were sometimes felled by the poisonous "ten-minute cognac," medicinal alcohol laced with sugar, water, and a few drops of real cognac for color. Nonetheless, generally Ridgway was pleased with his division's behavior (always a concern with the rowdy paratroopers). During the occupation, only two members of the division were court-martialed.[34]

The 82d's success began to tempt planners to ask it to do the impossible. For example, Ridgway had to combat a plan to send the 82d against one of the toughest of the fortified positions across the Volturno—a plan that failed to explain how the lightly armed 82d could take on an assignment that would be a challenge for a fully armored division. Ridgway managed to get the plan killed instead of his men. The 504th Regimental Combat Team did advance on October 27, 1943, through a gap between Clark's Fifth Army and Mongomery's Eighth Army in an attack across the Volturno that took it twenty-two miles in front of both armies. Ironically, its success led to the temporary breakup of the division. General Clark refused to release the 504th from the line to accompany the rest of the 82d to the United Kingdom for preparation for the Normandy invasion. Unwilling to lose one of the best units in the Army, Ridgway went outside channels and protested directly to General Marshall, who eventually ordered the 504th back to England to join the rest of the division. The regiment arrived back in England just a month before the invasion and had sustained so many casualties, particularly at Anzio, that it could not be refitted and retrained in time to participate in the cross-channel airdrop.[35]

The 82d's participation in the Italian campaign began to establish the unit's reputation for bravery. By far, the most effective use of airborne troops at this point proved to be as a highly mobile theater reserve. As planning for the invasion of Normandy commenced, there was little evidence that vertical envelopment by an airborne division was practical or effective.

NOTES

1. Ridgway, *Soldier*, 70; Taylor, *Swords and Ploughshares*, 50; Omar N. Bradley, *A Soldier's Story* (New York: Henry Holt, 1951), 126–127.

2. CBRP, 77–78.

3. Ridgway Diary, May 19–21, 1943, Ridgway MSS, Box 5a, Historical Record; Ridgway, *Soldier*, 68; CBRP, 74. Smith had previously assured Ridgway that Browning had been appointed purely as a staff advisor, not as his superior (Ridgway Diary, April 7–8, 1943, Ridgway MSS, Box 5a, Historical Record.

4. Bradley, *Soldier's Story*, 126.

5. CBRP, 77; Ridgway, *Soldier*, 68; Ketterson, 5–6.

6. Dwight D. Eisenhower, *Crusade in Europe* (Garden City, N.Y.: Doubleday, 1948), 172.

7. Eisenhower to the Combined Chiefs of Staff, July 10, 1943, DDE Papers, 2: 1249–1250.

8. Ridgway, *Soldier*, 72, 73.

9. Ketterson, 13, 14.

10. Gavin, OTB, 39–40; CBRP, 93.

11. CBRP, 96–98; OTB, 30–38.

12. Memo initialed by Ridgway, August 2, 1943, Ridgway MSS, Box 3, Personal File, January 42–November 43. For details of investigations of the 504th drop, see Ridgway Memo, August 2, 1943, Ridgway MSS, Box 3, Personal File, January 1942–November 1943; Ketterson, "82d Airborne," 7–8; DDE Papers, 2:1259.

13. Bradley, *Soldier's Story*, 132–133; Ridgway, *Soldier*, 73; CBRP, 102–103. On Ridgway's attempts to contact the Navy and antiaircraft units, see Ridgway Diary, Ridgway MSS, Box 5a. See also Eaton to U.S. Naval Forces, Northwest African waters, July 6, 1943; Chief of Staff to all corps and division commanders, July 16, 1943, Ridgway MSS, Box 3, PF.

14. Ridgway, *Soldier*, 69–70.

15. Eisenhower to Patton, July 12, 1943, DDE Papers, 2:1255–1256; Martin Blumenson, ed., *The Patton Papers, 1940–1945* (Boston: Houghton Mifflin, 1972–74), 2: 283.

16. Eisenhower to Marshall, July 17, 1943, DDE Papers, 2:1259.

17. Ridgway Memo, August 2, 1943, Ridgway MSS, Box 3, Personal File, January 1942–November 1943.

18. Eisenhower to Marshall, September 20, 1943, DDE Papers, 3:1440.

19. Ridgway to Eisenhower, July 26, 1943, Ridgway MSS, Box 3, Personal File, January 1942–November 1943; Gavin, OTB, 52–54; Ridgway, *Soldier*, 70, 71.

20. Ridgway, *Soldier*, 76; CBRP, 113.

21. James Gavin, interview with Clay Blair, January 4, 1983, 16, Clay Blair Collection, Box 32.

22. Ketterson, "82d Airborne," 42–53; OTB, 55–61; CBRP, 126–131.

23. Gavin, OTB, 58–63; Ridgway, *Soldier* 77–83; Ketterson, "82d Airborne," 49, 50.

24. Ridgway, *Soldier*, 80–82

25. Castellano to Ridgway, November 20, 1955; Ridgway to Castellano, December 20, 1955; Ridgway to Smith, December 5, 1955; Smith to Ridgway, December 15, 1955, Ridgway MSS Box, 5, Castellano Correspondence.

26. Ridgway, *Soldier*, 96–98.

27. Ketterson, "82d Airborne," 54–55; Ridgway, *Soldier*, 85–87; CBRP, 149–150.

28. CBRP, 150–151; Ketterson, "82d Airborne," 79.

29. Ketterson, "82d Airborne," 90; CBRP, 152.

30. Gavin, OTB, 70.

31. CBRP, 157; Eisenhower to Marshall, September 6, 1943, DDE Papers, 3: 1428; Eisenhower to Marshall, September 19, 1943, DDE Papers, 3:1436; Eisenhower to Marshall, September 20, 1943, DDE Papers, 3: 1439–1440; CBRP, 157–162. See also OTB, 71–73.

32. Ketterson, "82d Airborne," 72; Ridgway, *Soldier*, 88.

33. Gavin, OTB, 72, 73.

34. Ridgway, *Soldier*, 90, 91.

35. Ridgway, *Soldier*, 90, 92, 96.

CHAPTER 6

Narrating the 82d from Northern Ireland to Normandy

For conscientious officers like Ridgway, planning and training for the invasion of France were almost as physically demanding as the invasion itself. Some of his problems emanated from Supreme Headquarters, Allied Expeditionary Forces (SHAEF) where the head air planner, Air Chief Marshal Sir Trafford Leigh-Mallory, also gave American airborne officers headaches, predicting that the Germans would shoot down all their troop carriers. Gavin later ascribed Leigh-Mallory's pessimism to disdain for U.S. capabilities, and the air marshal apologized to Eisenhower after the successful drop.[1]

Other difficulties involved the training and discipline of Ridgway's division. When the 82d moved from Northern Ireland to Leicester-Nottingham area between February 14 and March 10, Ridgway had to cope with some serious discipline problems at the new post, which was near towns where the troopers mixed with civilians and soldiers from other units. The Leicester chief of police thanked Ridgway at least once for court-martialing a thief amongst the personnel of the All-American.[2]

Racial conflict exacerbated the paratroopers' disdain for the "straight leg" army. Dating between British women and African American service troops who had been stationed in the area for a long time enraged some soldiers in the 82d. On their first night in town, a black soldier stabbed a paratrooper.

False rumors spread that the paratrooper had been killed. Ridgway, who had anticipated trouble, visited every unit in the area:

> I told them that the troops who were there when we arrived were wearing the same uniform we were wearing, they were there under orders of competent authority. They were performing tasks just as essential to the war as the tasks we were performing. And though this matter of color might be one of the great problems that plagued our people at home, it was not our responsibility to try to settle it three thousand miles from home in the middle of a war.[3]

Ridgway doubled the number of MPs and patrolled the streets of Leicester himself on the first night. This approach to racial tension based on pragmatic military considerations also reflected Ridgway's corporatist ideology. He wanted people to get along and get on with the war effort without wasting time on racial division. Insofar as racism had become an obstacle to military efficiency, he found it objectionable. Ridgway worked to overcome these discipline problems and established good relations with the citizens of the town. In recognition of his efforts, the Leicester English-Speaking Union later presented him with a George III silver salver.[4]

Ridgway got so overworked that he fell ill with malaria (contracted long before in Latin America) and almost missed out on the drop. Nonetheless, on the night of June 5, 1944, Matthew Ridgway found himself loaded up with his own weight in gear on a C-47 (the military version of the famous DC-3) bound for the coast of Calvados in Normandy.

Ridgway had never before made a combat jump. Lying in bed before the action, he meditated on how to calmly submit to his fate, trying to induce the insouciance necessary to a commander in battle. His ideal of the detached commander was Zen-like—one reason he detested the official history that claimed that he had been "alarmed" during the battle.[5]

The planes, flying in a V of Vs, disappeared into a cloud bank. Some of them would scatter, impairing rapid assembly. Ridgway jumped from inside the plane's cargo bay as the green signal light came on. In the struggle to free himself from the cumbersome parachute harnesses, he dropped his pistol. Irritated as he groped around in the grass, he saw something moving and gave the challenge "Flash." Hearing nothing, he relaxed when he realized it was a cow. "I could have kissed her," he wrote, for the presence of a cow in the field meant that it was not mined.[6]

Soon he saw another movement in the shadows. This time the challenge was promptly answered. It turned out to be the same Captain Willard Follmer who had been the first paratrooper Ridgway had met after landing in Sicily. That time Follmer had lain on the ground with a broken ankle. This time he thought he had broken his back. Ridgway told him: "Well, I guess you never hope to see *me* again."[7]

Soon after, Ridgway found ten or eleven officers from his staff and set up headquarters in an apple orchard—appropriate enough, as the department of Calvados where they had landed is famous for its apple brandy. Unlike a typical infantry command post, though, Ridgway's D-day command post had little to command. All the long-range radios had crashed, so Ridgway had no idea whether the invasion was successful—he could not even contact most of his own units, let alone coordinate them. Perhaps the greatest achievement of paratrooper training is the individual initiative of the troopers in finding their units, assembling, and hitting targets of opportunity as they do so, without divisional coordination.[8]

As in Sicily, the troop carriers organized late and with insufficient training in how to carry paratroopers. They had not been sufficiently prepared for flack or for bad weather—and dispersed after hitting a cloud bank. This dispersal would work to the 82d's advantage in some ways—making the landings seem more formidable and numerous to the Germans—and to their obvious disadvantage in reducing their firepower.

Many gliders crashed or ran into the mined anti-airborne poles known as Rommelspargel, or Rommel's asparagus, reducing the division's firepower even further. Others fell into rivers, unexpectedly flooded by the Germans for defensive purposes. These measures deprived the division of much of its antitank artillery, radios, and motor transport. Subsequent glider operations were even more disastrous.[9]

As Ridgway could not perform the traditional functions of a division commander, he traveled by foot on the first day, relaying from his command post to wherever the fighting appeared to be most intense. The 82d's objective was to seize and hold the crossroads town of Ste. Mère Église and two causeways, La Fière and Chef du Pont, and to provide transportation routes for the infantry divisions coming over Utah Beach.[10]

The 2d and 3d battalions of the 505th Parachute Infantry Regiment, a component of the 82d, had fairly cohesive drops, and by 6 A.M. Lieutenant Colonel Edward C. Krause's 2d Battalion had secured the town, though they had no radio to notify their regimental commander, Colonel William E. Ekman. Lieutenant Colonel Benjamin H. Vandervoort, who had broken his leg in the jump, commanded the 3d Battalion from a wheelbarrow. In one of the most intelligent decisions of the action, Ekman ordered Vandervoort back to Ste. Mère, prudently detaching a platoon to protect the northern end of the town at Neuville-sur-Plain. That platoon made a valiant stand and blocked an assault on the town from the north while it was also under attack from the south, making good the defense of the town.[11]

The situation was much more difficult at the Merderet crossings. At La Fière, bad misdrops of the 507th and 508th Parachute Infantry Regiments complicated attempts to take the causeway. Part of the force that should have taken the bridge, a group under the command of the 2/507 commander, Charles Timmes, got pinned down by Germans and could only send a small patrol to Cauquigny, at the western end of the causeway. A group under the leadership of Lieutenant Louis Levy and Lieutenant Joseph Kormylo dug in at Cauquigny. On the other side of the bridge, the 505 forces did not know that Cauquigny was so lightly held; they thought U.S. forces were in control, having seen the orange smoke grenades used for recognition. Eventually, Levy and his little group, which the 505th on the other side failed sufficiently to reinforce, were driven back after fierce combat with German armor.[12]

Near the other side of the bridge, the Germans had set up a command post in an old stone farmhouse. After being initially repulsed by heavy fire, by the afternoon, the U.S. forces renewed their attack and consolidated their hold on Le Manoir. The situation from the Manoir side had seemed under control, and some of the forces that had participated in it went on to other objectives. But the counterattack at Cauquigny had left the troopers with only half a bridge.

By nightfall on D-day, June 6, the 82d was surrounded in a triangular airhead with points at La Fiére, Ste. Mère Église, and Chef du Pont. The division was running low on ammunition, with troopers venturing out into the night to pick up what they could from scattered airdrops. Ridgway was out of communication with the rest of the army. He had no way of knowing that Colonel Edson D. Raff's task force, which was supposed to link up with the 82d on D-day, was just four miles away, though he sent a runner, Lieutenant Colonel's Walter F. Winton, back to the 4th Division to apprise it of the 82d's situation—urgently in need of artillery, antitank guns, and tanks. Winton had to take Benzedrine after the heavy day of fighting to reach Major General Raymond O. Barton's command post. He delivered his message, then collapsed in sleep. Ridgway and Gavin also described how quickly they fell asleep that night, only to be awakened, in a sense, by each other. Gavin was awakened by a messenger from Ridgway's staff, saying that the general wanted to see him. When he reported, Ridgway was furious that Gavin woke him up; he thought a nervous Gavin had come seeking comfort. The misunderstanding cooled relations between the two men.[13]

On the morning of June 7, the Germans assaulted the 82d's positions in Ste. Mère and La Fière. Soon after the first contact with the beach invasion forces, Brigadier General Theodore Roosevelt Jr. visited Ridgway's command post. Roosevelt Jr., Ridgway's old friend from the Philippines, was aide-de-camp of the 4th Division. He had crossed no-man's-land to make contact and, as Ridgway put it, to "offer us all the help, guns and ammunition that we would need." Roosevelt died a few days later and was posthumously awarded the Congressional Medal of Honor. Help arrived around noon with Colonel James A. Van Fleet's 8th Regiment of the 4th Division and the Corps Commander, Major General J. Lawton ("Lightning Joe") Collins. Ridgway immediately had Vandervoort's men counterattack north, forcing a German retreat from the perimeter of Ste. Mère Église. At La Fière, another battalion of the 505 beat off another German attack across the bridge.[14]

D-day+2 would be another day of frustration. A battalion of the 325th Glider Regiment, at 75% strength after a rattling landing, attacked across an underwater ford across the Merderet. The battalion made contact with Timmes and was able to string a telephone line. The battalion, however, was scattered and wound up holing up in Timmes's orchard, failing in its mission to capture the western end of the La Fière bridgehead. They would not reach it until the next day.[15]

By D-day+3, Collins offered to attack across the causeway, but Ridgway would not hear of it and ordered a force under Gavin, augmented by artillery from the U.S. 90th Division, to force the causeway. It was not easy for Gavin to coax the men of the 325th's Third Battalion onto the causeway under heavy German fire. Gavin, who disliked reliefs, had to summarily relieve Charles Carrell, the battalion commander, who, according to Gavin, when told to "Go, Go, Go," replied that he couldn't go, saying, "I'm sick." Carrell denies this story. Ridgway, Gavin, and 507th executive officer Art Maloney forged out onto the crossing themselves. Ridgway even helped clear a burned-out German tank from the road: "I haven't the slightest doubt that if Gavin and I and the battalion commanders had not been there that crossing of the causeway would not have succeeded." He won a Distinguished Service Cross for the action.

The 82d had accomplished its basic missions despite the massive misdrop of much of the division and the catastrophic glider crashes. The 82d had sustained heavy casualties, and airborne doctrine held that they should then be pulled out of the line. Corps Commander Collins, like many commanders to follow, was reluctant to give up the tough veteran troops in his drive to solidify the Allied position in the Cotentin and asked to keep them in his line. In nasty hedgerow to hedgerow fighting, their losses were again heavy. The division continued to attack to the north of Ste. Mère, and then to the east. It took until June 16 to capture the town of St. Saveur-le-Vicomte, just ten miles east of Ste. Mère Église, which helped to seal off the Cotentin Peninsula.[17]

Although Gavin's unwanted visit to Ridgway on the night of June 6 had begun to worsen relations between the two generals, things got even cooler on July 3 when Ridgway agreed to the 82d's transfer to Troy Middleton's VIII Corps to add some experienced troops to his relatively green corps for the breakout of the Cotentin. Some officers, perhaps including Gavin, protested the decision, fearing that further fighting would so decimate the division that it could not be rebuilt. Some said that Ridgway was just trying to please his superiors. One of them, Colonel Edson Raff, commander of the 507th Parachute Infantry Regiment, accused Ridgway of being a "glory seeker" who "didn't give a damn about the men fighting for him." The 82d led the attack on La Haye-du-Puits, and, but for orders from the VIII Corps to wait for other units, might have captured it, though the division lost still more officers. After the fight, none of the original battalion leaders of the 507th, for example, would be left in command. The division was finally relieved on July 11.[18]

The 82d got through the Normandy battles with a reputation unparalleled for toughness and got the "cream" of volunteers from the States. The cost, however, was high—at least a 46% casualty rate, perhaps more. More than 4,000 men were casualties, including 1,142 killed in action, and more than 3,000 wounded or injured in action. Among the worst hit was the senior leadership. The division lost two of its four regimental commanders, and eight of twelve of its original battalion commanders; moreover only one of the twelve remained unwounded. Half of the men who replaced the original battalion commanders were wounded. Ridgway's superiors lavished praise on the division despite—perhaps even as a result of—the high casualties. Ridgway returned to England, where he would resume bureaucratic battles with the British over the future employment of U.S. airborne troops.[19]

The story of the Normandy invasion has been told many times. Of all the battles that Ridgway would fight, of all the positions of high command that he would occupy, he considered the narrative of Normandy to be the most central to his identity—the war story that he chose to begin his 1956 autobiography *Soldier*.[20]

After the battle, Ridgway began shaping a D-day narrative with an alacrity that suggests how crucial he believed it was to his own future and that of the Army. Less than three weeks after the return of his exhausted division to England from Normandy, Ridgway sent a Captain Barnett of the 505th Parachute Infantry Regiment back to the States on temporary public relations duty, as a reward for his valor in the action. The division equipped Barnett with a graphic presentation of the 82d's actions in Normandy. "In years to come," Ridgway wrote, "I believe this will become a saga—an epic of tenacity and purpose—an example of what one small division can accomplish when bound together with the unbreakable cement of mutual confidence, tried and proven in battle."[21]

Ridgway had already chosen the narrative's genre—that of saga or epic—and it is worth a moment's digression to examine what these forms actually were. Ridgway was undoubtedly using the secondary meaning given by the *Oxford English Dictionary* (2d ed.):

> **saga**. A narrative having the (real or supposed) characteristics of the Icelandic sagas; a story of heroic achievement or marvelous

adventure . . . Now freq. in weakened use, a long and complicated (account of a) series of more or less loosely connected events.

Ridgway was probably right to see saga as a synonym for the more inclusive epic, a poem "which celebrates in the form of a continuous narrative the achievements of one or more heroic personages of history or tradition." His continual emphasis on heroism may seem naive to a cynical post-Vietnam audience, but for officers of Ridgway's generation, heroism and self-sacrifice remained what they would call "enduring values." What is remarkable in Ridgway's declaration, however is the *corporate* nature of heroism: the coordinated corporate action of "one small division" that was "bound together with the unbreakable cement of mutual confidence."

Some aspects of the impending narrative were dispersed in letters. After the battle, Ridgway inundated his division's clerical staff with a flood of correspondence. Every family of every dead or missing soldier in the division—over four thousand of them—received a personally signed letter from the commanding general, which, according to Ridgway's former chief of staff, Ralph Eaton, created an unusual "family feeling" in the 82d.[22]

As Ridgway constructed the story, "The 'All-American Division' has accomplished every mission on or ahead of orders; has decisively beaten all enemy forces opposing it; has never lost ground gained; and goes into Army reserve with fighting spirit higher than ever," though it paid a high price in casualties for its achievment: 46 to 54% of its initial combat strength.[23]

After the war, Ridgway battled against more skeptical and critical narratives of the Normandy battles. In the first edition of *Utah Beach to Cherbourg*, one of the first draft official histories to come out, Ridgway was mortally offended by obvious inaccuracies in the narrative, such as the suggestion that he had come in by glider instead of parachute, that he was "alarmed" by the initial situation over the Merderet, that by D-day+1 "its D-Day mission was still unaccomplished," and that "the continued failure of the 82d Division to establish a bridgehead over the MERDERET and the 4th Division's slow progress towards its D-Day objective forced the first modification in the 7th Corps plan." Ridgway considered these choices of words to be unfairly negative, vitally affecting "the reputation of thousands of gallant dead and living members of the 82d Airborne division," and he successfully persuaded higher-ups in the Army brass to change some of the wording of the manuscript before the work was incorporated in the final official history. Eventually, the historical division, after attempting to defend itself, agreed to substitute "concerned" for "alarmed" and "continued difficulties" for "failure," though the Historical Division chief, Major General Harry J. Maloney, refused the other changes that Ridgway had wanted as "impractical" or "improper."[24]

Ridgway was properly mortified at the false reports that he had come in on a glider, instead of by parachute. He jumped in part because it was the best thing for the execution of the operation. Moreover, early in the planning for OVERLORD, Ridgway's British rival, Lieutenant-General F. A. M. "Boy" Browning, who hoped to get command of all Allied airborne forces, had virtually accused Ridgway of cowardice for taking a boat into Sicily instead of jumping himself. Gavin stoutly defended his boss, but one cannot but think that Ridgway's choice to jump into Normandy was motivated by a desire to give Browning the lie. Throughout the planning, Browning continued his machinations to break up the American divisions into battalions under British control. General Bradley, with backing from Generals Marshall and Arnold, countered Browning's power play and insisted on committing the American airborne on a divisional scale in Normandy.[25] After Normandy, the paratroopers had become the most prestigious and sought-after troops in the history of the Army. Substantial publicity at home enhanced their reputation. Generals Marshall and Arnold also pressed for large-scale use of paratroops. Eisenhower, with some prompting from Ridgway and Gavin, had finally decided on a larger form of airborne organization: The First Allied Airborne Army (FAAA), to be commanded by an American airman, General Lewis Brereton. Eisenhower's choice of a commander may have reflected his skepticism about large-scale airborne operations. Eisenhower, displeased with Brereton's performance as head of the 9th Air Force, wanted to kick the Air Force general upstairs. Sharing the peculiar dogmas of World War II–era airmen, Brereton had tended to concentrate more on strategic bombing, his first love, rather than on such mundane tasks as troop carriers or close air support for ground forces. Eisenhower hoped the new command would force Brereton to focus his energies on the problems of airborne troop carriers. Creation of the new airborne army also deflated Browning's ambitions—he would only be deputy FAAA commander under Brereton, though keeping control of British airborne forces in a corps. Ridgway would be elevated to commanding all the U.S. airborne divisions in the theater, as head of the XVIII Airborne Corps.[26]

Despite the opportunities offered by his new job, Ridgway hated giving up the 82d. Max Taylor, a frequent Ridgway critic, thought that Ridgway never really cut his emotional cord to the division. He was bound to over-supervise its commander. Taylor said he "used to thank god that I didn't get the 82d . . . I'd have been fired." Gavin took division control on August 10 and busied himself with setting up a new set of leaders for the division and integrating replacement troops.[27]

While Gavin rebuilt his division and Ridgway built a corps staff, German resistance in France was collapsing in front of General Bradley's breakout at St. Lô in July and the defeat of a Hitler-ordered counterattack at Mortain. Indeed some planned airborne operations were canceled because General Patton overran the drop zones before the airborne troops could be deployed. While the Allied armies drove across France, there was a split between Montgomery and Bradley over strategy. Bradley favored continuation of Eisenhower's strategy of advance upon a broad front into the Rhine and into Germany. Montgomery wanted a quick "stab at Berlin" by all four armies—concentrated, of course, under his command.[28]

Brereton proposed a drop called LINNET II on Aachen, to allow General Courtney Hodges's First Army to punch into Cologne. This also might allow a more rapid advance by Patton toward the Saar. An infuriated Montgomery denounced the plan, which advanced the U.S. armies instead of his own. Browning, who seems always to have maintained a nationalistic outlook rather than an Allied one, began to sabotage the plan from within FAAA, claiming that his "division commanders" would protest the mission violently. Ridgway bluntly told Brereton that this was nonsense, that his division commanders would "express an opinion in the formative stages, but once a decision had been made they would do 'a hundred per cent job of it.'" As a result of this conversation, Brereton relieved Browning, and Browning resigned, creating a politically dangerous situation because of Browning's direct relationship with Churchill. Eisenhower, fearing a split in the high command, canceled LINNET II but told Montgomery for the nonce that he would give more resources to Hodges and Patton. Brereton and Browning made up their differences; and after Browning withdrew his resignation, he was named to command what was then supposed to be a small Anglo-Polish drop to capture a bridge in Arnhem, The Netherlands, on September 7.[29]

By September 4, an overconfident Montgomery had blundered badly. He took the port of Antwerp, which would have relieved the supply problem, but failed either to dash to the Rhine at Arnhem before the Germans could improvise a defense or to make Antwerp a usable port by clearing the islands in the Scheldt estuary of German gunners. To the east, the retreating German forces, reorganized under Field Marshal Walter Model, began to slow the Allied advance. Montgomery realized that a two-division airborne assault on Arnhem would be insufficient. Over strong protests from Bradley, Montgomery persuaded Eisenhower to expand the jump to five divisions, the operation that became known as "Operation MARKET-GARDEN," dramatized in the book and movie *A Bridge Too Far*. The famous flaw in the plan was that it required Lieutenant General Sir Brian Horrocks's tank corps to advance sixty-four miles to Arnhem within two days to relieve the British 1st Airborne Division in Arnhem. Horrocks would have to cross numerous waterways on a narrow causeway. The causeway and the bridges would be taken by a "carpet" of airborne troops from the 101st Airborne and the 82d. Eisenhower assented largely for political reasons. He had been under pressure from Marshall and Arnold to make large-scale use of airborne troops and from London to do something about the V-2 launching sites in the area. The V-2s were one of Montgomery's primary selling points for the "Market Garden" plan.[30]

Ridgway, Gavin, and Taylor disliked both the plan and Browning. This disquiet was not limited to the Americans. Experienced British airborne officers were appalled at both the plan and Browning's staff, which, one officer wrote, "came straight from soft living in comfortable houses in England and had never done a single exercise." The Americans did get some modification of the plan. Montgomery and Brereton also agreed to a more compact drop. Ridgway, the left-out corps commander, was a "disappointed" man, who later described his role as "minor and passive." His 82d was in the biggest drop in history, and all he could do was to watch it as a spectator from a B-17 bomber. It appeared to be a textbook drop, and that night he went back to his bed in London. The next morning, fog kept Ridgway (as well as Allied air cover for the MARKET-GARDEN forces) grounded. It was not until September 19 that he was able to fly with Brereton to Antwerp, after Ridgway's pilot found a hole in the fog. The two generals then jeeped to Eindhoven.[31]

When they got to Eindhoven, it was jammed full of British motor traffic, a sitting duck for what was left of the Luftwaffe. Ridgway saw a single airplane overhead, which dropped two flares, and said to Brereton, "Lewis, I don't like the looks of this. Let's get the hell out of here." They jumped into the jeeps and went two blocks before "the whole world exploded." Ridgway barely disguised his disdain for "Lewis in his nice uniform, scrambling for the pistol he had dropped" as both generals hit the ground. In the confusion, they got separated and Brereton had to find his way back to England on his own.[32]

Finding himself blocked on every road after the air attack, Ridgway went to sleep. The next morning he and his aide, driver, and bodyguard started off again. They came upon advance elements of British armor, whose rapid forward movement was crucial to the relief of the beleaguered airborne. The armored column was stalled, allegedly because of enemy fire on the road ahead. Ridgway, already in pain because his trick back had gone out when he hit the dirt in the air attack, waited forty minutes and saw no attempt to clear the road. As he had no command status in the operation, he couldn't order the soldiers to do it. So he and his companions walked down the road for a mile and a half without a shot being fired at them and reached Taylor's and later Gavin's command post. The British column could have done the same thing and provided badly needed assistance. Their immobility further frustrated the powerless American general.[33]

When Ridgway showed up at Gavin's command post, Gavin was fighting on three fronts. He was much too busy to brief Ridgway, abruptly said hello, and handed him over to Walter Winton for a briefing. Ridgway, already in a bad mood from constant back pain and the appointment of Browning to command, later wrote Gavin and demanded an immediate explanation for the alleged discourtesy. Gavin refused to apologize. Instead, he wrote a letter explaining the military situation at the time and stating that he had believed he could rely on his previous friendly understanding with Ridgway. He also offered to resign. Ridgway decided to treat this as a complete apology. Later, he wrote that, under the circumstances, Gavin's behavior was understandable.[34]

MARKET-GARDEN was in the end a dismal failure that sacrificed the entire British 1st Airborne Division, despite the successes of the American paratroops. Ridgway, and other American officers, attributed this failure to the "sluggishness" of the British advance (though American armored divisions might not have moved any faster under the circumstances), to the questionable assumption that German resistance would be minimal, and finally to the plan itself, which landed the British 1st Airborne Division too far from its objective, the Arnhem bridge, without the realistic possibility of relief from heavier ground-based units.[35]

Russell Weigley, in a careful study of the battle, has argued that Montgomery has been too much abused for MARKET-GARDEN. The plan, in his opinion, was audacious; Montgomery lost the battle owing to failures in "tactical execution." If Brereton, for example, had allowed two drops a day instead of one, and if the 1st Airborne had been dropped right at the bridge and had established the bridgehead immediately, it might have been able to hold. In the end, Weigley holds Browning responsible, arguing that the more experienced Ridgway might have met with more success.[36]

NOTES

1. Ridgway, *Soldier*, 12; James M. Gavin, interviewed by Lieutenant Colonel Donald G. Andrews and Lieutenant Colonel Charles H. Ferguson, Senior Officers Debriefing Program, U.S. Army Military History Institute, Carlisle Barracks, Pa., May 29, 1975, Interview 2 (hereafter Gavin-Andrews Interview), 3.

2. Chief Constable Cole to Ridgway, May 6, 1944, Personal File, Ridgway MSS, Box 3.

3. Ridgway, *Soldier*, 100.

4. Leicester Branch English-Speaking Union Report for 1943–44, Personal File, Ridgway MSS, Box 3; Personal File; CBRP, 202.

5. Ridgway, *Soldier*, 3.

6. Ibid., 6.

7. Ibid.

8. Ibid., 7.

9. CBRP, 234–235.

10. Ridgway, *Soldier*, 10.

11. Ibid., 7–9, 82d Airborne Division "Operation Neptune," Ridgway MSS, Box 5; S. L. A. Marshall, *Night Drop: The American Airborne Invasion of Normandy* (Boston: Little, Brown, 1962), 22–39; CBRP, 243–244.

12. Booth and Spencer, 184–185; CBRP, 246–251; Marshall, *Night Drop*, 63–72.

13. Ridgway, *Soldier*, 10–11; Gavin, OTB, 111; T. Michael Booth and Duncan Spencer, *Paratrooper: The Life of James M. Gavin* (New York: Simon & Schuster, 1994), 187; CBRP, 257–258.

14. CBRP, 259–260; Ridgway, *Soldier*, 11.

15. 82d Airborne Division After-Action Report "Operation Neptune," Ridgway MSS, Box 5.

16. CBRP, 270, 273–276; OTB, 116.

17. CBRP, 286–287; After-Action Report, 12–18.

18. CBRP, 291–294; Booth and Spencer, *Paratrooper*, 201; Ridgway, *Soldier*, 15.

19. JB, 2:1:54; CBRP, 295; After-Action Report, 29–30, annex no.1D.

20. Ridgway, *Soldier*, 2.

21. Ridgway to General Thomas H. Handy, July 19, 1944, Personal File, Ridgway MSS, Box 3.

22. Quoted in CBRP, 296.

23. Ridgway, "Normandy Operations, 82d Airborne Division," July 10, 1944, Personal File, Ridgway MSS Box 3.

24. Ridgway to Chief of Historical Division, November 12, 1948; Maloney to Ridgway November 18, 1948; Ridgway to Haislip, December 2, 1948; Collins to Ridgway, December 4, 1948; Maloney to Ridgway, n.d. (after November 1948); Personal File, Ridgway MSS, Box 3.

25. Booth and Spencer, *Paratrooper*, 151.

26. Ridgway, *Soldier*, 107; Weigley, *Eisenhower's Lieutenants* (Bloomington: Indiana University Press, 1981), 288–289; CBRP, 298–301; James Gavin, interview with Clay Blair, January 4, 1983, 6, Clay Blair Collection, Box 32.

27. Taylor quoted in CBRP, 305.

28. For more on this strategic controversy, see Russell Weigley, *Eisenhower's Lieutenants* (Bloomington: Indiana University Press, 1984) and Forrest Pogue, *The Supreme Command* (Washington, D.C.: Government Printing Office, 1954).

29. CBRP, 320–326; Lewis H. Brereton, *The Brereton Diaries* (New York: Morrow, 1946), 338.

30. Weigley, *Eisenhower's Lieutenants*, 291–293.

31. Ridgway, *Soldier*, 108; CBRP, 331–336; British officer quoted in Martin Middlebrook, *Arnhem 1944: The Airborne Battle 17–26 September* (London: Penguin, 1994), 12. Ridgway to Taylor and Gavin, October 2, 1944. Ridgway expressed his "profound regret" at "having exercised no influence on the operation" (Ridgway to Marshall, October 5, 1944, both in Personal File, folder D, August–December, 1944, Ridgway MSS, Box 5a.

32. Ridgway, *Soldier*, 109–110; CBRP, 339.

33. Ridgway, *Soldier*, 110–111.

34. Booth and Spencer, *Paratrooper*, 232, 240–241; Ridgway quoted in CBRP, 340–341.

35. Ridgway, *Soldier*, 111.

36. Weigley, *Eisenhower's Lieutenants*, 319.

CHAPTER 7

From the Battle of the Bulge
to VE-Day

When German forces knocked the 106th and 28th Divisions back through the Ardennes, the Allied airborne forces again proved that their ability to deploy fast was more important than parachuting. Brigadier General Ralph Eaton, the XVIII Airborne Corps chief of staff, had received orders from the 1st Army to move the Corps into the increasingly gappy front on December 17 at 5:30 P.M. He promptly notified General Gavin, the senior officer on duty at the Corps command post in Rheims. The 82d and 101st, weary from six weeks of hard fighting in Holland, were comfortably billeted in the Champagne for refitting and replacement. Many of the troopers got passes to Paris, where, Gavin relates, one staff officer told another, "Those paratroopers are the smartest, most alert-looking soldiers I have seen." The other answered, "Hell, and, they ought to be, you are looking at the survivors." There had been so little expectation of a major offensive that Ridgway and most of his staff had gone back to England to inspect the training of the 17th Airborne. Maxwell D. Taylor, commander of the 101st, was back in Washington, lobbying to enlarge the hard-fighting airborne divisions to the size of a normal infantry division. No one had expected, after the weeks of punishment in Holland, that the 82d and 101st would soon be sent into the line for a month of some of the hardest fighting of the war. Gavin did not even know of Ridgway's and Taylor's absence until he got Eaton's call. No plans existed for the movement of the Corps.[1]

Gavin made instant arrangements to move the 82d and the 101st on the next day—the 82d to move one hour after daybreak, the 101st to leave at 2 P.M. Gavin then left in an open jeep on a "miserable" nine-hour drive to report to First Army commander Courtney Hodges at Spa. Hodges decided to commit the 82d north of the Bulge at Werbomont and the 101st to Bastogne.[2]

Ridgway, back in England, found out a little after 2 A.M. on December 18 that his Corps was about to be committed to battle. He immediately arranged for air transport and at 8:30A.M. his Corps staff was on the way from England to Rheims, despite the fog and rain. After landing at Rheims, he hurried to meet Eaton at the Corps advance command post in Épernay and got his orders from 1st Army to establish his Corps headquarters near Gavin's 82d Division at Werbomont. He set off on roads jammed with traffic, in fog so dense that he felt obliged to take the wheel from his driver, and spent the night at Troy Middleton's VIII Corps command post in Bastogne. Bastogne that night was full of soldiers in retreat, and Ridgway carefully noted the low morale of those who had filtered back from the front.[3]

Perhaps the best known story of the Battle of the Bulge is that of the "Battling Bastards of Bastogne"—the 101st Airborne—under Middleton's corps, not Ridgway's. When surrounded by German troops, who demanded his surrender, the American commander Brigadier Anthony McAuliffe replied "Nuts!" which, his subordinates explained to puzzled German officers, meant "Go to hell." The story made a sensation in the States, and the hard-fighting 82d has always been jealous of the publicity.

Ridgway was still traveling that night on roads that were thick with German patrols. By "god's guidance," Ridgway picked one of the two roads that had not yet been cut by the Germans on his way out of Bastogne and proceeded on towards Werbomont, pausing long enough to establish his command post. Then he rushed off to Spa to see Hodges, who informed him that the 82d Airborne and part of Maurice Rose's 3d Armored would be assigned to his corps, along with all other forces in the general area of Stavelot. The next day Hodges added the 30th Division, the 7th Armored, and the survivors of the badly mauled 106th and 28th Divisions. Using these forces, Ridgway would stabilize his six-mile-long corps front. It wouldn't be easy.[4]

Meanwhile, back at SHAEF, on December 19, General Eisenhower met with Bradley, Patton, and other senior commanders. At this meeting, Patton dramatically announced that he could attack toward Bastogne with three divisions in three days, as shown in the movie *Patton* (1970). The movie omitted Eisenhower's less than cinematic reply: "Don't be fatuous." The battle situation troubled Eisenhower. The next morning, Eisenhower appointed Field Marshal Bernard L. Montgomery to command all forces north of the Bulge. The normally phlegmatic Bradley, for one, was livid—he felt that such an appointment showed a lack of confidence in him as a commander, and he was not mollified by Eisenhower's recommendation that he be promoted to full general. But he could not deny that vital communication links had been cut between him and Hodges on the northern side of the Bulge—and this, plus the hope that Montgomery would throw British troops into the battle to help, was the main reason for Eisenhower's decision.[5]

As Eisenhower was making his decision to appoint Montgomery, the battle continued at the critical road junction town of St. Vith. Brigadier General Robert W. Hasbrouck, commander of the 7th Armored, sent Hodges a series of letters about the prospect that his forces might be cut off. Hodges met with Ridgway that day and approved his plan for an attack by elements of his corps to the southeast to relieve the pressure on St. Vith pocket and improve Hodges communications.[6]

Montgomery, however, had other plans and arrived at First Army with a tactless superior attitude that, as one American officer put it, was "apt to rouse the old South Boston Irish in us." As Gavin put it, "The Americans simply did not trust Monty." The British general horrified First Army by insisting that they "tidy up the lines" by withdrawing from St. Vith and pulling back the 82d and 3rd Armored to a more secure battle line.[7]

Hodges and his staff temporarily dissuaded Montgomery from yielding St. Vith because of the risk that the road junction would spur the Germans north to Liège. They couldn't stop Montgomery, however, from transferring Ridgway's proposed offensive to Collins's VII Corps, far to the west at Marche.[8]

The next day, December 21, brought some of the hardest fighting of the campaign along three places on the northern part of the Bulge. At St. Vith the Germans hit hard with more than three divisions. Bruce C. Clarke's Combat Command B of the 1st Armored Division was forced to contract its perimeter—losing nine hundred killed or captured in the process. Clarke, who was later promoted to full general, was bitterly critical of Ridgway's failure to withdraw earlier from St. Vith, as Montgomery had suggested the day before. That evening, Ridgway or his staff proposed circling the wagons. The plan called for the forces in St. Vith to retreat to a fortified "goose egg" like that at Bastogne. Bruce Clarke later charged that Ridgway wasted precious time pursuing this concept, which, Clarke maintained, could not work with an armored division, which required considerable logistical support and a good road net. Clarke and his superior, Brigadier General Robert W. Hasbrouck, commander of the 7th Armored, thought that Montgomery had been right, that the division should have retreated two days before. As Clarke and some historians have painted it, Ridgway was excessively gung-ho and resisted ordering a withdrawal until the very last minute.[9]

It is true that Ridgway, along with Hodges and most of First Army staff, opposed Montgomery's initial suggestion of withdrawal from St. Vith, and it also seems to be agreed upon that the continued defense of St. Vith was invaluable in slowing the progress of the German offensive. By the night of December 21, however, Ridgway himself reported to First Army Chief of Staff William B. Kean Jr. that "I seriously doubt the ability of [Hasbrouck] and his teammates to hold." Perhaps Ridgway recognized the goose egg strategy for what one historian has called it—"a very temporary expedient." The XVIII Corps commander continued: "I would like to authorize their withdrawal back to the 82d area tonight." Kean approved the withdrawal order, which was discretionary with Hasbrouck. The next day, December 22 at 12:25 P.M. Ridgway approved Hasbrouck's request to withdraw. Montgomery's order to withdraw was not issued by First Army until 2 P.M.[10]

One serious problem within the St. Vith salient had been the chain of command. The commander of the largest force in the salient was Brigadier General Robert W. Hasbrouck, an experienced and competent veteran. Ridgway and Hodges viewed him as de facto commander within the salient. Hasbrouck, however, was outranked by Major General Alan W. Jones, commander of the 106th Infantry Division, which had been shattered in the first days of the Bulge offensive. Jones, depressed over the loss of more than half his division and of his son—presumed captured or killed in one of his own cut-off regiments—was not functioning at the level that Ridgway expected of division commanders. Jones may also have been suffering from the first stages of a heart attack, which might explain his erratic behavior. Initially, Ridgway tried to regularize the command arrangements in a routine order by putting Jones in charge of the salient. This has been seen by some writers as a "relief" of Hasbrouck, though at the time neither man saw it as such, and Hasbrouck continued to be in *de facto* command. On the 22d, when Ridgway traveled to his and Hasbrouck's command post to supervise the withdrawal of American forces from the salient, Ridgway found that Jones was detached and apathetic and relieved him on the spot, putting Hasbrouck in command. Ridgway also made William M. Hoge deputy commander of the 7th Armored division. This action gave Hoge command authority over Bruce Clarke, who had made no secret of his dislike for Ridgway.[11]

Gavin strongly criticized the relief of Jones. He considered it bad for morale to relieve a green commander the first time he made a mistake. Jones suffered a severe heart attack the day after his relief, which seemingly confirmed Ridgway's judgment that he was not up to running the difficult and dangerous withdrawal.[12]

There was considerable skepticism within the salient about whether the withdrawal could be made without significant loss. Even Ridgway's close friend Hoge was not a believer. Ridgway arranged a meeting with him, and when Hoge asked, "How can you?" Ridgway replied, "We can and we will." It would have been much more difficult if a cold front on the morning of December 23d had not frozen the muddy roads, easing passage for armor and motor transports, while at the same time allowing for formidable Allied air support to cover the retreat. While Ridgway's claim that not a man was lost is an exaggeration, there can be no question of the success of the retreat from St. Vith. Moreover, the criticism that the withdrawal orders should have come earlier seems obviated by the assessment of some military historians that the stand in the St. Vith salient significantly channeled and slowed the German advance.[13]

Further to the west, December 22 brought more attacks by German divisions seeking an outlet north toward Liège. This time the attack came at Hotton. The attack was contained by Rose's 3rd Armored and paratroops from the 509th and the 517th Regiments after a bloody fight at Soy. As Rose rushed to meet the threat at Hotton, however, he opened a gap on the right flank of Gavin's 82d, at another key crossroads town, Fraiture. Gavin was deeply concerned that the gap might be exploited by renewed attacks by German forces that had bypassed St. Vith and were looking for another outlet north. Gavin reinforced the Fraiture crossroads with a company from the 325th Glider Regiment, later adding a battalion brought from the 504th Parachute Infantry Regiment.[14]

By the next day, December 23, the fight on Gavin's right was getting white hot. He jeeped to Manhay, a crucial town on the road north to Werbomont, which was supposed to be the command post of the 3rd Armored, and found it deserted, guarded by one MP. With no armor protecting his left flank, he sped to corps headquarters. Ridgway tended to spend days away from his command post, trying to be at the most intense points of the battle. During his absence, his chief of staff, Brigadier General Ralph P. Eaton, bore a huge responsibility. Eaton told Gavin to deal with the situation on his own. They had an argument, perhaps partly over jealousy that Gavin had received so much publicity as commander of the 82d. Eaton reminded Gavin that he owed Ridgway, who had fought hard to get him the 82d, and later described him as "a black Irishman looking out for number one who was upstaging Ridgway." Gavin later criticized Ridgway's staff system, claiming that the corps staff did nothing while its commander was away.[15]

That night, despite Eaton's tiff with Gavin, Ridgway ordered Hoge's exhausted Combat Command B of the 9th Armored Division, to take positions on Gavin's right, and later added the 7th Armored, blocking the road from Manhay. He also asked Hodges for an additional infantry division. By the next morning, the corps considered the situation on Gavin's right to be "urgent."[16]

The morning of the 24th, Ridgway met the emergency with energy and resolve. At 6:15 A.M. he assembled his corps staff, assuring them that he had told the Army commander that "the situation is normal and entirely satisfactory." Implicitly acknowledging the battle weariness of the troops from St. Vith, he assured his staff that "the enemy has thrown in his last reserves, and this is his last major effort in the West in this war. This Corps will halt that effort and attack and smash him." He asked the corps staff to disseminate his "utter confidence" in the battle's outcome. After the meeting, he personally called the commanders of the 106th Division, the 7th Armored, and the 30th Division to tell them that this was the "last dying gasp" of the German army. The American soldiers might be tired, but he wanted it made clear to his men that "we are going to lick the Germans here, today."[17]

Well, not quite. Though Ridgway had had attack plans, the Germans threw his forces on the defensive with a massive attack at Manhay. That afternoon Montgomery went to see Ridgway and with his agreement ordered a withdrawal to close up the spread-out forces of the 82d. Gavin agreed with the move, though he worried about the morale effects on a division that prided itself on never having relinquished any ground gained. Worse yet, the 3d Armored and the tired 7th Armored bungled the retreat and lost the important crossroads town of Manhay.[18]

Christmas Day saw Ridgway in the front lines trying to implement a grim order from a worried First Army to retake Manhay whatever the cost. What Ridgway saw of the understandably exhausted soldiers from the 7th Armored did them little credit in his eyes. He relieved a 2d lieutenant who was leading his men to the rear because they had run into heavy fire and replaced him with a sergeant who volunteered to lead the men back into combat. When German artillery fire drove a nearby sergeant hysterical, Ridgway tried to snap him out of it, then had his driver march him to the rear, with orders to shoot if he tried to escape. What was left of the division proved unable to retake Manhay that day. Ridgway described the battle to Bill Hoge as "last night's fiasco," which he attributed to incompetent leadership, especially in the 424th Infantry Regiment.[19]

The day after Christmas, Ridgway massed his artillery, lobbed 8,600 rounds into the town and ordered the 3/516 in to take possession of the ruins. By December 26, the German offensive was spent. Ridgway's corps would participate in the offensive to move the Allies back to the Siegfried Line. It would take the corps three weeks of hard fighting. After refitting, the 7th Armored would not return to St. Vith until January 23. Once again, perhaps owing in part to General Montgomery's caution, the U.S. forces failed to cut off and destroy the German Army.[20]

The Battle of the Bulge made Ridgway's reputation as a corps commander. In early December, he was untried at that level, and a memo by Eisenhower to Marshall ranking his senior officers put Ridgway as number 31 out of 32. After the Bulge, Eisenhower rated Ridgway as one of the three top officers who deserved the next open army command. Just as Ridgway hoped to add to this reputation as a great corps commander by driving on into Germany, however, he was halted and diverted into action to capture the Roer Dams at Schmidt. Then Allied Headquarters recalled him to England to plan a series of airborne operations, codenamed VARSITY, CHOKER II, and ARENA. He and Hodges had tried to resist his reassignment, but to no avail.[21]

VARSITY, the only one of these plans ever executed, called for an airdrop in support of General Montgomery's crossing of the Rhine. CHOKER II was a similar operation designed to help Patch's Seventh Army get across the big river on the Southern Front. Ridgway was most interested and challenged, however, by ARENA—a plan for a massive drop of an airborne army into the Kassel-Padersborn area on May 1, which, it was thought, might just cause the collapse of the Reich.[22]

Bradley's Twelfth Army Group upstaged Montgomery when Brigadier General Bill Hoge, still commanding Combat Command A of the 9th Armored Division, captured intact the Ludendorff Bridge at Remagen on March 7. With the subsequent exploitation of this impromptu crossing, Hodges and Patton would get to Padersborn long before any troops could be airlanded there, obviating both CHOKER II and ARENA.[23]

Montgomery had insisted on bringing Ridgway and his corps headquarters in for the VARSITY operation. Some historians attributed Montgomery's demand for Ridgway as a tacit admission of his error in giving the MARKET-GARDEN command to Boy Browning. Ridgway was, however, in for a shock when he visited General Miles Dempsey, the British Second Army commander. Dempsey presented Ridgway with a prearranged plan for VARSITY that repeated many of the mistakes of MARKET-GARDEN. The British general also declared, to Ridgway's irritation, that he planned to hold onto the XVIII Airborne Corps for as long as possible after the crossing. This declaration contravened Ridgway's understanding with General Eisenhower that he would be released quickly for other operations.[24]

Ridgway and Brereton were abashed, both by Dempsey's audacity in trying to grab Ridgway's corps for the rest of the war and by the impracticability of the plan—which depended, like MARKET-GARDEN on optimistic estimates of the speed that Dempsey's army could advance. The plan also failed to account for the limited logistic support available to First Allied Airborne Army. The volatile Brereton wanted to appeal to Eisenhower immediately, but his chief of staff, Floyd Parks, cooled him down. Brereton then ordered Ridgway to devise an alternative plan and presented it on February 19 to SHAEF chief of staff Lieutenant General Walter Bedell Smith and Montgomery's chief of Staff, Francis "Freddie" De Guingand. Smith told him to work it out with Dempsey but made it clear that the corps would be released early for employment elsewhere.[25]

Ridgway did go back to Dempsey, and they were able to compromise. One objective, an attack on Wesel, was eliminated in order to keep the operation on a sustainable scale. Dempsey gave absolute assurance of a linkup with the paratroopers within forty-eight hours; and to help assure this linkup, the drop would be made *after* Dempsey had crossed the Rhine. To avoid friendly fire, moreover, the British commander promised to forgo the use of his artillery between 9:30 A.M. and 1:30 P.M.[26]

On March 24, at 6 A.M., the operation took place in slightly hazy weather, which disrupted some of the drops. The British 4th and 5th Brigades were placed almost right on their drop zones. They lost 10 of 121 planes, 7 more crash-landed, and some 70 were damaged.[27]

The Americans from Brigadier General William "Bud" Miley's 17th Airborne had less luck getting to their drop zones. Coutts's 513th Parachute Infantry Regiment had a particularly harrowing time in the new C-46 troop transports, which, when hit in their wing gasoline tanks, flared up and burned the fuselage. Nineteen of their seventy-two planes were lost to German flak. Ridgway afterward banned the use of the C-46 for parachute drops. Many of Coutts's men were also dropped in open fields and raked by German machine gun fire.[28]

Ridgway crossed the Rhine to meet his forces on an amphibious-tracked vehicle and drove off into the forest in search of his division commanders. At one point, he came upon a German soldier in a foxhole, eyes open, aiming right at him. Fortunately for Ridgway, the soldier proved to be dead. A short while later, he heard a noise, which proved to be an American paratrooper sitting on a commandeered farm horse, wearing a silk top hat. The trooper started at meeting a no-nonsense general, known for demanding that his men shave every day, even in combat. He did not know whether to salute, dismount, or what, until he saw that Ridgway was laughing his head off. The incident is important because it reveals a certain ideological boundary that marks off Ridgway's attitude toward what he considered "American"—a healthy individualism and the need for discipline combined with individual initiative, which Ridgway contrasted with the mythical blind peasant obedience of the German soldier.[29]

Later that night, returning from Bols's command post, Ridgway and his party encountered a German patrol as they detoured off the road to get around a burned-out jeep. Ridgway hit the forest floor and started firing with his Springfield. When he rolled over to reload, he luckily put his head against the wheel of the jeep, which protected him when a fragmentation grenade exploded right under the vehicle. Ridgway was slightly wounded, with a crescent-shaped piece of metal lodged in his shoulder. It did not bother him much, so, against doctor's advice, he left it in. After the explosion, there was a silence, and the Germans retreated. Ridgway aimed at a figure in a ditch whom he almost shot, but challenged him first. He turned out to be American, leading Ridgway to observe that the paratrooper, used to being alone and surrounded, has to be very careful about whom he shoots at—another valorization of individualism within the framework of disciplined cooperation.[30]

Eisenhower and Brereton were buoyed by the success of VARSITY. Despite misdrops and heavy casualties, the divisions involved managed to assemble within two hours and accomplished their missions, destroying an entire German division within five hours. Ridgway was proud of the drop, though he believed its cost was dear compared to the gain. It is far from certain, however, whether the loss of planes and highly trained paratroopers was worth a mission that might have been relatively easily accomplished by the overwhelming ground forces at hand.[31]

VARSITY also helped turn Ridgway into a star. *Time* highlighted his craggy profile on its April 2, 1945 cover, against a stylized background of parachutists and planes. The caption read: "General Ridgway of the U.S. Airborne—his fighters cross barriers on bridges of silk." The magazine described Ridgway as "a Roman senator" who lived "like a Spartan hoplite" creating an image of Ridgway as a paragon of republican simplicity who practiced the most complex of combat conceits—envelopment from the air.[32]

After the VARSITY landings helped secure the Rhine bridgehead, the XVIII Airborne Corps drove clean to Münster by April 2. Ridgway may have been disappointed yet again when, instead of driving deeper into Germany, he was called upon to assist in the reduction of the German armies that had been bypassed and surrounded in the Ruhr and, according to historian Russell Weigley, that had little strategic importance.[33]

The attack, which Brereton called "the largest double envelopment in military history," began on April 4. Perhaps worried that troops would be wary of aggressiveness, not wanting to get killed in the last days of the war, Ridgway told his commanders, "It isn't sufficient just to imbue the infantry with the offensive spirit. I want every man in the division . . . imbued with this idea: That this Corps is going forward here to destroy that German force in the Corps zone in the minimum of time, and the greater the pressure, the shorter the time, and the less the loss." Despite Ridgway's exhortations, and the hopelessness of the German position, the operation still took two weeks.[34]

As Ridgway's intelligence chief, Colonel Whitfield Jack noted at the outset, "the psychological warfare aspects of the situation" were "pregnant with possibilities." Troops were equipped with leaflets outlining in German and English the procedure for unconditional surrender; and when the envelopment was completed, Ridgway tried twice to lessen the bloodshed by presenting Model with a surrender demand. Indeed, Model's chief of staff, General Karl Wagener, had been urging Model to ask Hitler for permission to surrender. Model, who had criticized Field Marshal Friedrich von Paulus for surrendering at Stalingrad—the first violation of the tradition that no German field marshall should ever surrender—discharged much of his army and dissolved his command.[35]

Ridgway, somewhat ethnocentrically, sent Model another letter, alluding to Robert E. Lee's surrender in the American Civil War and how it had enhanced his honor. Instead, the Generalfeldmarschal went off into the woods and shot himself. His chief of staff returned with Ridgway's emissaries and surrendered, as did tens of thousands of German personnel in the next two days. Allied intelligence had estimated that there were between 80,000 and 100,000 German troops in the Ruhr. Instead, Allied forces took over

317,000 prisoners—more than the Red Army took at Stalingrad. Eisenhower was extremely pleased with the operation and endorsed Bradley's recommendation for Ridgway's promotion to lieutenant general, which became effective on June 4.[36]

The collapse of the Third Reich was imminent, but not yet accomplished. In the last days of the war, there would be one more mission for Ridgway, occasioned by Montgomery's slowness in getting to the Elbe. Eisenhower feared that the Russians would beat Montgomery to Wismar and march into Denmark, and he assigned Ridgway's XVIII Airborne Corps to stop them. The mission was a curious politico-military hybrid, goading one ally, the British, to move across to the Baltic in order to prevent the advance of another ally, the Soviets. In a very real sense, the operation was the first battle of what would come to be called the Cold War. It was also a unique military problem.[37]

Montgomery outlined the mission on April 21. Afterward, Ridgway went to see Bradley, who gave him top priority in the choice of divisions for the mission. Ridgway picked Gavin's 82d Airborne, Hasbrouck's 7th Armored, Bryant E. Moore's 8th Infantry Division, which had served him well in the Ruhr, and Bols's 6th Airborne, a British division, which was already up north with Dempsey. The first problem was to move all those divisions—more than 50,000 men—up north, which Ridgway did by April 29. The next problem was getting them past the traffic jams of Dempsey's army in order to close with the Soviets.[38]

In order to get around Dempsey, Ridgway decided to make his own crossing of the Elbe at Bleckede. By 1 A.M. on April 30, two battalions of the 505th Parachute Infantry Regiment, 82d Airborne, warily crossed the Elbe in canvas assault boats. Within a few hours, the 505th had secured the beachhead, though German artillery began to pound the engineers who were building a bridge for the rest of the infantry. Ridgway believed that the engineers had taken cover and stopped work (though some of the engineers later denied it). To encourage them to continue, Ridgway walked out on the bridge and determined that there was little danger from the shells exploding near the bridge in the water, though his aide-de-camp, Don Faith, later reported being "scared pink" while on the bridge. Ridgway chewed out the engineer commanders; if the bridge did not get finished soon, the 505th would be annihilated. The engineers got the 1,180-foot bridge finished in fifteen hours—"As fine a performance as I've ever seen," Ridgway later wrote. For his trip out on the bridge, Ridgway won a second Silver Star and a chewing out from Eaton for risking his life so late in the war.[39]

Two days later, the XVIII Airborne Corps had thrust the sixty miles to Wismar and accepted the surrender of 359,796 German soldiers, including fifty generals. "I believe that never has the element of TIME, so vital a factor in military operations, been more completely or effectively exploited"

Ridgway later wrote. This mass surrender followed news broadcasts of Hitler's suicide on May 1, as Germans in the area sped to become prisoners of the Americans rather than of the Soviets.[40]

On the march from the Elbe, General Dempsey asked Ridgway if, for prestige reasons, he would let Bols's division, a British unit, be the first to meet the Red Army. At first, Ridgway said no, fearing that it would slow him down; but after consideration, he reversed himself. Gavin, however, sneaked patrols into Wismar on May 2, an hour before Bols arrived. By the time Ridgway's XVIII Airborne Corps arrived in Wismar, it was face to face with the Red Army.[41]

One of the commanders' first priorities was demarcation between both the U.S. and Red Armies, and between American soldiers and the German populace. The two armies soon established a one-kilometer "neutral zone" between them, though they drank (a lot) and partied together, at least until the Soviet political commissars arrived. As far as the Germans were concerned, Ridgway issued strict nonfraternization orders.[42]

Gavin was one of the first to find out about the concentration camps. Installed at the magnificent palace of the Grafs von Mecklinberg-Schweringen in Ludwigslust, Gavin accepted the surrender of local German forces. Two days later, he heard that the mayor of the town and his wife and daughter had killed themselves. Their deaths seemed inexplicable until soldiers discovered the nearby Wobelein Concentration Camp. Gavin later recounted:

> One could smell the Wobelein Concentration Camp before seeing it. And seeing it was more than a human being could stand. Even after three years of war it brought tears to my eyes. Living skeletons were scattered about, the dead distinguishable from the living only by the bluish-black color of their skin compared to the somewhat greenish skin, taut over the bony frames of the living. There were hundreds of dead about the grounds and in the tarpaper shacks. In the corner of the stockade area was an abandoned quarry into which the daily stacks of cadavers were bulldozed. It was obvious they could not tell many of the dead from the living.[43]

Wobelein was not an extermination camp like Auschwitz. Most of its prisoners were politicals. Its inmates, recently moved from the East as a result of the Russian advance, had been starved in part because of the mayor's failure to share the town's food supply with them. Gavin called in doctors to feed the living intravenously and forced the leading citizens of the town to bury the dead in the park in front of the palace. Then he ordered the entire town to attend the memorial service conducted by Colonel Harry

Cain (later a Senator and, in the early 1950s, chair of the Subversive Activities Control Board). Ridgway attended the service and in his memoirs quoted Cain's speech at length:

> "The Allies shudder," Cain told the people of Ludwigslust, assembled over the graves, "because they never dreamed or visualized that human leadership, supported by the masses, could so debase itself as to be responsible for results like those who lie in these open graves. The civilized world shudders on finding that a part of its society has fallen so low."[44]

When Ridgway would use the word "civilization," as he frequently did in the Cold War years, to draw a boundary with the Soviets, it was no longer quite the positive, conquering imperial civilization of progressivism. Civilization for Ridgway was read against the barbarism he had seen in the camps. In his mind, the brutalities of Nazism were integrally connected to the process of boundary-making with the Soviets.

NOTES

1. Gavin, OTB, 203–204; 82d Airborne Division, "Belgium: The Story of the Bulge," Ridgway MSS, Box 5 (hereafter Belgium unit history); XVIII Corps (Airborne) Operations Reports, Ardennes, December 19, 1944 to February 13, 1945, March 1, 1945, Folder "WWII Lessons Learned" (hereafter OR, Ardennes), Ridgway MSS, Box 7. On Taylor's success in Washington, see Marshall to Ridgway, December 18, 1944, and on Ridgway's work with the 17th Airborne division back in England, see Ridgway to Eaton, December 10, 1944, both in Personal File, Folder D, August–December 1944, Ridgway MSS, Box 5a.

2. Gavin, OTB, 203–204; CBRP, 363; Belgium unit history, 4.

3. Ridgway, *Soldier*, 112: CBRP, 365; OR, Ardennes, 1, 2.

4. "Narrative of Events," HQ XVIII Airborne Corps, Box 5a, Bulge Diary, 1.

5. John S. D. Eisenhower, *The Bitter Woods* (Nashville, Tenn.: Battery Press, 1969); Hugh M. Cole, *United States Army in World War II. The European Theater of Operations. The Ardennes: Battle of the Bulge* (Washington, D.C.: Department of the Army, 1965), 423–424; CBRP, 369–370.

6. CBRP, 377–378.

7. CBRP, 378–379; Gavin, OTB, 194; Eisenhower, *Bitter Woods*; Weigley, *Eisenhower's Lieutenants*, 503–506.

8. CBRP, 378–379; Gavin, OTB, 194; Eisenhower, *Bitter Woods*; Weigley, *Eisenhower's Lieutenants*, 503–506.

9. Eisenhower, *Bitter Woods*, 299; Cole, *Battle of the Bulge*, 406–407; J. D. Morelock, *Generals of the Ardennes: American Leadership in the Battle of the Bulge* (Washington, D.C.: NDU Press, 1994), 325–326.

10. "Record of General Ridgway's Conversation with General Kean," December 21, 1944, Corps Diary, Ridgway MSS, Box 5a; Cole, *Battle of the Bulge*, 407.

11. CBRP, 386; Ridgway, *Soldier*, 120. See also Hasbrouck to Blair, February 5,

1984, Clay Blair Collection, Box 32; Ridgway to Shaw, January 12, 1984, and Ridgway to Gavin, October 6, 1978, Ridgway MSS, Box 3, Correspondence with Gavin regarding *On to Berlin*.

12. Gavin, OTB, 232–233; CBRP, 388; Hasbrouck to Blair, February 5, 1984, Clay Blair Collection, Box 32.

13. Ridgway, *Soldier*, 120. The best account of the withdrawal from St. Vith is in Cole, *Battle of the Bulge*, 412–422. On the significance of the stand at St. Vith, see also Eisenhower, *Bitter Woods*, 304.

14. Gavin, OTB, 231–232; Cole, *Battle of the Bulge*, 378–379, 388–389.

15. Quoted in CBRP, 392; JB, 1:83, 84.

16. Bulge Diary, December 24, Ridgway MSS, Box 5a; CBRP, 393; Gavin, OTB, 237–238; Cole, *Battle of the Bulge*, 399, 580, 583.

17. Memo, December 24, 1944, Ridgway MSS, Box 5a.

18. On Montgomery's visit, see Bulge Diary, December 24, 1944. On Gavin's attitude, see Gavin, OTB, 239; Cole, *Battle of the Bulge*, 587–589; Eisenhower, *Bitter Woods*, 358–359; CBRP, 399.

19. Ridgway, *Soldier*, 121–122; Summary of Testimony of Major General Ridgway in the Case of 2d Lt. Loring Bergman, Company "C," 23d Armored Infantry Battalion, December 26, 1944, Folder D, October–December 1944, Ridgway MSS, Box 5a; Ridgway to Hoge, December 25, 1944, Personal File, Folder D, October–December, Ridgway MSS, Box 5a.

20. CBRP, 398–399; Cole, *Battle of the Bulge*, 598. Eisenhower, *Bitter Woods*, 430.

21. Weigley, *Eisenhower's Lieutenants*, 758–759; CBRP, 434; Eisenhower to Marshall, January 4, 1945, DDE Papers, 4:2427. On Februrary 1, Eisenhower ranked Ridgway sixteenth among all the general officers in the ETO; the only corps commander ranked higher was J. Lawton Collins (Butcher Diary, February 1, 1945, DDE Papers, 4:2466–67).

22. CBRP, 445–447.

23. See Weigley, *Eisenhower's Lieutenants*, 626–639.

24. Weigley, *Eisenhower's Lieutenants*, 647; CBRP, 441–443.

25. CBRP, 443. *Brereton Diaries*, 396–997.

26. CBRP, 443–444.

27. Ibid., 457.

28. Ibid., 457–459.

29. Ridgway, *Soldier*, 134–135.

30. Ibid., 136–137.

31. CBRP, 466.

32. *Time*, April 24, 1945.

33. Weighley, *Eisenhower's Lieutenants*, 678.

34. CBRP 475; "Report on Operations, XVIII Corps (Airborne) Reduction of Ruhr Pocket, 1 April 1945 to 18 April 1945," May 4, 1945, (hereafter "Report on Operations") Lewis H. Brereton, Ridgway MSS, Box 7; The *Brereton Diaries* (New York: Morrow, 1946): 421.

35. Ridgway, *Soldier*, 139–140; CBRP, 484–486; Ridgway Diary, April 3, 1945, Ridgway MSS, Box 5a.

36. Ridgway, *Soldier*, 140; Ridgway Diary, April 3, 1945, Ridgway MSS, Box 5a; CBRP, 486; Weigley, *Eisenhower's Lieutenants*, 680. Note that the actual estimates of German strength in the pocket Ridgway initially gave at his briefing for division

commanders (those cited here), were significantly below even the low estimates of 125,000–150,000 quoted elsewhere. On the hams, see Montgomery to Ridgway, May 1, 1945, Eisenhower to Ridgway, May 2, 1945, Personal File, April–May, 1945, Ridgway MSS, Box 3.

37. Weigley, *Eisenhower's Lieutenants*, 719–720; CBRP, 488.

38. CBRP, 490–492; Report on Operations, 2.

39. Ridgway, *Soldier*, 144; Report on Operations, 3; CBRP, 493–494.

40. Gavin, OTB, 285–288; CBRP, 495; Report on Operations, 2.

41. Ridgway, *Soldier*, 145.

42. Memorandum: Relation of Troops with Civil Populace, May 8, 1945, Historical Record, Ridgway MSS, Box 5a.

43. Gavin, OTB, 288.

44. Ridgway, *Soldier*, 148. See also Ridgway's similar address, given at Haganow, May 8, 1945, Personal File, April–May 1945, Ridgway MSS, Box 3.

CHAPTER 8

The Perils of Peace:
Matthew Bunker Ridgway and
the Postwar Order, 1946–1947

The time given to an unprepared selected victim by a potential aggressor may in the future be measured not in years, not in months, but in days. I hope that word "unprepared" may strike every American brain with the impact of a blow.[1]

—Matthew Bunker Ridgway

When his XVIII Airborne Corps reached the Elbe, in May 1945, Ridgway contacted a Soviet corps commander and one other general whose forces were stationed opposite his own. He ordered his officers to pay courtesy calls on the Soviets and told them, "I should like the guiding policy to be one of friendliness and tolerance, with firmness where our own rights or relations are concerned." The general himself maintained friendly, but wary, relations with the Soviet officers whom he met in Germany. When General D. I. Smirnov, the Soviet corps commander, had just been painfully injured in a car accident, Ridgway earned Smirnov's friendship by arranging American medical treatment for him. While Ridgway treated Smirnov with respect, he could easily turn to stereotyping other Soviet soldiers. On Smirnov's first visit, Smirnov brought with him a General Dzinet, "whose only social function," according to Ridgway, "was to try to intimidate me."

Ridgway never saw Dzinet after that first visit. "He never smiled, never shook hands, but stood by the side of his commander, glowering at me—one of the most formidable-looking creatures physically I have ever seen. I could not help but think what an excellent target he would make, seen over the sights of my Springfield, though of course, I was careful not to let this feeling be reflected in my manner." This description, in which he transforms the officer into prey to be shot with his hunting rifle, shows how Ridgway remained suspicious of the Soviets, willing to characterize some as barbarians, even at the moment of triumph of the U.S.–U.S.S.R. alliance.[2]

After victory in Europe, Ridgway flew to the Pacific to prepare his XVIII Airborne Corps for the invasion of Japan. By the time he landed, the war was over. After returning to Washington in late 1945, General Marshall made Ridgway commander of U.S. forces in the Mediterranean. Demobilization of the U.S. Army in this year became a key episode in his understanding of the limitations placed on U.S. power by the lack of public support for a large peacetime army. He deplored the American soldiers' and the public's unwillingness to maintain forces in Europe long enough to reduce or prevent Soviet hegemony in the East, and he criticized the "points" system of demobilization. Under that system, the most experienced soldiers were shipped home first, leaving Ridgway to administer Italy with poorly motivated raw draftees.[3]

In January 1946, General Eisenhower ordered Ridgway to leave the Mediterranean for London, to serve as his personal representative to the United Nations Military Staff Committee (MSC). Eisenhower considered the UN job one of the most important in the military establishment. Ridgway's appointment as Eisenhower's personal representative to the MSC was strong evidence that Eisenhower appreciated Ridgway's abilities. "We must make this organization work," wrote the Chief of Staff in December 1945, shortly before appointing Ridgway.[4]

Ridgway moved on to his new duties at the convening meeting of the Security Council in London. His transfer orders arrived as a welcome surprise on New Year's Day, 1946. An honored guest in London, he used the opportunity to get back in touch with many old comrades of the war. He enjoyed the company of members of the delegation to the General Assembly, such as Senator Arthur Vandenberg, Senator Tom Connally, John Foster Dulles, Adlai Stevenson, Eleanor Roosevelt, and Ralph Bunche. "I still remember how," he wrote in his memoirs, "as the three senior military officers arrived for the first meeting there in London, the people gathered in the streets, cheered and applauded. In their faces you could read their bright hope that here, in these councils, a war-sick world could find a formula for peace. I too felt that hope in my own heart."[5]

GI demonstrations, which Ridgway found profoundly disturbing, marred his London visit. For example, on January 20, 1946, 500 GIs marched on Claridge's Hotel in London, where the U.S. delegation to the UN was housed. The GIs called for a more democratic army and faster discharges. Eleanor Roosevelt, then a UN delegate, promised to aid them. Similar incidents occurred in Frankfurt and in the Pacific Theater.[6]

The GI demonstrations marked a definite limit to U.S. military power, which rapidly melted away after the war, leaving the Soviets as the unchallenged land power in Europe. Ridgway, who considered the rapid demobilization a serious, if politically inescapable, error, believed that the abrupt decline of U.S. forces was due to a social weakness that damaged army morale, led to the loss of tons of poorly guarded materièl owing to abandonment and theft, and lessened America's deterrent against another European war. He wrote General Eisenhower, calling for a civilian inquiry, which became the Doolittle Board—a body that democratized the Army a bit too much for Ridgway's taste.[7]

The Military Staff Committee of the UN Security Council, created by Article 43 of the United Nations Charter, was intended to be the vehicle for commanding the Council's military forces. At the time it was first conceived, the UN was not yet an organization for world peace, but still a military alliance against the Axis Powers, whose main purpose was to provide an organ for continued collective military action against "aggression." Unlike the League of Nations, the United Nations Organization would back its resolutions with the armed force of the Great Powers. The MSC was officially to be composed of the chiefs of staff of each armed service of the five Permanent Members of the Security Council or their representatives.[8]

The U.S. Representatives to the MSC quickly set up offices in the Henry Hudson Hotel on West 57th Street. Ridgway attended numerous social functions, and his old commander, Major General Frank McCoy, supplied him with courtesy cards at the Harvard and University Clubs and arranged membership in the Knickerbocker Club at his request so that the MSC's senior Army officers might have a pleasant place to dine with their foreign colleagues. Ridgway frequently commuted to Washington for his secondary assignment as Chair of the Inter-American Defense Board and to confer with Army Chief of Staff Dwight David Eisenhower.[9]

The MSC was a frustrating assignment. The members could not come to agreement, in part because of increasing Cold War tension, in part because the charter provisions for UN military forces, which Secretary of State Cordell Hull had made deliberately vague to assure ratification, proved to be almost impossible to implement. Through the fall of 1946, Ridgway followed the general climate of debate and became increasingly antagonistic toward the Soviet Union though not toward individual Soviet officers. After nearly eleven months of unsuccessful negotiations, Ridgway wrote Marshall that "the M.S.C. has dogged along like a hound on a dusty country lane," attributing the lack of progress to Soviet inflexibility, despite the fact that Ridgway and the Joint Chiefs of Staff opposed virtually every effort of State Department officials to modify the American position.[10]

Ironically, the American United Nations Military Staff Committee officers also held to a rigid position. The Joint Chiefs of Staff and the State Department kept those officers on as short a leash as the Soviet representatives, though the Americans never acknowledged their own rigidity. They were convinced that, as a matter of military technique, the proposals they offered were the only effective way to organize a Security Council force, a view which defined the essentially political questions raised by the U.S.S.R. off the agenda. In his 1956 memoirs, writing at a time when the death of Stalin renewed hope for disarmament, Ridgway quoted his favorite poet, Rudyard Kipling, to dismiss the Soviets as an untrustworthy, uncivilized, and dangerous enemy. "As I looked at the pictures of Mr. Bulganin and Mr. Khrushchev in the papers, I could not but remember the sage advice of Mr. Kipling, who urged, 'Make no truce with Adam-zad—the Bear who walks like a man.' "[11]

As early as 1947, Ridgway represented the Soviets as masters of illusion, capable of tricking a naive U.S. public into surrender, with their attractive-sounding proposals for disarmament. Commenting on the 1947 UN negotiations on multilateral security and disarmament, Ridgway told Major General J. R. Deane, a veteran of the Moscow embassy, that "we are in it with all we have, and shall give it our continuous best efforts, but we must exert an equal effort to combat the ceaseless and insidiously clever Soviet attempts to disguise their aims, to dispel our suspicions and to exploit our all but childish ingenuousness."[12]

The MSC negotiations went nowhere, though the committee has continued to meet monthly for the last fifty years in order to set its next meeting and adjourn. Many other structures, both within and without the UN, emerged to administer armed action for collective security. Most probably the inherent weaknesses of the scheme outlined in the UN Charter, which prevented the formation of a force in 1946, will continue to prevent the operation of such a scheme today.[13]

In addition to his MSC duties, Ridgway also worked closely with Major General Leslie Groves to advise the Baruch Group (named for its chair, financier Bernard M. Baruch), which was studying the international control of atomic energy. While he did little to further the negotiations, Ridgway did gain from the job a new familiarity and expertise with atomic weapons, writing Marshall of his excitement about working in a "completely uncharted field."[14]

The Baruch Plan was unacceptable to the Soviets because it would have internationalized the regulation of nuclear power reactors and prevented them from developing an atomic bomb, while preserving the American monopoly indefinitely. Ridgway, like the rest of the U.S. government, was unaware that the U.S.S.R. was only three years from developing its own atomic device. Had the U.S. government been aware, it would have been clear that the "carrot" of the plan, the sharing of atomic power technology, was not very worthwhile to the U.S.S.R., which would explode its own atomic device in 1949, while Soviet nationalists found the "stick"—inspection of atomic facilities and subjection to atomic retaliation if they developed their own bomb—humiliating. For his part, Ridgway believed the Baruch Plan was a matter of neutral international public interest—only evil or perversity could prevent the Soviets from perceiving it.[15]

Ridgway added professional military expertise to support the plan already favored by Baruch, particularly on that aspect of Baruch's plan that called for atomic retaliation against violators of the proposed prohibition of atomic weapons development by other countries. Ridgway's support helped Baruch override the objections of other officials, such as Undersecretary of State Dean Acheson and Atomic Energy Commission Chairman David Lilienthal, who had written the first version of the plan so that it would depend on technological means of enforcement, rather than inspections and sanctions, correctly predicting that the Soviets would inevitably reject the punitive features of the Baruch Plan.[16]

REDUCTION OF CONVENTIONAL ARMS

Ridgway, along with the other MSC delegates, attended a meeting with the Baruch group on August 22, 1946, which discussed proposals pending in the UN for conventional disarmament. He strongly opposed extending the United Nations Atomic Energy Commission discussions to other types of weapons, perhaps because he believed America had already given up too much of its conventional capacity.[17]

Public pressure for the reduction of conventional arms led Ridgway to use his considerable talents to prevent U.S. moves toward disarmament. His formulation of the problem, in a memo titled the "M.S.C Report No. 8," solidified U.S. policy against a brief flirtation with disarmament proposals in December 1946. Ridgway met with Major General Lyman L. Lemnitzer on November 12, 1946, asking him to clarify the State-War-Navy agreements with regard to conventional disarmament. Lemnitzer told Ridgway that the military representatives to the State-War-Navy Coordinating Committee strongly opposed conventional disarmament and had convinced the State Department to adopt their views. "For example, [State] originally held to the idea that it was possible for us to engage with other nations in discussing disarmament and that progress could be made in eliminating 'offensive' weapons, etc." The committee agreed on three preconditions to any U.S. negotiation for conventional disarmament: (1) adoption of a plan for the international control of atomic weapons, (2) conclusion of peace treaties with Germany and Japan, and (3) conclusion of agreements for a Security Council military force. The Army steadfastly opposed conventional disarmament because its officers wished to use arms aid to influence allies in Asia and Latin America. They also feared that the United States could be "subjected to severe criticism" as the world's largest arms vendor."[18]

Strengthening American allies militarily, the Joint Chiefs of Staff argued, would help keep peace and contain communism. Some officials, like Ridgway, favored extension of influence by arms shipments to Latin America. Refusing to negotiate conventional disarmament seemed politically and morally untenable, however, to UN Ambassador Warren R. Austin, a late convert to the Cold War. Austin went so far as to protest to Byrnes personally, proposing a draft speech that referred to a future U.S. disarmament proposal. Byrnes, with President Truman's concurrence, slapped down the proposal. "First, we will get to the atomic thing and have a showdown on that" he declared, postponing a decision on conventional disarmament. The same day that Byrnes told Austin he wanted a showdown, however, Alger Hiss wrote Acheson that it would "not be feasible simply to oppose any Assembly resolution on the subject of disarmament."[19]

A combination of strong public support for disarmament, and a slight thaw in the Cold War (the Soviet-American agreement to negotiate peace treaties with several ex-Axis states) led the Americans to compromise. On December 14, 1946, the UN General Assembly passed a disarmament resolution. The measure expressed the hope of the Assembly for an agreement combining the Soviet approach of outlawing nuclear weapons with Baruch's plan of safeguards and urged speedier establishment of UN military forces as the key to disarmament. The conciliatory moment quickly faded. Ridgway helped articulate a consensus within the American security bureaucracy that disarmament proposals were little more than clever Soviet manipulation of public opinion. Of the major policy makers of the time, only Austin and Eisenhower seem genuinely to have considered conventional disarmament as an option, and Eisenhower did little to act on his conviction until he became president.[20]

General Marshall, meeting with the War and Navy Secretaries on January 29, believed it important to persuade the public that disarmament was wrong: "We have a good propaganda base out of what happened after the last war. We disarmed unilaterally and the results are still fresh in American memory. It is important for us to prepare our proper propaganda." The group decided to assemble a group of important editors and publishers to explain their position.[21]

Ridgway's influence in the fight against disarmament was palpable at this cabinet-level meeting, where Robert Patterson, the Secretary of War, wanted "to draw the line" on disarmament. Undersecretary of State Acheson, in contrast, felt that the United States should not adhere to any fixed position. Patterson countered Acheson's position by circulating Ridgway's MSC Report No. 8, which provided strong ideological ammunition to the opponents of disarmament negotiations. Report No. 8 solidified opposition to disarmament within the government and enhanced Ridgway's reputation as a policy maker far beyond his official rank of lieutenant general, a position derived from his close association with Secretary of State George C. Marshall as well as his reputation as a crack corps commander in World War II.[22]

Ridgway insisted that Soviet disarmament proposals formed part of "an integrated plan to bring about unilateral disarmament by the U.S. under the guise of a plan for the general regulation and reduction of armaments by all nations; to strip us of our present technological, managerial and scientific superiority; and to elevate the U.S.S.R. to the position of the dominant military power in the world."[23]

Dean Acheson told Ridgway that his report "made policy." For the duration of the Truman Administration, the United States avoided disarmament negotiations. Report No. 8 had a lasting effect on Ridgway. Ten years later, he wrote in his memoirs that the Soviets' "one great motivating idea is [still] the same—by guile or subterfuge, or force if need be, to bring this nation to its knees." In 1975, at a time of Soviet-American "détente," he remarked that "Soviet behavior patterns have not changed one iota since then so far as their objectives are concerned."[24]

Ridgway argued that the Soviets were dangerous illusionists, manipulating "U.S. national conscience" to compel the United States to comply with one-sided, unverified arms reduction agreements. His report is a manifesto for military preparedness. He uses technical military language about objective "capabilities" to disguise an analysis that was based on political assertions rather than any neutral technical criteria. "Well known U.S.S.R. moral codes and conduct indicate the following as capabilities with a high degree of probability." Such Soviet "capabilities" included: (1) efforts to secure one-sided arms agreements on atomic weapons, while producing its own bombs clandestinely, (2) an attempt to secure UN approval of measures that would place U.S. forces on a level of numerical and technological parity with the Soviets, forcing the U.S. to forego its technological advantages, and (3) infiltration of the industrial structure to "paralyze" American national systems of communication, transport and fuel distribution, which was really more a matter of political organizing than espionage. This estimate is a good example of Ridgway's tendency to endow the Soviets with more power than they actually had.[25]

The Ridgway Report put a stop to further conventional arms negotiations. Partisans of "positive" proposals for disarmament failed. Yet Report No. 8 remained secret, while the government continued to waffle in public. By mid-1947, however, officials who supported disarmament could be red-baited. When Wilder Foote, press officer to UN Ambassador Warren R. Austin, sent an appeal to start negotiations through the bureaucracy, General Lemnitzer wrote Ridgway that "the writing of such memoranda borders on the subversive and seriously jeopardizes U.S. security."[26]

Ridgway's increasingly negative view of the Soviet Union profoundly affected his ideological image of American society, as it developed through the 1940s. Ridgway understood that the atomic age would bring vast constitutional changes to the American state. "Automatic or immediate retaliation with atomic weapons implied a drastic fundamental change in our form of government. If retaliation is to follow with sufficient speed to promise success, the war-making power of the U.S. [Congress] must be transferred from it and vested in another and different agency." He also believed that American society had to be more organic to insure its own safety.[27]

Social harmony and teamwork in the name of national security were basic to Ridgway's social vision. This is because modern war is based on logistics, on the transfer of industrial power to its armed forces in time of peace as well as in time of war, as Paul Virilio, a French philosopher, has observed. Ridgway put it in slightly different terms. "We depend upon [our industrial potential] more than upon any other factor for our national preservation."[28]

Ridgway perceived that the military necessity of maintaining industrial production was fundamental to American security. In the spring of 1946, he asked Eisenhower to mount a study on the protection of U.S. industrial potential, noting the success of industrial subversion used by the Germans against Russia in 1917 and used "defensively by Stalin in 1919 [sic]" (Ridgway probably meant 1939). He believed that to prevent industrial subversion, the armed forces had to be in communication and negotiation with all segments of society involved in production, much as he believed they had been in World War II.[29]

Ridgway linked class harmony directly to preparedness in a speech he gave to the Women's Society of Manhasset, Long Island, a few months after he wrote Report No. 8, warning of Soviet efforts to unilaterally disarm the United States. The speech unequivocally demanded rearmament as a national priority. "The time given to an unprepared selected victim by a potential aggressor may in the future be measured not in years, not in months, but in days. I hope that word 'unprepared' may strike every American brain with the impact of a blow."[30]

Yet preparedness was not enough. Society must be organized for "teamwork on the greatest American scale," as it had been, at least according to Ridgway, during World War II. In 1947, however, he observed that "today that teamwork is inoperative. In part this is due to factors inherent in democracy, in part to the exploitation by hostile elements of our freedom of the press to confuse the issues, divide our counsels, seize upon every divisive element and destroy the team." He encouraged the Manhasset women to develop quasi-critical faculties to suppress opinions that might threaten the cohesiveness of the team. True security, he argued, "calls for the best each of us can contribute . . . in the education of those who by faulty reasoning or for other causes do not see the issues as they are. It calls for painstaking analysis to detect the specious and hostile arguments in press and radio. It calls for self-dedication to the task of education in things American. It calls for selfless devotion to the task of destroying in this nation things un-American."[31]

Ridgway's rhetoric about "teamwork" seems commonplace enough, but it contains within it an assumption of the subordination of individual and class interest to the work of the "team." Ridgway believed that organized labor was one of the most important potential disruptors of America's "inoperative" team effort. A remarkable conversation between Ridgway and Eisenhower in 1946, a year of unprecedented labor unrest, on the subject of industrial sabotage reveals Ridgway's concern to get workers to join the team:

> I referred to the fact that we had in the Army today set aside a very great and powerful segment of America—labor—from which we as Army officers stayed almost entirely aloof . . . we must seek through personal acquaintances to understand their points of view and by exchange of views to assist in solving the nation's problems. I [Ridgway] remarked that the only alternatives in the case of men like John L. Lewis, whom it was our natural tendency to condemn, were either to sit down and talk or stand up and shoot, and between those two alternatives there was only one choice.[32]

Ridgway thought officers should help balance relations between social classes in order to maintain the production necessary to fight the Cold War. Military logistics required class harmony. As U.S. Army representative to the MSC, and as an advisor on arms control and disarmament negotiations, Ridgway urged negotiators to eschew flexible positions on arms control and disarmament questions because he believed that preparedness and not disarmament would best serve American security in the face of a perceived threat from the U.S.S.R., a country he believed to be duplicitous and dangerous. Security, he believed, should once again be America's top priority, as it had been during the war. In order to achieve the industrial capacity and military might necessary to protect the United States, he thought that individuals and social classes must subordinate their own demands and interests to U.S. security needs.

NOTES

1. Ridgway speech before the Women's Society of Manhasset, Long Island, New York, March 10, 1947, Ridgway MSS, Box 10.

2. Ridgway, *Soldier*, 149; Ridgway to Division Commanders, April 25, 1945, Ridgway MSS, Box 3. Ridgway to Lieutenant General D. I. Smirnov, September 14, 1945; Gavin to Ridgway, September 29, 1945; Ridgway to Gavin, November 19,

1945, Ridgway MSS, Box 8. See also Ridgway to Dempsey, May 3, 1945, Personal File, April–May 1945, Ridgway MSS, Box 3.

3. Ridgway, *Soldier*, 158.

4. Ibid., 168; DDE Papers, 7:634 has an excellent note on the Military Staff Committee.

5. Ridgway, *Soldier*, 163–164.

6. Ridgway to Eisenhower, January 18, 1946, and Eisenhower to Ridgway, March 15, 1946, DDE Papers, 7:782.

7. Ridgway, *Soldier*, 165–166; Eisenhower to Ridgway, March 15, 1946, DDE Papers, 7:782; R. Alton Lee, "The Army Mutiny of 1946," *Journal of American History* 53 (December 1966): 555–571, 563.

8. United Nations Charter, Articles 43, 47.

9. Ridgway to McCoy, March 27, 1946 and McCoy to Ridgway, April 17, 1946, Frank Ross McCoy MSS, Box 51, Library of Congress.

10. For an extended and more extensively documented discussion, see Jonathan Soffer, "All for All or One for One: The UN Military Staff Committee Negotiations," *Diplomatic History* 21 (Winter 1997): 45–69; Ridgway to Marshall, October 28, 1946, Ridgway MSS Box 8a.

11. Ridgway, *Soldier*, 309.

12. Ridgway to Major General J. R. Deane, February 17, 1947, Ridgway MSS, Box 10.

13. Soffer, "All for One or All for All," 68, 69; *New York Times*, January 8, 1992.

14. Gregg Herken, *The Winning Weapon: The Atomic Bomb in the Cold War, 1945–1950* (New York: Knopf, 1980), 167; Ridgway to Marshall, October 28, 1946, Ridgway MSS, Box 8a.

15. For accounts of the Baruch Plan, see Larry G. Gerber, "The Baruch Plan and the Origins of the Cold War," *Diplomatic History* 6 (1982): 69–95; Lloyd Gardner, *Architects of Illusion: Men and Ideas in American Foreign Policy, 1941–1949* (Chicago: 1970), 171–201; Herken, *Winning Weapon*, 154–161, 169–191; Jordan A. Schwartz, *The Speculator: Bernard Baruch in Washington* 1917–1965 (Chapel Hill: United Nations Charter Press, 1981), 490–507. On Ridgway and the Baruch Plan, see Ridgway, *Soldier*, 170–172; Ridgway to Marshall, October 28, 1946, Ridgway MSS, Box 8a.

16. Herken, *Winning Weapon*, 155–157.

17. M.S.C.-Baruch meeting, August 22, 1946, *Foreign Relations* 1 (1946): 885.

18. M.S.C.-Baruch meeting, *Foreign Relations* 1 (1946): 885; Lemnitzer to Ridgway, November 14, 1946, Ridgway MSS, Box 8a.

19. Austin-Byrnes conversation, *Foreign Relations* 1 (1946): 1053, 1054; Hiss to Acheson, November 29, 1946, *Foreign Relations* 1 (1946): 1073, 1074. On Austin's delayed conversion, see George T. Mazuzan, *Warren R. Austin at the U.N., 1946–1953* (Kent, Ohio: Kent State University Press: 1977), 94.

20. Ridgway to Eisenhower, May 31, 1946, Ridgway MSS, Box 8a. Regarding Eisenhower on disarmament, see Rusk to Peterson, January 16, 1947, *Foreign Relations* 1 (1947): 349.

21. Minutes of a meeting of the Secretaries of State, War, and Navy, January 29, 1947, *Foreign Relations* 1 (1947): 381–386.

22. Minutes of a meeting of the Secretaries of State, War, and Navy, January 29, 1947, *Foreign Relations* 1 (1947): 381–386. The editors of *Foreign Relations* noted that

Secretary Patterson transmitted General Ridgway's memorandum to the Secretaries of the State and Navy Departments at the suggestion of his Special Assistant, Dean Rusk. In his acknowledgement of Febuary 18, Secretary Marshall declared that he was "in agreement with General Ridgway's statement of the Soviet objectives" and likewise agreed "with his conclusions." The secretary of state further remarked that he was "taking steps to have Senator Austin and his principal assistants, as well as the officers of the Department of State who deal with these matters, informed of General Ridgway's views and of my agreement with them." Copies of this memorandum and the correspondence between the secretaries were enclosed in instruction 1740 to the embassy in the Soviet Union on Febuary 27. See FR 1947, 1:401–404.

23. Report No. 8, February 3, 1947, Ridgway MSS, Box 8a., reprinted in *Foreign Relations* 1 (1947): 402–404.

24. Report No. 8, February 3, 1947, Ridgway MSS, Box 8a., reprinted in *Foreign Relations* 1 (1947): 402–404; Ridgway, *Soldier*, 172; Ridgway to Col. James Agnew, November 10, 1975, Ridgway MSS, Box 31.

25. Ridgway, M.S.C. Report No. 8, Ridgway MSS, Box 8a.

26. Lemnitzer to Ridgway, April 23, 1947, Ridgway MSS, Box 8a.

27. Ridgway to Eisenhower, M.S.C. Report No. 3, June 10, 1946, Ridgway MSS, Box 8.

28. Paul Virilio and Sylvère Lotringer, *Pure War*, trans. Mark Polizotti (New York: Semiotexte, 1983), 8, 9, 14; Ridgway to Eisenhower, May 31, 1946, Ridgway MSS, Box 8a.

29. Ridgway to Chief of Staff Regarding Protection of U.S. Industrial Potential, May 31, 1946, Ridgway MSS, Box 9. In reality, labor was given little power in government agencies responsible for war production. Business predominated. See P. A. C. Koistinen, "Mobilizing the World War II Economy," *Pacific Historical Review* 42 (1973): 443–478. The reference to Stalin in 1919 is puzzling; I suspect Ridgway meant 1939–40, the time of the Hitler-Stalin Pact, when then-Major Ridgway was actively planning in anticipation of putative communist sabotage of U.S. industry (see memo for the Chief of Plans Section, December 12, 1939, Ridgway MSS, Box 2).

30. Ridgway speech before the Women's Society of Manhasset, Long Island, New York, March 10, 1947, Ridgway MSS, Box 10.

31. Ridgway speech before the Women's Society of Manhasset, Long Island, Manhasset, Long Island, N.Y. March 10, 1947. In a long conversation with Eleanor Roosevelt at the UN, in which Roosevelt mused that women in this country had no notion of what women had suffered in the areas where the war had been fought, Roosevelt asked Ridgway if he thought returning veterans would speak about what they had seen. Ridgway replied that the ones who had seen the most were likely to talk the least and were those who had undergone the most profound changes inside themselves (Ridgway, "Memo to File, Herschel Johnson Dinner," October 31, 1946, Ridgway MSS, Box 8a).

32. Ridgway, memo of conversation with Eisenhower, c. November 1946 Ridgway MSS, Box 8a.

CHAPTER 9

Ridgway and the Latin American Military: The Truman Years

Shortly after World War II ended, President Truman asked General Marshall to recommend his best combat officers for duty as ambassadors. Truman's request was a huge step toward the militarization of diplomacy, though it is doubtful he gave the matter much thought. Before the war, officers like McCoy and Ridgway who received important diplomatic assignments were exceptional. After World War II, Truman viewed the general officer corps as a pool of diplomatic talent and unexpectedly offered Ridgway the ambassadorship to Argentina. The prospective appointee, who was known throughout the military for many fine qualities, but not particularly for his tact, visited the president, protesting that he lacked diplomatic skills. Truman oddly insisted that anyone with three-star rank must have picked up some diplomatic skills.[1]

Ultimately, Ridgway rejected the job. He was not wealthy enough to run the expensive Buenos Aries Embassy. More important, he supported rearmament of the Argentine Army, contrary to the position of Undersecretary Dean Acheson and Assistant Secretary of State Spruille Braden. Acheson and Braden wished to punish President Juan Perón, ostensibly for his sympathy with Fascism, but also, as David Green has argued, because Acheson and Braden opposed Perón's independent nationalist stance.[2]

Ridgway feared that if he were posted to Argentina he would have no chance to move State Department policy on arms aid toward the position he had helped formulate at the War Department. He realized that Braden and other anti-Perónists in the State Department would do their utmost to undermine his position and credibility as soon as he got to Argentina.[3]

Ridgway supported Argentine rearmament because he believed that standardization of arms throughout Latin America would enforce the dependence of Latin armies on the United States. As Ridgway described it in his memoirs: "Our military establishment is their model, and the U.S. Army, particularly, is the model for the armies of most of the Latin-American republics. And it is their armies which excercise the controlling influence over their governments." The end of the war naturally undermined the U.S. military's ascendency in determining U.S. policy in Latin America, as did Truman's increased reliance on the State Department, which had been often ignored by FDR.[4]

Acheson and Braden argued that arming Perón would reward the Argentines for their recalcitrance at the expense of loyal allies like Brazil and would weaken democratic forces in the region. Although Braden knew Ridgway from his secret mission to Colombia before the war, the Assistant Secretary was horrified at the prospect of sending a military man as ambassador to Argentina. Braden thought the Argentines would perceive the appointment as an endorsement of military rule.[5]

Ridgway steered clear of the whole imbroglio and instead took command of U.S. forces in the Mediterranean (see chapter 8). By the beginning of 1946, Ridgway was back on the Latin America beat, assigned to chair the Inter-American Defense Board (IADB), an international group of military officers formed under the auspices of the Pan American Union. Ridgway traveled to Washington once a week to deal with Board affairs and courted one of the secretaries, the future Penny Ridgway, while living in New York and working for a second time as U.S. Army representative on the United Nations Military Staff Committee.[6]

The leading student of the IADB has noted that the Board was a largely ineffectual organization because the United States preferred to make bilateral deals for military aid, over multinational packages formulated by the Board. The main purpose of the Board was public relations to make Latin Americans feel that they could influence North-South military policy.[7]

Many subsequent U.S. officers on the IADB reported their frustration with the do-nothing Board. But Ridgway noted during his tenure as chairman that most of his problems came from Lieutenant General Carlos Von der Becke, a former commander-in-chief of the Argentine armed forces. Almost immediately after his inauguration, Perón sent Von der Becke to Washington to negotiate an arms deal—a difficult job, given the strained relations between the two countries. Although Argentina had agreed to the hemispheric defense goals of the Act of Chapultepec of 1945, Perón's tolerance of former Axis agents was a major obstacle to better relations with the United States.[8]

The son of German immigrants, Von der Becke was regarded by his peers as a professional soldier, considered neutral in the struggles between pro- and anti-Perónist generals. He tended to admire authoritarianism, and as a proud Argentine he wished to remain independent of U.S. influence. Former U.S. Ambassador Spruille Braden was less diplomatic: "He was one of three brothers, all rabid Nazis. He was also amazingly stupid." Even Ambassador George Messersmith, a critic of Braden's blunt style, referred to Von der Becke as "the dumb Prussian."[9]

Von der Becke, for his part, found his IADB tour of little use. Shortly after his arrival in Washington, he dined with some U.S. officers, including Ridgway, who grilled the Argentine on the issue of totalitarianism. As an evangelist of democracy, Ridgway tried, without success, to make the Argentine see the light of liberalism, eliciting polite agreement from the Argentine general "that any nation which sought to eliminate ideas by killing those who advanced them would inevitably meet disaster." When Army Chief of Staff General Dwight D. Eisenhower relayed warnings "that we were taken in by Von der Becke," Ridgway replied that he "did not feel we were; that I thought there was no question but that Von der Becke himself was taken in by Perón and his ideas."[10]

Ridgway and Von der Becke continued their rhetorical tussle at a plenary meeting of the IADB. Ridgway's speech stressed the commitment of the American republics to liberalism—"the right of every individual to develop his mind and his soul in the way of his own choice, free of fear and coercion—provided only that he does not interfere with the rights of others." Von der Becke, on the other hand, carefully avoided challenging the U.S. general's liberalism, while pricking him by stressing the importance of Latin American nationalism. Von der Becke complained that because of the small amount of lend lease aid given to the region "the Latin American countries have seen their relative position in the scale of material power lowered."[11]

Von der Becke continued to get increasingly annoyed at Ridgway, partly because the Argentine general seemed incapable of understanding the limited sphere of military authority in the United States. He complained to Sumner Welles that Ridgway would not see him alone. Ridgway replied that he would try to soothe the Argentine's sensibilities. Yet when Von der Becke broached to Ridgway the idea of setting up a bilateral defense board between the United States and Argentina, Ridgway told him that was a political matter for the Argentine embassy, though Von der Becke insisted that in his country this would be a military matter. Nevertheless, U.S.–Argentine relations did improve throughout 1947, especially when Argentina finally expelled some former Nazis. Ridgway thought the improvement in relations occurred because the United States sent the Argentines more sympathetic ambassadors, such as George Messersmith. Dean Acheson, on the other hand, believed that policies more critical of the Argentine government, which he had promoted, had forced their hand. Using noticibly gendered language to insinuate fickleness and irrationality, Acheson told Ridgway that the Argentines were becoming more pro-American "because of the constant pressure we were applying, but that was the only reason, and that it wouldn't move if Messersmith continued to make love to it." Soon after this conversation, reports arrived that the Soviets were "wooing" Argentina with promises of arms. Congress, however, proved reluctant to reply with an arms program for Latin America.[12]

THE INTER-AMERICAN MILITARY COOPERATION ACT

Implementing the 1945 plan for standardization of arms throughout the hemisphere required the ability to ship cheap arms south. This ability expired as World War II surpluses disappeared. The War and Navy Departments then went to Congress for additional authority to provide military aid to Latin America through the Inter-American Military Cooperation Act, which was introduced in 1946.

The U.S. military had dominated arms export policy during the war. In 1943, the Joint Army and Navy Advisory Board on American Republics, which had been created the year before at Ridgway's insistence, urged the use of lend lease to standardize the armaments used throughout the hemisphere.[13]

In July 1945, the War and Navy Departments received reluctant State Department approval for a policy to use the Surplus War Property Act to "begin the indoctrination, training and equipment of the armed forces of the other American republics." But the State Department had exacted several provisos that expressed the hesitations that ultimately prevented the adoption of the Inter-American Military Cooperation bills. The State Department, and particularly Dean Acheson and Spruille Braden, worried that arms sales might create military establishments beyond the means of nations to support them and that the arms might be used to threaten neighboring countries or to suppress internal dissent. In his memoirs, Braden charged that arms exports to Latin America were a "military racket." He claimed that the Pentagon wanted to draw down its inventories in order to ask Congress for money to buy new weapons. The State Department also insisted on giving final approval to any arms shipment plan.[14]

By December 1945, the State Department stopped all shipments to Argentina, the Dominican Republic, Haiti, Honduras, and Nicaragua and limited shipments to Bolivia and Paraguay. An internal debate followed between the War and Navy Secretaries, who wished to resume shipments, and State Department officials, who wanted to keep the lid on them. Eventually, Secretary of State James Byrnes sided with Secretary Patterson of the War Department and James Forrestal at Navy, resulting in the introduction of the Inter-American Military Cooperation Act of 1946. It sailed through committee but, owing to the press of legislation, never made it to the House floor.[15]

Until General George C. Marshall became Secretary of State, the bill seemed dead because Braden opposed it and Secretary Byrnes had thought that aid to Greece and Turkey was a much higher priority. As chair of the Inter-American Defense Board, Ridgway began a strong lobbying effort to resurrect the defeated bill. First, he asked his boss, Army Chief of Staff Eisenhower, to speak to Secretary Marshall about the matter. A month later, Ridgway checked with Eisenhower, who reported that the secretary of state remained noncommittal.[16]

In the meantime, Ridgway sent a memo to the White House, on March 30, 1947, signed by him and his colleagues in their capacity as U.S. delegates to the IADB, urging "prompt resubmission" of the act to Congress. Failure to pass the act would weaken inter-American defense cooperation, especially since U.S. officials had been promising such a program since 1939. Ridgway transposed the prewar threat of Axis influence into a threat to the Monroe Doctrine, warning that "non-American nations are now endeavoring to increase their military influence in these Republics, as the expense of ours and the supply of the military needs of these Republics from non-American sources is already a possibility, the serious implications of which are apparent."[17]

Ridgway's lobbying campaign was a partial success. On May 1, 1947, Secretary of State Marshall approved the bill, and transferred responsibility for its passage from the unsympathetic Assistant Secretary Braden to Assistant Secretary John H. Hilldring, a former general who supported it. The decision led to Braden's resignation.[18]

This time, the bill came under heavier scrutiny from conservative isolationists and liberal Democrats. Both Marshall and Eisenhower testified in favor of the bill. Marshall recalled his 1939 trip to Brazil, when it was "almost impossible" to export armaments to the Brazilian armed forces, despite their strong cooperation. "Throughout all of those affairs we were very severely embarrassed by the lack of just such legislation as is now proposed to your committee." Eisenhower also harkened back to the difficulties with Latin America at the outset of the war, and, significantly, he attacked the notion that arms shipments might contribute to the formation of a military-industrial complex. "I think this thing of the munitions makers or the industrialists of the United States pushing us into war is a myth that all of us ought to smash."[19]

Ridgway also testified in favor of the bill. His testimony was challenged by conservative representatives who fretted that the arms might fall into the hands of revolutionaries, as well as liberals such as Helen Gahagan Douglas who worried that the shipments would increase internal repression and direct resources away from the poor. Douglas argued that "we are not going to sell our way of life to the people of the South American countries through a sale of arms, but through the kind of programs that will help the people of these countries to fight disease and help them generally to achieve a higher standard of living." When Ridgway replied that the War Department acknowledged "the vital importance of the economic factor in these things and of the need for sanitation and public health and social welfare," he echoed the old reform tradition of Wood and McCoy; but unlike them, he insisted that rearmament should be America's first priority.[20]

Ridgway was not entirely convincing when he answered Douglas's questions that dealt with the problem of U.S. arms being used to increase internal repression by Latin American military establishments. "I do not believe the character of the armament in the possession of a government is a major determinant in the degree of oppression that government can impose upon its population. If a form of government has a certain type of armament, even though it is obsolete and intends to oppress its people and remain in power and divert the resources of that country to its own advantage, I do not think it makes much difference whether it is an 1879 gun or a 1941 gun. They will do it anyway. That is my personal opinion"—an opinion that seems to have changed since he lauded the effectiveness of techological advantage in the counterinsurgency against Sandino twenty years before.[21]

For Ridgway, "the whole question summarizes around this matter of strengthening a political system, the inter-American system." The "political system" he meant was an alliance dominated by the United States. Despite America's admitted dominance, Ridgway insisted that "the whole machinery is defensive" though he agreed to the proposition that making the Latin American armies dependent on the U.S. for spare parts would give the United States "a great deal of control over the situation."[22]

A few months after his congressional testimony, Ridgway returned to Rio as an alternate delegate to a conference at which the various American nations signed the Inter-American Treaty of Reciprocal Assistance, an alliance that provided that an attack on one American nation would be an attack on all. The Rio Pact was a prototype for the North Atlantic Treaty, though, unlike NATO, it did not result in the deployment of troops. Ridgway's role at the conference was minor; he provided military advice to the delegation and kept the Joint Chiefs informed about developments at the conference. According to Ridgway, the United States tried to keep the Rio treaty as general as possible, perhaps because it was anxious to fend off Latin requests for economic aid. The treaty created no permanent military command organ, thus obviating one of the primary tasks of the IADB in preparing for the conference. However, Ridgway did not seem overly disappointed and praised the treaty in his memoirs.[23]

In the spring 1948, Ridgway traveled to Bogotá with his new bride, Mary

Princess Anthony Ridgway, to attend the Bogotà Conference, which would establish the Organization of American States as a regional security organization under the United Nations Charter. The Organization of American States replaced the Pan American Union as an inter-American forum. During the conference, a riot, known as the Bogatàzo, erupted in response to the assassination of a populist Colombian politician, Jorge Gaitàn. Ridgway had been so wrapped up in the details of the inter-American defense system that the assassination initially meant little to him. The illusion of unity was critical to the genesis of both the Organization of American States, NATO, and the American alliance with Japan and was not to be disrupted by local politics. After an interruption, the delegates continued to meet in the suburbs as the capital burned.[24]

Not comprehending the significance of the assassination, Ridgway drove to his office with his orderly Sergeant Cooke. Even six stories up, the noise of the riot soon distracted the two men. They went to the windows and saw people "destroying automobiles, smashing windows, breaking into liquor and hardware stores, and just every indication of a riotous performance." Ridgway, in mufti, decided to rejoin Penny at their hotel. Deciding that he was safer unarmed, he deliberately left his .45 in the safe, a decision he later regretted, and stood on the street corner. He approached a man carrying a red flag, "quite obviously one of those labor leaders," and asked him if there was any reason he could not walk up to his hotel. The man told him "that the best thing I could do was to get off the streets and get out of sight." But he ignored the crowds and no one threatened him with violence. He arrived at the hotel safely, but in a combat mind-set.[25]

From their room, Penny stared down at the burning city and said with more curiosity than fear: "Do you see what they are doing? They can't do that." Ridgway, expecting the electricity to go out, sent the bellboy out to buy all the candles he could find. The bellboy returned in an hour, as the sun was setting, and Ridgway distributed candles to some of the other guests, including Argentine General Carlos Von der Becke, who apparently admired the U.S. general's resourcefulness under quasi-combat conditions. He came to Ridgway's room in the dark to get some candles, apparently quite frightened. Though Von der Becke had caused Ridgway considerable political trouble in the past, "he softened quite a bit after that."[26]

As the crowd surged into the lobby of his hotel, Ridgway tore two legs off the bottom of a table, gave one to Penny and stood behind the door with the other. "The first son-of-a-bitch that comes in this door, I'll get him," Ridgway told his new bride. Always practical in combat, he had decided that if he had to kill an intruder, he would have to dispose of the body down the elevator shaft if he could. Fortunately, the crowd never came up the stairs because the hotel manager presciently diverted them to the wine cellar.[27]

Then the Mexican ambassador, an old friend, took General and Mrs. Ridgway to the American embassy in his car, which sported a Mexican flag.

As they passed down the street, the flag prompted chants of "viva Mexico, viva Colombia." At the American embassy, the Ridgways found asylum with Ambassador Willard Beaulac who, as Ridgway noted, "had been in every darn trouble spot in Latin America." The ambassador generously put the general and his wife in his master bedroom. Ridgway organized a miniature command post with Penny as message center chief and G-2. Information poured into the embassy, which had radio communications with the Canal Zone in case the personnel needed to evacuate. From a house in the suburbs where he had been assigned as quarters during the conference, Secretary of State Marshall ordered Ridgway to rescue a group of delegates stranded in the barracks of the Presidential Guard battalion and gave him four officer-delegates from Colombia, Argentina, Brazil, and Paraguay to do the job. Ridgway asked the senior general of the Colombian military for a light tank and a bus. The tank commander assigned to him was completely unprepared and drove so fast through the streets that Ridgway thought he was trying to lose him. Despite the Colombian officer's recalcitrance, the American general reached the barracks and brought the beleaguered diplomats to safety in the suburbs.[28]

The conference continued to meet in private homes and approved the charter of the Organization of American States. The rioters, though not primarily communist, were supported by the Colombian Communist Party. In reaction, the Americans induced the other delegates, who were horrified by the riot, to pass strong U.S.-sponsored anticommunist resolutions. After the first few days of rioting, the President of Colombia ordered the Army into Bogotà, where it killed many people. The Bogotàzo was the start of several years of bloody civil strife between Liberals and Conservatives, known as "La Violencia."

When the Ridgways returned to Washington in mid-April, the incoming Army Chief of Staff General Omar Bradley called Ridgway in and offered him a choice of commanding either a continental army, or the Caribbean theater. Ridgway eagerly chose the Caribbean. "It proved to be a happy choice," he wrote, "for in all my career, I never had a quieter, more pleasant tour of duty." He took over the command from General Willis D. Crittenberger on July 28, 1948.[29]

The Caribbean command had small military responsibilities but large political ones. Ridgway noted that "the importance of the command is all out of importance to its size, and the commander-in-chief of the Caribbean, and his component service commanders exercise a tremendous influence on the military establishments and, therefore on the political regimes of the Latin-American republics." The boundaries of the command were large. With headquarters at Quarry Heights in the Canal Zone, the commander was responsible for U.S. military forces from the Galapagos to the Antilles.[30]

U.S. defense policy, as formulated in 1945, was predicated, as Ridgway noted, on two major considerations: "First to maintain the area as a source of vital strategic materials, and accordingly, to ensure the production and transportation of these materials to our processing areas. Second, to discharge our military obligations, implied and actual, stemming from announced national policies ranging from the Monroe Doctrine to the Inter-American Treaty of Reciprocal Assistance." The Army also hoped that stronger Latin militaries would decrease the diversion of U.S. personnel to that theater in the event of another world war.[31]

Congress, however, failed once again to approve arms aid to Latin America, which was the keystone of the proposed plan. The most the Army could do was to facilitate the provision of arms from expensive commercial sources. The lack of arms supply worried Ridgway, particularly as Argentina and Venezuela were beginning to purchase arms from Europe, including Czechoslovakia, Sweden, and Belgium. Independent of Cold War considerations, Ridgway warned General Bradley that "the vicious circle of non-American arms procurement, non-American military missions and influence, and anti-United States feeling can begin all over again and in the absence of wise and timely action on the part of the United States Government, I think it will."[32]

In the postwar world, Venezuela, the site of massive U.S. investment in oil production, began to replace Panama as the number one defense priority. Oil and bauxite became more important than ship transport, owing to the development of a "two-ocean navy." Ridgway took a special trip to Venezuela, where he visited oil installations and met with executives of U.S. corporations to coordinate plans for defense of the oil fields. Back in Washington, security agencies considered other plans for more direct intervention. The Central Intelligence Agency sent a team to Venezuela to study oil plant security. Ridgway pushed for an agreement with the Dutch for the defense of refineries in Aruba, and the Joint Chiefs of Staff studied "the political implications of using Puerto Rican troops for occupation purposes in Dutch and Venezuelan territory."[33]

The Puerto Rican element of Ridgway's command was another key to the maintenance of North American control of the Caribbean region. The mission of U.S. Antilles far exceeded the defense needs of the island, including the maintenance of a regular army cadre for the "wartime purpose of exploiting Puerto Rico's large resources in military manpower." If necessary, Puerto Rican units could be called in to maintain a mobile strike force ready to go to any "troubled critical spot" in the Caribbean area or to cope with "subversive activities and civil disturbances beyond the scope of the National Guard."[34]

The Panama Canal was at the center of American ambitions in the Caribbean when it was acquired in 1904; and control over the canal, while less important than during World Wars I and II, was a jealously guarded privilege. The canal was both the rationale for, and a key tool of, U.S. naval dominance.[35]

Few Panamanians would have termed the late forties, one of the most turbulent periods of Panamanian history, a trouble-free "Panama Idyll," as Ridgway did. There were two main sources of friction between the United States and Panama in the late forties: military bases outside the Canal Zone and racial discrimination in employment. Starting in 1940, the United States occupied 114 small installations and some larger ones for the defense of the canal. The leases for these bases expired at the end of the war, and the United States tried to renew them in 1946. When Panama refused to renew, the United States returned over 100 of the sites, but continued to occupy Rio Hato airbase and 13 other sites. Negotiations continued, with the Panamanians demanding "joint authority" over the sites, which was unacceptable to the United States. Finally, in December 1947, the United States obtained a ten-year renewable lease for Rio Hato and a five-year renewable lease for the remaining sites. This agreement provoked the resignation of Foreign Minister Ricardo Alfaro and led to massive student demonstrations. The Panamanian Assembly rejected the treaty by a vote of 51–0, and the United States evacuated the bases.[36]

Ridgway, faced with the task of defending the Canal Zone with the bare minimum of forces, had little sympathy with Panamanian nationalism at the time, although he later became one of the most prominent military supporters of Jimmy Carter's 1978 Panama Canal Treaty. At the beginning of 1949, he met with U.S. Ambassador Monnett Davis to inquire about the possibility of reopening base negotiations. Davis replied that such negotiations were not practicable. He attributed opposition to the bases to communist influence, particularly in the schools and universities—a gross exaggeration. Davis drafted a proposed policy, in which Ridgway concurred, for avoiding further negotiations on the bases, noting that the United States could, under its 1936 treaty with Panama, unilaterally take the bases in a defense emergency.[37]

Another major area of friction was wage discrimination between North American workers, placed on a "Gold Roll," who earned a minimum of $1.07 per hour, and Panamanian workers on a "Silver Roll," who received 44–66 cents per hour. While the State Department pushed for full equality in wages and benefits, Ridgway placed budgetary considerations above principles of equal pay. He feared that if Panamanian employees of the military establishment (as opposed to employees of the canal) received equal pay for equal work, then the military would have to do the same for local workers all over the world. Acceptance of the principle of equal pay for equal work threatened "major dislocations" in "other important United States interests here and in other overseas areas." He supported integration of Canal Zone facilities and cosmetic reforms, such as abolition of the invidious "gold" and "silver" rolls, without changing the wage differential. Ridgway thought that employee complaints were only partly justified, and implied that many of the complaints originated from communists when he suggested that the grievances were "deliberately intended to injure relations with Panama."[38]

Matt and Penny loved life in the torrid zone. They found Panama "a delight both to the eye and to the spirit." Penny took up painting and, as an accomplished outdoorswoman, accompanied the general on fishing trips in Panama, as well as on official trips to Ecuador, the Galapagos, and Argentina. In 1949, she also gave birth to a son, Matthew Bunker Ridgway Jr. Ridgway wrote, "I just can't imagine a man more blessed than I, there among those friendly people, in a climate like morning in Paradise, with a fine new son to bear my name, and a noble, wonderful woman for my wife."[39]

It is hard to realize from these bucolic descriptions that Panama had undergone a coup d'état during this period, perhaps because Ridgway had supported the victor, José Rémon. Rémon, who headed the Guardia Nacional, overturned the 1948 election of Arnulfo Arias and took power. While the Americans maintained only loose relations with the Guardia, U.S. Army intelligence, under Ridgway's command, helped prevent a countercoup by Arias's brother Harmodio.[40]

Ridgway maintained a closer, if more circumspect, relationship with Argentina's Juan Perón and his wife. He and Penny traveled to Buenos Aires to represent the U.S. military in Argentine independence ceremonies in July 1949.[41] Socially, the trip was a big success. President and Mrs. Perón received the Ridgways repeatedly. Argentine newspapers carried pictures of Évita and Penny on the front page, and in numerous public appearances Perón accorded General Ridgway precedence above all others present, except the Brazilian minister of war. "Penny and Évita are now 'buddies,'" Ridgway wrote to General George C. Marshall, noting that a number of things could be done to improve U.S.-Argentine relations. Ridgway also got in a minor bit of trouble for accepting a decoration and a sword from Perón. Ridgway felt that to refuse would be discourteous and that accepting the decoration was a proper method for promoting closer relations. But from the Pentagon, Paul Freeman warned Ridgway that the decoration had brought bad publicity, and that there "was some feeling on the top level that it is indiscreet for senior officers who are advocating military aid for a country to accept its decorations." Eventually, Ridgway had to turn the decoration and the sword over to the Adjutant General. Ridgway had hoped that he could at least keep the sword.[42]

Ridgway was enthusiastic about prospects for cementing Argentina firmly into the inter-American defense system. He urged General Bradley to pass on his report to Marshall and to General Eisenhower. (Though Eisenhower had left the service for Columbia University, Ridgway presumably wanted to enlist his prestige in prevailing over the opponents of military aid at the State Department.) Ridgway argued explicitly that, for reasons of state, the United States should choose to support the military, which "for the predictable future appears almost certainly to continue to be the most potent single element with which foreign governments must reckon," over Argentina's poor. For Ridgway, this was not a matter of morality. He observed that Argentina "is a military state. Whether we Americans think it right or wrong is immaterial. It is a cold reality which seems likely to endure."[43]

His recommendations for action included training of Argentine officers in U.S. military schools, better U.S. military missions, and invitations to more of Argentina's "men of influence" to tour the United States. He also advocated increased arms aid. Ridgway's aim was ideological as well as military. He feared that the Argentine military, though anticommunist, might turn toward the Soviet Union unless stroked by the U.S. military: "By our decision now we shall determine whether we enter this asset in our record book in black in days of future crisis, or by diverting into hostile hands record it at some future date 'in the red' of battle losses of American lives and treasure." The goal of the military aid program should not necessarily be democratic doctrine, but rather the Monroe Doctrine—to exclude European influence from the Western Hemisphere. At a time when the Argentine military was apparently correctly rumored to be sheltering Nazi fugitives and remained one of the last bastions of pro-Fascist sentiment, Ridgway's realism was controversial. He tried, however, to suggest that cooperation would eventually serve the end of democracy: "If we wisely choose, we can, in time, eliminate from the Argentine armed forces the last effective influence of non-American military doctrine; replace non-American sources of arms with our own; implant in the Argentine people a sturdy respect for our own; and, in time of future trouble, have some reasonable assurance of a strong, helpful and willing ally instead of an uncertain and troublesome neutral, or even possibly of an open enemy."[44]

Ridgway's impassioned plea for aid to Argentina made little impression in Washington. General Bradley informed him that Latin America "is a low priority compared to Europe." All of Ridgway's important suggestions for increased aid and a closer relationship were rejected, at least until the Korean War forced policy makers, again fearful of another world war, to reconsider measures for hemispheric defense.[45]

NOTES

1. JB, 2:3:1–3; John Child, interview with Ridgway, May 10, 1977 (hereafter Child Interview) (Ridgway MSS), 3.

2. David L. Green, *The Containment of Latin America* (Chicago: Quadrangle 1971), 7:246–252.

3. Child interview, 14; Jesse H. Stiller, *George S. Messersmith: Diplomat of Democracy*. (Chapel Hill: University of North Carolina Press, 1987), 229.

4. Ridgway, *Soldier*, 184; Chester J. Pach Jr., *Arming the Free World: The Origins of the United States Military Assistance Program, 1945–1950* (Chapel Hill: University of North Carolina Press, 1991), 35–42.

5. Spruille, Braden, *Diplomats and Demagogues* (New York: Arlington House, 1971), 360; Gary Frank, *Juan Perón v. Spruille Braden: The Story Behind the Blue Book* (Lanham, Md.: University Press of America, 1980), 95.

6. U.S. Congress House of Representatives, Committee on Foreign Affairs, *Hearings on H.R. 3836, The Inter-American Military Cooperation Act*, 80th Cong. 1st sess. June 23–July 2, 1947, testimony of Ridgway, 85.

7. See John Child, *Unequal Alliance: The Inter-American Military System, 1938–1978* (Boulder, Colo.: Westview Press, 1980), 1–5; Child, interview with Ridgway 9, Ridgway MSS.

8. Child interview with Ridgway 9, 10; Alberto Conil Paz and G. Ferrari, *Argentina's Foreign Policy, 1930–1962* (South Bend, Ind.: University of Notre Dame Press, 1966), 140.

9. Child interview with Ridgway, 10; Robert A. Potash, *The Army and Politics in Argentina, 1945–1962* (Stanford, Calif.: Stanford University Press, 1980), 9; Braden, *Diplomats and Demagogues*, 316.

10. Ridgway Diary, October 21, 1946, Ridgway MSS, Box 8a.

11. Speeches of Ridgway and Von der Becke to IADB on Its Fifth Anniversary, March 22, 1947, Ridgway MSS, Box 8a.

12. Sumner Welles to Ridgway, June 25, 1947, and Ridgway to Welles, July 2, 1947, Ridgway MSS, Box 8a; Ridgway Diary, July 30, 1947, Box 8a; Ridgway Diary, February 14, 1947, and Lt. Col. Walter Winton to Chief of Staff, March 13, 1947, Ridgway MSS, Box 8a.

13. Chester J. Pach Jr., "The Containment of U.S. Military Aid to Latin America, 1944–1949," *Diplomatic History* 6, no. 3 (Summer 1990): 226–228.

14. Ibid., Stephen G. Rabe, "Inter-American Military Cooperation 1944–951," *World Affairs* 137, no. 2 (Fall 1974): 132, 136; Braden, *Diplomats and Demagogues*, 364–365.

15. "Inter-American Military Cooperation," 137: The bill was numbered HR 6326 and S2153.

16. Pach, "Containment," 234–237; Ridgway Diary Memos, February 18, 1947, and March 22, 1947, Box 8a, Ridgway MSS.

17. Ridgway to Secretary, Presidential Staff Charged with Legislation, March 30, 1947, Harry S. Truman Papers, White House Central Files, Confidential, Harry S. Truman Presidential Library, Independence, Missouri.

18. Pach, "Containment," 238; Rabe, 140; Braden, *Diplomats and Demagogues*, 367.

19. U.S. Congress, House, Committee on Foreign Affairs *Hearings on H.R. 3836, Inter-American Military Cooperation Act*, 80th Cong., 1st sess. June 23–26, July 2, 1947, Marshall Testimony, 7, Eisenhower Testimony, 50.

20. Ibid., 86.

21. Ibid.

22. Ibid., 87, 93.

23. Ridgway, *Soldier*, 174; Pogue, *Marshall*, 4:381–384; Child Interview, 20.

24. Ridgway, *Soldier*, 178; JB 2:3:24, 25. The Bogotàzo began on April 9, 1948.

25. Ridgway, *Soldier*, 178; JB 2:3:27.

26. Ridgway, *Soldier*, 178, 179; on Von der Becke, Child Interview, 10.

27. JB 2:3:24–29.

28. JB, 2:3:29–30; Ridgway, *Soldier*, 180; Pogue, *Marshall*, 381–384.

29. Ridgway, *Soldier*, 182; Ridgway, 201 Files, Ridgway MSS, Box 1.

30. Ridgway, *Soldier*, 183; Ridgway to Barbey, July 27, 1948, Ridgway MSS, Box 1.

31. Proposed Latin American Program, March 8, 1948, Ridgway MSS, Box 1.

32. Freeman to Ridgway, July 8, 1948, Ridgway MSS, Box 13; quoted in Freeman to Ridgway, April 6, 1949, Ridgway MSS, Box 1; Ridgway to Bradley, September 1, 1949, Ridgway MSS, Box 1.

33. Hanson Baldwin, "Canal Role Defense Cut: Bauxite and Oil Are Now the Key Factors in Naval Caribbean Strategy, Study Finds," *New York Times*, March 4, 1949; Ridgway to Wedemeyer, January 20, 1949, Ridgway MSS, Box 13; Memo on Venezuela Tour, August 16, 1949 and Memo on U.S. and Bethlehem Steel Interests in Venezuelan Iron Ore Deposits, August 16, 1949, Ridgway MSS, Box 14; C.I.A., Freeman to Ridgway, November 16, 1948, Ridgway MSS, Box 13; Freeman to Ridgway, April 6, 1949, Ridgway MSS, Box 1.

34. HQ U.S. Army Forces to Maj. Gen. Porter, February 19, 1949, Ridgway MSS, Box 13.

35. J. Michael Hogan, *The Panama Canal in American Politics* (Carbondale: Southern Illinois University Press: 1986), 31.

36. Walter LeFeber, *The Panama Canal: The Crisis in Historical Perspective*, 2d ed. (New York: Oxford University Press, 1989), 79–81; Defense Site Negotiations, n.d., after December 1947, Folder, Misc., Ridgway MSS, Box 13.

37. Memcon, February 16, 1949, Ridgway MSS, Box 13. For examples of exaggeration of communist influence, see LaFeber, *Panama Canal*, 80.

38. LaFeber, *Panama Canal*, 83; Ridgway to Secretary of the Army, November 29, 1948, *Foreign Relations* 9 (1948): 688; Memorandum by the Acting Assistant Chief of the Division of Central American and Panama Affairs, December 8, 1948, *Foreign Relations* 9 (1948): 689; Ridgway to Bradley, October 30, 1948, Ridgway MSS, Box 12.

39. Ridgway, *Soldier*, 184, 185.

40. LaFeber, *Panama Canal*, 87.

41. Ridgway to Chief of Staff, U.S. Army, Report on Argentine Trip, July 27, 1949, Ridgway MSS, Box 1.

42. Ridgway to chief of staff, U.S. Army, Report on Argentine Trip, July 27, 1949, Ridgway MSS, Box 1; Ridgway to Marshall, July 19, 1949, Ridgway MSS, Box 11; Ridgway to Freeman, July 20, 1949, Ridgway MSS, Box 11; Freeman to Ridgway, July 25, 1949, Ridgway MSS, Box 11; Adjutant General E. F. Witsell to Ridgway, July 21, 1949 and Ridgway to Witsell, July 21, 1949, Ridgway MSS, Box 15.

43. Ridgway to Bradley, July 28, 1949, Ridgway MSS, Box 13; Ridgway to chief of staff, U.S. Army, Report on Argentine Trip, 27 July 1949, Ridgway MSS, Box 1.

44. Ridgway to chief of staff, U.S. Army, Report on Argentine Trip, July 27, 1949, Ridgway MSS, Box 1.

45. Pach, *Arming the Free World*, 62; Bradley to Ridgway, August 13, 1949, Ridgway MSS, Box 11.

Matthew Ridgway, age 12, with sister and friends, 1907. Courtesy of the U.S. Army Military History Institute.

"The Black Knight of the Hudson" USMA Cadet Matthew B. Ridgway, West Point, 1917. Courtesy of the U.S. Army Military History Institute.

Major General Matthew B. Ridgway, commander of the 82d Airborne Division, walks with General Dwight D. Eisenhower, North Africa, 1942–43. Courtesy of the U.S. Army Military History Institute.

Mary Princess Anthony (Penny) Ridgway, General of the Army George C. Marshall, and General Matthew B. Ridgway, n.d. (probably in Washington, D.C., May 1952). Courtesy of the U.S. Army Military History Institute.

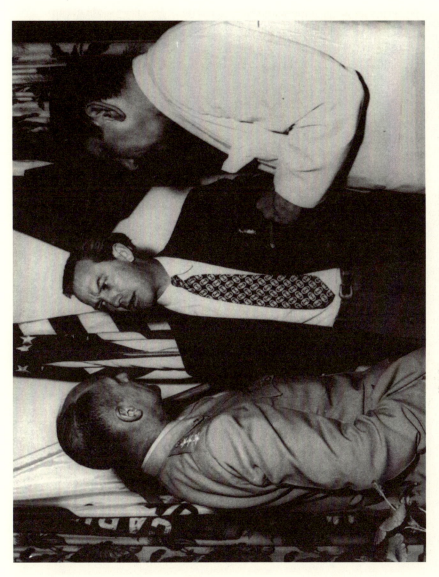

Caribbean Defense Commander, Lt. General Matthew B. Ridgway confers with Congressman L. Mendel Rivers and Governor Luis Muñoz Marín, El Torro Officers Club, Fort Brooke, Tampa, Fla., 1949. Courtesy of the U.S. Army Military History Institute.

Lieutenant General Ridgway, commanding Eighth Army, confers with visiting General Mark W. Clark, Korea, February, 1951. Courtesy of the U.S. Army Military History Institute.

General Matthew Ridgway turns over Supreme Allied Command, Europe (SACEUR) to General Alfred M. Gruenther, Paris, July, 1953. Courtesy of the U.S. Army Military History Institute.

Army Chief-of-Staff Matthew Ridgway gives a shooting lesson to his son, Matthew B. Ridgway Jr., at the firing range at Fort Belvoir, Va., August 31, 1954. Courtesy of the U.S. Army Military History Institute.

CHAPTER 10

The Korean War

When his orders came through, Ridgway was not happy about trading the Caribbean Command for an office in the Pentagon and the dry-sounding title of Deputy Chief of Staff for Administration. He found the Washington atmosphere "stultifying." In Quarry Heights, Canal Zone, he was *the* theater commander. At the Department of Defense, he was just one of many generals. Washington duty was sure to be hard on his wife, Penny, too. Most of the wives of high-ranking officers in Washington were older and envied her youth. These women resented her marriage into high rank. She had skipped the thirty years of tribulations incident to a long career as an officer's wife, which they thought all the more galling because her first husband had been an enlisted man.[1]

Still, there were compensations. Though Ridgway probably did not know it, General Omar Bradley, an old friend, had moved Ridgway to the Pentagon in order to groom him as future Army chief of staff, an assignment held at the time by J. Lawton Collins. Ridgway and Collins had been classmates at West Point, but they were more rivals than friends. Ridgway had lost the race to succeed Eisenhower as chief due to his lack of Pentagon experience, and perhaps because of his "controversial" second divorce and remarriage.[2]

The Ridgway home, Quarters Five, at Fort Meyer, also compensated for the unpleasantness of Washington duty. Lieutenant-General Albert C. Wedemeyer, his predecessor, wrote him that Quarters Five had "perhaps the loveliest view from the front porch that one could find on the perimeter of Washington." Wedemeyer also informed him that he was entitled to "two boys" from a "colored" servants detachment of soldiers on the base that had "excellent material for cooks and houseboys." Although Ridgway said nothing and accepted the perquisite without comment, he would later initiate action that ultimately destroyed the army's system of segregation that reduced African American soldiers to "houseboys."[3]

The Ridgways boarded a steamship to New York, arriving in Washington by rail on September 14, 1949. That day, rainwater samples from contaminated clouds confirmed that the Soviet Union had exploded its first atomic device. Along with the victory of the Chinese Communist armies, and the accusations of atomic spying against the Rosenbergs, the announcement of the Soviet atomic tests inaugurated the most fear-filled period of the Cold War.[4]

As a deputy chief of staff, and a well-known hero of World War II, Ridgway was frequently asked to give speeches, in which he delineated his corporatist ideological framework in an effort to moblize support for Cold War military spending. His delivery was more arresting than amusing. He later observed: "There was never anything of the showman in me and never anything of the jokeman. I can't make a speech and be funny, and I never tried, because it would just fall flat."[5]

In a talk to the Women's Patriotic Conference on National Defense, a coalition of patriotic women's organizations, Ridgway stressed the lack of rationality inherent in the world situation. "Confusion of thinking will continue to perplex us," he observed. That audience included many right-wing women, such as the Gold Star Mothers who had pressed hard for demobilization. Ridgway appealed to them for a return to Victorian values of self-sacrifice, faith, and civic virtue. Implicitly criticizing hedonistic consumerism as an obstacle to winning the Cold War, he prognosticated that "it will not be by the EASY life that we shall survive." In one of his few explicit discussions of virtue, he told the women at the conference to fix their thoughts upon "the subordination of the self to service, the willingness to sacrifice all for others, courage, moral stamina, physical endurance, and the will to fight for principle while life remains."[6]

Ridgway entangled his notion of virtue as collective self-sacrifice with a corporatist ideology calling for social harmony and consensus—a prerequisite, he believed, for national security. In discussing plans for World War III, he told an audience at the Armed Forces Staff College that "only by the combined, skillful, balanced employment of Army, Navy and Air; of industry and science; of labor and management; of our people and our allies; welded into one all-inclusive, persevering effort, can we both win the war and more important still, the peace to follow."[7] He favored imposition of mobilization controls on the economy and the use of federal troops to end a railway strike that threatened to impede the war effort during the critical situation in Korea in December 1950.[8]

Ridgway's concern for social harmony followed naturally from his understanding that industrial capacity had become the indispensable element of warfare. He appreciated the importance of technological change. Nevertheless, he opposed enthusiasts of air power who would downgrade the role of the foot soldier in favor of a pushbutton war. Instead, he argued that the increasingly lethal nature of the technological battlefield made the morale and civic virtue of the soldier more critical to successful operations. In fighting a rearguard action against the domination of the battlefield by technological values, Ridgway ironically anticipated the preoccupation of late-twentieth-century strategists with motivating the human soldier to function in the "increased stresses to which new weapons will subject them in tomorrow's combat."[9]

He disdained discussion of "the marvels of future combat." He understood that for all its importance, technology alone would not win wars, that the soldier himself had to be trained, even modified, to meet the demands of battle: "We won't win just because we have the best gun. We must also have the best man behind that gun—one far superior to his individual enemy in intelligence, discipline, alertness and toughness of spirit."[10]

Ridgway's concerns for morality, class harmony, and self-sacrifice for common interests in security, as well as his concerns about the limits of technology in war, continued to be his recurring major themes throughout the 1950s. These themes would inform his campaigns for more U.S. and allied defense spending, and his criticisms of U.S. military policy. Corporatist ideology enabled Ridgway to explain many of the contradictions between his life as a warrior and his life as a bureaucrat.

THE POLITICS OF THE PENTAGON, 1949–1950

As the army's "general manager," Ridgway held a wide variety of responsibilities. He made extensive comments on Army planning for World War III. Along with twelve other generals at the apex of the Army command, Ridgway met weekly with Secretary of the Army Gordon Gray. He continued to keep a hand in Latin American affairs and administered the Army's day-to-day business at a time of widespread skepticism about the usefulness of the foot soldier in the atomic age. He also had to contend with the merciless budget axe of Secretary of Defense Louis Johnson, the chief skeptic. Budget cutting may well have been justified, but Johnson was not a man of sufficient authority or subtlety to persuade military officers that it was.[11]

Johnson favored a military strategy based on an atomic blitz against the U.S.S.R., mostly because it seemed the cheapest strategy. In the budget contests between rival services, this meant more money for the Air Force and cuts for the other services. He cancelled the building of the "supercarrier" *United States,* which provoked the "revolt of the admirals" when senior naval officers complained to Congress. Johnson also upset Army officers when he withheld from President Truman the May 1949 Harmon Report, which raised questions about the effectiveness of an air-atomic blitz. As Congress became a forum for titanic battles between the United States Navy and the United States Air Force, land forces were largely ignored.[12]

During this period, most military planners assumed that the next war would be a struggle for control of the periphery of the Eurasian landmass. Plans, such as DROPSHOT, a long-term plan for war in 1957 and OFF-TACKLE, the plan for immediate world war, presumed that the ambitious global objectives of the planners could be attained by means of atomic attack.[13] Despite the reservations of prominent generals such as Bradley and Gruenther, these plans moved forward, primarily as a reflection of the budgetary priority granted to atomic weapons over land forces.

After the Korean War started, speculation about World War III became a public preoccupation. By this time, Ridgway had become identified in the eyes of the public as an almost generic symbol of American military power. *Collier's* magazine bought a full-page in the *New York Times* advertising its October 27, 1951, issue that presented views of numerous authors on the "Preview of the War We Do Not Want," subtitled "Russia's Defeat and Occupation, 1952–1960." In the foreground is a soldier holding a bayoneted rifle. There is a grenade on his lapel—a Ridgway trademark—and his features are recognizably Ridgway's. According to his helmet, he is a "military policeman of the United Nations occupation forces." The background is a map of Eastern Europe and the U.S.S.R. Moscow flies a UN flag and is labeled "Occupation Headquarters." Ridgway, who at the Pentagon had repeatedly opposed the irresponsible brandishing of U.S. military power, was reduced by the magazine's art department to a symbol of American military imperialism.[14]

Contrary to his militant public image, Ridgway challenged the reliance of war plans on atomic weapons "on the grounds that we might win military operations, but would destroy what was left of Western European civilization and bankrupt our own people." He called for more imaginative offensive use of land forces based on the use of mobility and surprise, as opposed to the type of strategy used for the Normandy invasion—building up one great base for support of an effort in a predetermined military direction. Such a strategy, he argued would better serve America's strategic objective in another world war—economic improvement—a crude extrapolation from the nation's World War II experience with military Keynesianism.[15]

Despite his call for a new strategy, the narrative that Ridgway constructed for a third world war still sounded like a curiously optimistic reprise of World War II, with the United States substituted for Britain as an island redoubt. "We may have to take a first strike and retaliate, and it will be hard to survive "the long period of buildup," he observed. The beginning of the war would be "a period of maximum stress on field commanders" and "a period of soul-searching for our statesmen who, putting aside every lesser end, must seek to lead our nation and our world to something far better than any from which even as victors we have yet emerged following a global war."[16]

When war actually came, it would be completely different from what either Ridgway or *Collier's* had imagined. The ongoing strife between North and South Korea escalated into a full-scale war on June 25, 1950; and by June 30, President Truman had committed U.S. combat troops. Though Truman tried to convince the world that this was merely a "police action," the action involved a large chunk of America's available combat forces. When Ridgway heard the news of the North Korean offensive, he rushed back to Washington from Carlisle Barracks, where he and Penny had been on a junket inspecting both the Pennsylvania National Guard and the beautiful countryside. In short order, he became General J. Lawton Collins's chief advisor and executive on Korean matters, briefing the chief of staff and the secretary of the Army daily and personally overseeing the supply of critical materials, such as the new 3.5-inch bazookas needed to stop Soviet-made North Korean tanks.[17]

In 1950, the United States had made no contingency plans for a defense of South Korea. Indeed, President Truman committed combat troops more as a reflex application of the Truman Doctrine than as a carefully debated policy decision. Most major war planning, such as Operation DROPSHOT, had been geared to World War III—an attempt to maintain control of the littoral of the Eurasian landmass on a worldwide basis. Military planners interpreted the march south of the North Korean People's Army as part of a grand design by Stalin. They thought the Russians wanted to gain an advantage for a world war, perhaps by diverting U.S. troops to the Korean Penninsula—then considered relatively unimportant in American geopolitical strategy. In fact, the initiative for the attack came from North Korean leader Kim Il Sung, as part of an ongoing civil war. Though the move was cleared with Stalin and Mao, who promised aid, it was not ordered by them.[18]

Ridgway continued to fear that the Korean War might escalate into World War III; and consistent with his corporatist ideals, he favored a full mobilization of the U.S. economy. It seemed to him that American mobilization for the Korean War was unduly limited by the reluctance of the American people to sacrifice what he saw as their cushy lifestyle. In the very first days of the war, General Dwight D. Eisenhower, then president of Columbia University, "dropped by" to visit Ridgway at the Pentagon and offered to lobby Truman for a partial mobilization, internal security measures, and the use of atomic weapons in Korea and to allow General Douglas MacArthur, the Far East Theater commander, to operate north of the 38th parallel.

Eisenhower also suggested replacing MacArthur as commander. In his diary, Ridgway wrote that "Ike expressed the wish that he would like to see a younger general out there, rather than, as he expressed it, 'an untouchable' whose actions you cannot predict, and who will himself decide what information he wants Washington to have and what he will withhold." Ridgway agreed with Eisenhower's various suggestions and strongly encouraged him to see the president.[19]

In a meeting with Ridgway and General Mark Clark, Army Secretary Frank Pace expressed his opinion that the primary mission of the armed forces should be in Europe, not the Far East, an argument that assumed that a third world war was still in the making. He argued that "unless we are prepared either for defeat or for an indefinite continuation of living under the constant threat of Russian bullying, we have got to accept the fact of a lower standard of living, in order to create the military strength which will permit us to call a halt to this bullying and challenge its power once and for all." General Ridgway told Pace he agreed with him completely. Concerned that consumerism would feminize and ruin American youth, he called for "a national effort to combat the softening influences to which our youngsters were exposed from birth on."[20]

Ridgway still desperately wanted to get out of Washington, in part because he was bitterly critical of President Truman's "criminal neglect" in failing to develop a coherent grand strategy.[21] One suggestion that he offered in order to break the policy logjam was to appoint a committee of three to five individuals of "demonstrated intellectual capacity," "with a nationally recognized chairman," who would determine America's war objectives. Once this elite group made the decisions, "general acceptance" could be "obtained from our people, were sufficient effort made to draw it." The plan reveals once again the degree to which Ridgway's politics rested upon the idea of a neutral and unitary public interest that could be ascertained by experts. Ridgway had a particular expert in mind, noting that Eisenhower, who was then in the process of setting up the American Assembly at Columbia University, might be the best person to select the group. With Collins's blessing, Ridgway spent a half hour briefing Eisenhower, who said "he liked and would use the idea." Secretary of the Army Frank Pace also liked the idea and promised to show it to Ford Foundation Chairman Paul Hoffman."[22]

Ridgway's frustration with the plans for World War III contained a rationale for the as yet unarticulated doctrine that war should somehow be limited to be effective. Total war benefited no one; it would destroy Western Europe and most of Russia. He called for a complete revision of U.S. policy and war strategy to preclude the destruction of Soviet cities. In the case of victory, Ridgway believed, the United States should give terms that would avoid humiliating the Soviets and leave them with a reasonable standard of living.[23]

Ridgway's attitude as assistant chief of staff toward the possibility of taking command in Korea also suggests that he continued to anticipate world war, a fear that subsided only briefly after the Inchon landings. Returning from a trip to Tokyo with General Lauris Norstad and Averell Harriman, Ridgway expressed grave reservations over Eighth Army Commander General Walton Walker's lack of leadership, acceptance of a mediocre staff, and unsound base organization. Ridgway also endorsed MacArthur's controversial plan for an amphibious landing at Inchon Harbor. Probably unbeknownst to him, Norstad and Harriman recommended to Collins that Ridgway replace Walker in command.[24]

At the time, many observers thought Ridgway was angling for the job. In a meeting with Collins alone, Ridgway avoided expressing interest. Collins "discussed the question of command in Korea, and he made the statement that Van Fleet was the natural selection" but coyly told Ridgway that "of course you could do it too." In keeping with the tradition that it was gauche to lobby too hard for a combat command, Ridgway answered "in a matter of fact tone" that he "would prefer to fight in Europe"—still a plausible reply. Collins obviously wanted to cool down Ridgway's desire for a Korea command, telling him, "I am planning to put you in [Vice Chief] Haislip's place when he retires within a year and if I send you to Korea, you might be so involved I couldn't get you out."[25]

By the beginning of December, the rout of Eighth Army by the Chinese made the possibility of World War III less of an academic matter. President Truman began a huge military buildup, requesting a $16 billion supplemental appropriation, but Ridgway was still angry about Washington's slowness in mobilizing. At one meeting of the Joint Chiefs with Secretary of State Dean Acheson present, Ridgway vigorously protested talk of a UN-brokered cease-fire. "The JCS [Joint Chiefs of Staff] had a responsibility to the American people and to God," he exclaimed, to accelerate the buildup of U.S. forces "in anticipation of further Soviet inspired aggression, including Soviet hostilities."[26]

Still convinced that World War III remained imminent, Ridgway privately recommended even more drastic action to hunker down for a big war: evacuation of U.S forces from Korea, putting the economy on a wartime footing, and reallocation of forces between the Far East and Europe, as needed. Ridgway also suggested, for internal security reasons, that the government "Clamp down immediately and rigidly on disclosure of information of value to the enemy" and "forbid, under severe penalties, any recrimination among senior officers," an attempt, no doubt, to prevent General MacArthur from stirring up criticism of the Joint Chiefs.[27]

The depth of the war scare in a jittery Pentagon is suggested by the interruption of a three-service briefing just as General Marshall had called for "calmness" owing to reports "that a large number of unidentified planes were approaching the northeast U.S., and that there was no reason to believe them to be friendly." It turned out that there was no threat—whether they were U.S. Air Force planes returning from Europe or a flock of geese is uncertain from the record. The fear of total war in this period was so great that the message went all the way to the Joint Chiefs of Staff without confirmation. The situation was so critical that on December 18 Ridgway briefed the president on provisions for continental defense and U.S. plans to defend itself "by offensive action on other continents," noting that if war occurred immediately it would take at least a year to provide any major support to NATO.[28]

Ridgway's tribulations in Washington were cut short on a cold winter evening, three days short of Christmas 1950. After a grueling fourteen-hour workday, Matt and Penny were relaxing over cocktails with old friends. Just before midnight, he received a call from General Collins informing him that the Eighth Army commander, General Walton Walker, had died in a car crash and that Ridgway was to proceed to Korea as soon as possible. Ridgway agreed to go and put on a smile as he left the phone, determining not to tell Penny until he brought up her coffee the next morning, so that she could have a good night's sleep. (He did not know until 1975 that Collins and MacArthur had selected him as Walker's understudy in advance, so the news of Walker's death and his appointment must have been shocking.) Yet his smile was not entirely feigned. After all, he had just gotten the combat command he coveted. He would develop a reputation for working miracles.[29]

In December 1950, the war in Korea had proven a disaster for the Americans. The Chinese army had succeeded in pushing Eighth Army into a disorganized retreat. The Joint Chiefs of Staff seriously debated withdrawing U.S. troops from Korea, altogether in anticipation of a wider war. *Time* magazine was so dejected that its editors could not find an individual to name as Man of the Year, choosing instead the American GI, "Destiny's Draftee." Destiny's draftees were not a happy lot when Matt Ridgway arrived to take command. He convinced them to fight, and they advanced, but as with Ulysses S. Grant, there would be a price in blood for his fine generalship.[30]

RIDGWAY IN KOREA

> All of this business of restoring the fighting spirit . . . it is a multitude of little details, gentlemen. The synergistic effect over a long time is what works the miracles to them.[31]
>
> —Matthew B. Ridgway

By the day after Christmas (Tokyo time), Ridgway had reached Tokyo, where he conferred with his theater commander, General Douglas MacArthur. The two men had known each other since the early 1920s. MacArthur, then superintendent of West Point, gave Ridgway, then a young Spanish language instructor, the prestigious position of Director of Athletics—a push that helped launch the younger man's career. They had seen each other only twice since those days. When Ridgway flew to the Pacific after VE-Day in order to transport his XVIII Airborne Corps there, only to hear while in the air of Japan's surrender, MacArthur had courteously offered Ridgway a seat on the battleship *Missouri* for the surrender ceremonies. Ridgway gallantly declined, believing that his place should be held by an officer who had fought in the theater. The second time they saw each other was in August 1950 when Ridgway traveled to Tokyo to report to the Joint Chiefs of Staff on the plans for the Inchon landing, which Ridgway supported despite the worries of other military men.

Ridgway disagreed, however, with many other decisions that the senior general made in the course of the war. Ridgway was not too shy to recommend to General Hoyt Vandenberg, then Air Force chief of staff, that MacArthur be sacked for insubordination if he ignored directives from the Joint Chiefs, long before Truman did the deed. Nonetheless, Ridgway had always found MacArthur "fascinating and compelling," and MacArthur returned his respect. MacArthur did not feel he had to look over Ridgway's shoulder in the way in which he had shadowed Walker. He told Ridgway, "Form your own opinions and use your own judgment. I will support you. I will assume responsibility. You have my complete confidence." He gave Ridgway complete command of all forces in Korea, which ended the much-criticized split in command of land forces between Walker's Eighth Army and General Edward Almond's X Corps. Ridgway asked if MacArthur would have any objection if the former attacked at a time when most of Eighth Army expected to withdraw. MacArthur broke out in a broad grin and said, "Do what you think best, Matt. The Eighth Army is yours."[32]

Ridgway immediately flew to Seoul. His longtime aide, Walter Winton, later described the situation in those first weeks: "Weather terrible, Chinese ferocious, morale stinko." There Ridgway began the task of turning a dispirited army in retreat into a confident army moving forward—his most famous feat of generalship. In fifty-four days, he changed the war from a rout of his own army to a war of attrition at a defensive line more or less of his own choosing.[33]

General of the Army Omar Bradley said later, "It is not often in wartime that a single battlefield commander can make a decisive difference. But in Korea, Ridgway would prove to be the exception. His brilliant, driving, uncompromising leadership would turn the tide of battle like no other general's in our military history." Historian James F. Schnabel called it a "military miracle." Chinese commanders echoed Bradley's assessment. According to historian Michael Schaller, "They credit him with identifying their logistic weakness and employing air and artillery attacks in limited counteroffensives that devastated the ranks of the People's Volunteers. By avoiding the grandiloquent rhetoric and strategy of MacArthur, Chinese military historians admit, Ridgway broke their offensive power."[34]

The American Civil War was very much on Ridgway's mind as he toured each Eighth Army installation. While Ridgway claimed to be an admirer of Lee, his pragmatic revisions of both strategy and tactics seem more in the tradition of the dogged Civil War General Ulysses S. Grant. He wrote to X Corps commander Edward N. Almond: "We still have far to go to attain the standards of toughness of body and soul of American troops, who, as you so well remember, in each of several civil war battles, with fewer men engaged than we now have in line, suffered in a few hours double the number of casualties than this command has had in six months of fighting."[35]

Ridgway understood from his travels that his army was not yet in a position to go on the offensive, and he gave orders to continue the retreat. One priority was to reinstill an offensive spirit in officers and enlisted men. This often meant a tightening of procedures and discipline that some GIs were apt to refer to as "chickenshit." He avoided wholesale sacking of officers, except, perhaps, at the division commander level, but he could be absolutely ruthless, particularly if he wanted to set an example. In a highly publicized incident, Ridgway relieved Colonel John R. Jeter, the G-3 of I Corps when Jeter presented the corps's defensive plans, as ordered. Ridgway asked, "Where are your attack plans?" Jeter had none. The relief was capricious and probably unfair to Jeter personally; it was certainly unpopular among staff officers. The story, however, quickly circulated throughout Eighth Army. Thereafter, its officers always thought about attack as well as defense. Ridgway also decided to axe many of his senior division commanders and replace them with younger men. These younger men included such well-known World War II figures as Hobart "Hap" Gay, who had been at Patton's side when "Old Blood 'n' Guts" was killed in a car accident, and William B. Kean, who, as First Army chief of staff during the Battle of the Bulge, had worked closely with Ridgway. Fearing a congressional investigation, the Pentagon treated the returning generals like conquering heroes— they were decorated and the newspapers were told that they were being rotated back to positions of major responsibility.[36]

When he arrived in Korea, the strategic situation was so desperate that Ridgway asked permission to use poison gas against the Chinese in case of evacuation of the penninsula. Despite his concerns about the strategic effects of an air-atomic blitz, Ridgway did not believe atomic, chemical, or biological weapons were inherently evil. MacArthur denied the request for gas because "U.S. inhibitions on its use are complete and drastic" and allies would likely protest.[37]

Though retreating, even abandoning, Seoul in the face of a new Chinese offensive, the Army commander ordered units to maintain contact with the enemy and to kill or wound as many as possible. From the beginning, Ridgway went from camp to camp, jumping out of his jeep to tell officers, "I am not here to get real estate, I am here to defeat the enemy," adding "and you are going to do it now." Historian Roy Appleman, who served in Korea at the time, dryly commented, "This performance did not impress most of the viewers." Despite the 1970s TV image of MASH (Mobile Army Surgical Hospital) doctors as semipacifists, Ridgway made it a priority to visit all the hospitals and tell the doctors, "The minute you get a man here start instilling in him the eagerness to get back to his unit," explaining that "a man who has been trained is worth several times the raw replacement that you get for him." Ridgway also understood the potential power of nurses to motivate men, as symbols of family back home and the girl-next-door whom they were fighting for: "The nurses could play a hell of a part in this because a woman is trying to tell this wounded man . . . build up in him a pride in what he had done and the desire to get back with his buddies there as soon as possible, it has an electric effect on him."[38]

Defeating the enemy meant inflicting maximum Chinese casualties. Ridgway, understanding how to use the American advantage in firepower, turned the Korean War into a war of attrition, much as Grant had done in the Civil War. In addition, Ridgway revised tactics, ordering road-bound GIs to fan out and climb the hills and rearranging the lines so that each unit would become mutually supporting. This tactic made Allied lines much more difficult to penetrate.[39]

Ridgway's new strategy received wide publicity and praise on the home front. When the Chinese onslaughts temporarily stopped, *Life* reported that "U.N. officers were hopeful" that Ridgway's attrition strategy "might be paying off." Though the *Times* quoted unnamed military experts as worried that the Chinese manpower advantage could still drive the Eighth Army back to Pusan, by early February the dominant view in the Pentagon was that U.S. forces could stay in Korea indefinitely—which, of course, they have.[40]

Ridgway evacuated Seoul on January 4, 1951, in the face of a Chinese offensive that began on New Year's Eve. Owing to the limited logistical capacity of the Chinese forces, their offensive ran out of steam by January 7, and Ridgway ordered armed reconnaissance patrols, followed by larger armed reconnaissance operations, to keep contact with the Chinese army. By January 18, General Collins, after an inspection visit, reported that Ridgway had vastly improved the situation. Washington observers like General Bradley considered the Collins report a turning point. Within a week, the Eighth and Republic of Korea (ROK) armies would begin a series of offensive operations, some of which bore controversial names like Operation KILLER and Operation RIPPER, suggesting the savage warfare that Ridgway expected his troops to wage. In little over a month, U.S. troops regained the banks of the Han, retaking Seoul on March 14–15. Eighth Army continued to advance just far enough beyond the 38th parallel to take high ground for a defensive line called "Line Kansas." After this drive, there were no major retreats by either side. The war became a bloody stalemate.[41]

RIDGWAY'S COMMAND STYLE: THE IDEOLOGY OF MORALE

One of the most important changes that Ridgway made upon assuming command was closer communication between the Eighth Army staff and the front. Ridgway kept a small forward staff and moved his forward command post out of the city of Taegu into the field. Ridgway moved staff officers from the rear, "where they were very comfortable," closer to the battlefield, where they could better understand the situation of "fellows up front being shot at." At first he camped out at the command post at I Corps and virtually took over the corps command. (One reason for doing this was to improve the performance of the corps commander, Lieutenant General Frank Milburn, an old friend whom Ridgway did not want to sack.)

After six weeks, Ridgway was able to set up a command post on a bluff with a panoramic view of the Han River, a bit away from the smell of fertilized fields. He made the tent more homelike with pictures of his family and wrote Marshall that having his official family—McCleary, Moorman, Surles, and Winton—along also made him feel at home on the battlefield. Given the stupendous expenditure of ammunition on the front, it was perhaps ironic that Ridgway also wanted to hunt some of the ducks and geese that he saw by the riverbank. Yet for Ridgway, at his finest hour, there was a sort of odd balance between the beauties of nature and the glories of God, between the symbolic presence of the family back home and the actual presence of the homosocial "family" of combat, both with Ridgway at the head.[42]

Ridgway moved fast when he landed in Korea, traveling from unit to unit even before obtaining proper winter clothing. First, accompanied by U.S. Ambassador John Muccio, Ridgway paid a visit to President Syngman Rhee of the Republic of Korea, impressing Rhee with his determination. "I'm glad to see you Mr. President, glad to be here, and I mean to stay"—words that heartened the South Koreans, as the Pentagon and Foggy Bottom were full of talk of withdrawal.[43]

Traveling by light plane, helicopter, and jeep, Ridgway visited all corps and division headquarters within forty-eight hours of his arrival, "except one over on the east coast," and determined quickly that the army was incapable of offensive action. According to his pilot, Mike Lynch, Ridgway "was like a cat on a hot tin roof where combat was concerned." One time, the general decided to land behind enemy forces during a U.S. paratroop drop. Lynch had to land on a dike, wipe out an enemy machine nest and capture four enemy prisoners before he could take off again, all while Ridgway calmly walked around the drop zone, assessing the effectiveness of the airborne operation. While Ridgway demanded the best possible staff work to confirm his information, "he chiefly relied on his own two eyes," though Lynch did not tell Ridgway what he had been doing while the general was busy assessing the drop. He left him to read about it in the after-action reports.[44]

The presence of the commanding general encouraged rank-and-file troops, who could see Ridgway shivering with them in the frigid Korean winter. After Ridgway took command, all the other general officers shivered as well, when, for safety reasons, he forbade anyone to travel in a combat zone in a closed car, instead of an open jeep. Ridgway used his travels to find out about specific gripes of the rank-and-file soldier. Corporal Randle M. Hurst, a guard in one of Ridgway's jeeps, observed: "Obviously the General is a great go-getter. He doesn't smoke and can't stand the smell of tobacco. He is extremely courteous to enlisted men. He expects the same courtesy in return." Ridgway's prompt response to the complaints of his troops lifted morale. The mess tent of each unit was one important stop on his trips. He improved the quality of food on the front, requesting more rations from the United States and ordering kitchens brought closer to the front so combat troops could get hot food. When he found that one unit had no envelopes to write home, he had envelopes flown in by helicopter.[45]

Ridgway also emphasized liaison with and publicity for the contingents from other UN countries. He was willing to modify standard U.S. army logistics to meet a wide variety of needs for each nationality and made dietary changes to improve morale in the non-U.S. contingents. These orders were an interesting reflection of the diverse cultural preferences of the UN forces. The French and Dutch, for example, shunned American white bread; they got bread ingredients instead along with an added issue of 100 lbs. of dehydrated potatoes weekly. Filipinos wanted Philippine rice, if possible; the Thai would get Siamese rice and double the normal issue of spices. The Thai shunned, however, grapefruit segments, citrus fruit and tomato juices, beets, dry cereal, sweet pickles, and cake mix. The Turks got fresh fruit and spinach instead of sweet potatoes, lima beans, and corn. Both Turks and Greeks got extra bread, but the Greeks insisted on their own olive oil. "I think our logistic support from Japan out was magnificent," Ridgway later noted.[46]

Nonetheless, Ridgway understood that men would not fight on bread alone. Ridgway worked hard at the ideological as well as the physical mobilization of his men. He himself observed that his troops fought not for him but "for themselves, with pride rekindled, and with a determination that they would never again take the sort of licking they had accepted a month before." Such a change must, in part, be ideological. In his first inspection, Ridgway noticed that the "bewildered" army was not sure why it was fighting in Korea. So he told them, in a January 21 memo entitled "Why We Are Here." Ridgway considered this document of great importance. "It came from the heart, at a critical time in the evolving transformation of the spirit of the Eighth Army. It came from the soul. It was not a long-studied, carefully-written document. It was dictated within a few moments during a quick visit to my rear echelon command post from my battle command post 200 miles to the north."[47]

"Why We Are Here" in some respects is one of the most important and remarkable documents of the war, in spite of—perhaps because of—its clichés. Appleman, whose work explicitly excludes political and ideological concerns, claims that few soldiers saw the memo, but the evidence he cites was all after the fact. All replacements coming to Korea were required to read it. In any case, the circular had a tremendous impact in the United States. *Life* quoted it extensively on its editorial page, with favorable comment. The *New York Times* reported it in a dispatch that was more an editorial than a news article. *Time* presented the paper in a condensed version, juxtaposed with even more warlike quotes from General MacArthur.[48]

Contemporary intellectual historians have been much interested in the sources of GI's political obligation to the state and in the relation between discourses concerning savage war and corporatist ideology. Michael Walzer has argued, for instance, that in a liberal society, men risk their lives only for private obligations, as opposed to a straightforward obedience to the State.[49]

Cultural historian Robert Westbrook, in two articles, has argued that for the rank-and-file World War II soldier, the defense of family interests was the primary source of military obligation. GI Joe, Westbrook indicates, was fighting to protect Betty Grable—the symbolic embodiment of the girl-next-door. Even political motives such as the defense of what Franklin Roosevelt called "the Four Freedoms" were, in popular culture, completely intertwined with concern for the security of the family. This concern, Elaine Tyler May has argued, translated itself during the early Cold War into a passion for "domestic containment"—a family both defended and bounded by the curtilage of their suburban lawn.[50]

Walzer's idea that in a liberal polity public obligations derive from private ones is obviously dissonant with Ridgway's predominantly corporatist outlook. In appealing to his men, Ridgway copes with this dissonance by bifurcating the sources of his soldiers' political obligation. His first answer to the question "Why do we fight?" is rooted in organic conservative doctrines of obedience: The troops are in Korea because properly constituted authority put them there. Such authority "is conclusive because the loyalty we give, and expect, precludes any slightest questioning of these orders."[51]

The answer to the second question "What are we fighting for?" according to Ridgway, "is of much greater significance" and "one to which every member of this command is entitled to a full and reasoned answer," presumably to legitimate his bald assertion of authority in the first part. Reflecting his new military strategy, he argued that the issues are not primarily "real estate," or even "Korean freedom." After all, the Rhee government, though capitalist, could not precisely be described as democratic. The UN troops are, Ridgway argues, fighting for their own national existence, based on an opposition between an atheist authoritarianism and Christian liberal solicitude for individual rights:

> The real issues are whether the power of Western civilization, as God has permitted it to flower in our own beloved lands, shall defeat Communism; whether the rule of men who shoot their prisoners, enslave their citizens, and deride the dignity of man, shall displace the rule of those to whom the individual and his individual rights are sacred; whether we are to survive with God's hand to guide and lead us, or to perish in the dead existence of a Godless world.[52]

In "Why We Are Here," Ridgway deletes the explicit references to Christianity that were so prominent in his rhetoric while at the Pentagon. Instead, he talks of "God" and "Western Civilization." Perhaps sensitivity to non-Christians (such as the Turks, many Koreans, and many Americans) among the UN Forces spurred the change from more explicitly Christian rhetoric.

The opposition between "Western civilization" and the "men who shoot their prisoners, enslave their citizens, and deride the dignity of man" shows the lingering influence of Progressivism in Ridgway's thinking as late as 1950. This trope is a prime example of what Richard Slotkin has called the discourse of "savage war." Slotkin shows how the myth of "savage war" was used by Progressives like President Theodore Roosevelt to justify and extend the emerging corporate capitalist order. The myth legitimates violence as the source of true manhood—an escape from feminized Victorian civilization, while at the same time clearing the path for such civilization and the rule of a new managerial class. In "Why We Are Here," Ridgway fit the reasons for fighting the Korean War into a time-honored appeal to the manifest destiny of Americans to "civilize" the frontier, coupled with a reference to the very real mistreatment of UN prisoners by the North Koreans, which placed Korean conditions neatly into a three-hundred-year American tradition about the horrors of captivity by Indians.[53]

While the ideology of savage war worked well to motivate troops at the front, it sometimes upset both the brass and the folks back home. To arouse the fighting spirit of his men, Ridgway attached savage code names to his plans, such as Operation KILLER and Operation RIPPER. Secretary of War Frank Pace subsequently warned him that such names "do not find favor with the American people." Ridgway later learned that Republicans had complained that the Truman Administration had no strategy for eliminating the communists from Asia and was only interested "in killing Chinese." In view of heavy U.S. casualties at this stage of the war, the civilian leadership of the armed forces felt that the goal of maximizing enemy casualties lacked political "sex appeal." They wanted Ridgway to play down the war's savage aspects, which did not play well in either Peoria or London. Ridgway, however, was "not convinced that the country should not be told that war means killing" and was "by nature opposed to any effort to 'sell' war to people as an only mildly unpleasant business that requires very little in the way of blood." Despite his misgivings, he changed Operation KILLER and Operation RIPPER, to the more positive Operation COURAGEOUS.[54]

Appeals to family security and to civilizing the frontier had a direct nexus with the promotion of corporate liberalism. From the time of the Spanish-American War, expansion of international trade and equal access to capital for all nations was an important pillar of attempts to centralize and stabilize the U.S. economy. If Americans did not have the discipline to "civilize" the rest of the world, they might share the fate of those "fear-driven people we have just witnessed [fleeing] across the Han, and continue to witness in other areas." Unless Korea could be brought under control, a savage world might eventually "engulf our own loved ones in all its misery and despair."[55]

Ultimately, Ridgway realized what the cultural historians have been telling us: The authority of the State was not enough in and of itself to convince soldiers of their obligation to the army. Thus, the paradox presents itself that Ridgway, despite his more corporatist view, had to present sacrifice as individual interest in the defense of the family if his task of legitimating the war were to succeed; he constructed the opposition of civilization versus savagery to bridge that ideological gap. He himself may have preferred an organic social order in which duty would emanate from those vested with authority to maintain the security of society. Ridgway, however, was sophisticated enough to understand that most of his men did not share his penchant for a coordinated society, nor was national security their top priority in life. When Ridgway arrived in Korea, he quickly divined that Kilroy had little motivation to stay on the peninsula, because he did not know why he was there. In "Why We Fight," the general used the alternative political language of liberalism—an appeal to the defense of the GI's private interests, such as defense of family and property, which he knew would bolster morale by trying to give every private soldier a stake in the war's outcome.

NOTES

1. Ridgway, *Soldier*, 191; Blair, *The Forgotten War* (New York: Times Books, 1987), 561; JB, 2:3:39.

2. Blair, *Forgotten War*, 19.

3. Wedemeyer to Ridgway, September 1, 1949, Ridgway MSS, Box 15.

4. Ridgway, *Soldier*, 189; Herken, *Winning Weapon*, 302.

5. On humor, see JB, 1:2:41.

6. Ridgway, "Address to Women's Patriotic Conference on National Defense," January 27, 1950, Ridgway MSS, Box 15. The capital letters are in the original text.

On the struggle between consumerist and Victorian values, see Daniel Horowitz, *The Morality of Spending: Attitudes Toward the Consumer Society in America, 1875–1940* (Chicago: Ivan R. Dee, 1992), xxvii, 114.

7. "The Role of the Army in the Next War," address to the Armed Forces Staff College, February 15, 1950, delivered as "The Moral Is as to the Physical" to the Fourth Annual National Industry-Army Conference, New Orleans, Louisiana, February 27, 1950, Ridgway MSS, Box 15.

8. Ridgway Diary, December 15, 1950, Ridgway MSS, Box 16.

9. "The Role of the Army in the Next War," address to the Armed Forces Staff College, February 15, 1950, delivered as "The Moral as to the Physical" to the Fourth Annual Industry-Army Conference, New Orleans, Los Angeles February 27, 1950. Ridgway MSS, Box 15.

10. Ibid.

11. Curtis to Ridgway, November 2, 1949, Ridgway MSS, Box 15; "Latin American Affairs," Ridgway MSS, Box 15, passim.; JB, 2:3:34. On Truman and Johnson, see Blair, *Forgotten War*, 4–10, 15–17. For more on Johnson's ineffectiveness in the pre–World War II War Department, see Pogue, *Marshall*, 18.

12. Herken, *Winning Weapon*, 285–294.

13. On OFFTACKLE and DROPSHOT, see Herken, *Winning Weapon*, 283–298; see also Anthony Cave Brown, ed., *Dropshot: The United States Plan for War with the Soviet Union in 1957* (New York: Dial Press, 1978), a reprint of the plan with speculative comments by the editor. On the doctrine of defense in depth at the Eurasian littoral, see Melvyn Leffler, "The American Conception of National Security and the Beginnings of the Cold War, 1945–1948," *American Historical Review* 89 (April 1984): 346–400, 350, 357.

14. Herken, *Winning Weapon*, 288; *New York Times*, October 19, 1951.

15. "Memo for Chief of Staff from General Ridgway. Subject: Dropshot," January 25, 1950, Ridgway MSS, Box 15. For a critique of Ridgway's views, see Walter Millis, *Arms and Men: A Study in American Military History* (New York: Capricorn, 1956), 356. On popular ideologies associating war with prosperity, see Michael Sherry, *In the Shadow of War: The United States Since the 1930s* (New Haven: Yale University Press, 1995), 76.

16. "The Role of the Army in the Next War," address to the Army Staff College, February 27, 1950, Ridgway MSS, Box 15.

17. Ridgway, *Soldier*, 192; Ridgway to chief of staff, July 10, 1950, conference memo, July 22, 1950 and "Daily Briefings: Memo," July 6, 1950, Ridgway MSS, Box 16.

18. Blair, *Forgotten War*, 82–83; William Steuck, *The Korean War: An International History* (Princeton, Princeton University Press, 1995), 31–46; Kathryn Weathersby, "Soviet Arms in Korea and the Origins of the Korean War, 1945–1950: New Evidence from the Russian Archives," Cold War International History Project Working Paper, No. 8, November 1995; Melvyn Leffler, *A Preponderance of Power* (Stanford, Calif.: Stanford University Press, 1992), 366.

19. Ridgway Diary, June 28, 1950, Ridgway MSS, Box 16. At the meeting, "in commenting upon General MacArthur," Leffler argues that the U.S. military thought Soviet weakness precluded a world war. Ridgway was never part of this consensus, and Leffler himself implies that the consensus broke up after the start of the Korean War (Leffler, *Preponderance of Power*, 367–368).

20. Ridgway Diary, memo, July 11, 1950, and memo of meeting between Ridgway and chief of Staff J. Lawton Collins, August 14, 1950, Ridgway MSS, Box 16.

21. Ridgway to chief of staff, October 12, 1950, Ridgway MSS, Box 16.

22. Ridgway to chief of staff, October 12, 1950, notation on cover by Ridgway; Ridgway Diary, October 30, 1950, Ridgway MSS, Box 16.

23. Ibid.

24. Memo of meeting between Ridgway and Chief of Staff J. Lawton Collins, August 14, 1950, Ridgway MSS, Box 16; Harriman-Norstad recommendation in Robert Smith, *MacArthur in Korea* (New York: Simon & Schuster, 1982), 207.

25. Memo by Ridgway of conversation, August 16, 1950, Ridgway Papers, Box 16.

26. Ridgway Diary, December 3, 1950, Ridgway MSS, Box 16; Matthew B. Ridgway, *The Korean War* (Garden City, N.Y.: Doubleday, 1967) (hereafter TKW), 62; Dean Acheson, *Present at the Creation* (New York: Norton, 1969), 475.

27. Ridgway, notes on current situation and action required, December 3, 1950, Ridgway MSS, Box 16.

28. Ridgway Diary, December 6, 1950, Ridgway MSS, Box 16; briefing of president by Ridgway, December 18, 1950, Ridgway MSS, Box 16.

29. Ridgway, *Soldier*, 193–198; TKW, 79–81.

30. *Time*, January 1, 1951.

31. Matthew B. Ridgway and Walter F. Winton Jr., "Troop Leadership at the Operational Level, excerpts from transcript of a seminar at the U.S. Army Command and General Staff School, Ft. Leavenworth, Kansas, May 9, 1984, reprinted in *Military Review* 70, no. 4 (April 1990): 64.

32. Ridgway, *Soldier*, 152, quoted 201; Appleman, *Ridgway Duels for Korea*, 5–6. For Relations with MacArthur and suggestion for MacArthur's relief, see TKW, 75–78. On Ridgway's assumption of command, see TKW, 81–84.

33. Ridgway and Winton, "Troop Leadership," 64.

34. See Ridgway and Winton, "Troop Leadership," passim; Blair, *Forgotten War*, 712; Lt. Col. James F. Schnabel, "Ridgway in Korea," *Military Review*, March 2–14, 1964. Michael Schaller, *Douglas MacArthur: The Far Eastern General* (New York: Oxford, 1989), 228, citing an unpublished paper by Jonathan Pollack of the RAND Corporation entitled "The Korean War and Sino-American Relations."

35. Ridgway to Almond, January 2, 1951, Ridgway MSS, Box 17.

36. Blair, *Forgotten War*, 574. The incident received a lot of press play but was often misreported. The *New York Times* mistakenly reported that Ridgway had dressed down a British officer. On Pentagon reaction to replacement of the division commanders, see William B. Breuer, *Shadow Warriors: The Covert War in Korea* (New York: John B. Wiley & Sons, 1996), 120.

37. MacArthur to Ridgway, January 7, 1951, Ridgway MSS, Box 20, Korean War special file; Ridgway to Dr. Edward H. Litchfield (Chancellor, University of Pittsburgh, who had requested Ridgway's opinion to inquire about the propriety of chemical and Biological Warfare research on his campus), October 13, 1955, Ridgway MSS, Box 32.

38. Appleman, *Ridgway Duels for Korea*, 10; Greg MacGregor, "Front Line General," *New York Times Magazine*, March 4, 1951; hospitals and nurses, JB 1:2:99. Craig Cameron found that nurses undermined Marine morale and unit cohesiveness

in World War II, perhaps reflecting a greater alienation from civilian life in the Marine Corps than in the army (see Craig Cameron, *American Samurai: Myth Imagination and the Conduct of Battle in the First Marine Division, 1941–1951* (Cambridge: Cambridge University Press, 1994), 79.

39. Ridgway, *Korean War*, 88–97; *Newsweek*, January 8, 1951.

40. *Life*, February 5, 1951; *New York Times*, January 28, 1951; *Newsweek*, February 5, 1951.

41. Blair, *Forgotten War*, 646; TKW, 101–143 255. For detailed accounts of the battlefield action, see Walter Hermes, *Truce Tent and Fighting Front: United States in the Korean War* (Washington: Center of Military History, 1966) (reprint 1992); Billy C. Mossman, *Ebb and Flow, November 1950–July 1951*: United States in the Korean War (Washington: Center of Military History, 1990); Appleman, *Ridgway Duels for Korea*; and John Toland, *In Mortal Combat: Korea, 1950–53* (New York: Morrow: 1991).

42. Appleman, *Ridgway Duels for Korea*, 9; Ridgway and Winton, "Troop Leadership," 64; Ridgway to Marshall, March 12, 1951, Ridgway MSS, Box 17.

43. TKW, 84.

44. Ridgway and Winton, "Troop Leadership," 58, 67; TKW, 85–87; Blair, *Forgotten War*, 581; Appleman, *Ridgway Duels for Korea*, 439; John Toland, *In Mortal Combat*, 423.

45. Hurst quoted in Appleman, *Ridgway Duels for Korea*, 9; envelopes telegram CG EUSAK to CG, 24th Infantry Division, January 20, 1951, Ridgway MSS, Box 17; Ridgway, *Korean War*, 86–87.

46. Davis to Ridgway, March 15, 1951, Ridgway MSS, Box 21; "Magnificent" Ridgway and Winton, "Troop Leadership," 64.

47. Ridgway, *Korean War*, 86, 106. A copy of the memo can be found in the appendix of that book, which shows the importance Ridgway attached to it. The original "Memo for Corps, Division, Separate Brigade or RCT commanders and Commanding General 2d Logistical Command," January 21, 1951, is in Ridgway MSS, Box 21. See Ridgway's reply to questionnaire of Capt. William J. Whitner to Ridgway, June 10, 1957, Ridgway MSS, Box 20, which is also the source of the final quotation on the dictation of the memo.

48. Appleman, *Ridgway Duels for Korea*, 156–157; "The Issue Is Now Joined," *Life*, February 5, 1951; *New York Times*, January 23, 1951; *Time*, February 5, 1951.

49. Walzer, *Obligations*, 82, 97, 98; Westbrook, "American Women," 587–603; "Fighting for the American Family: Private Interests and Political Obligations in World War II," in Richard Wightman Fox and T. J. Jackson Lears, eds., *The Power of Culture: Critical Essays in American History* (Chicago: University of Chicago Press), 195–222. On the Cold War family as a security arrangement, see Elaine Tyler May, *Homeward Bound: The Family in the Cold War* (New York: Basic Books, 1988).

51. "Memo for Corps, Division, Separate Brigade or RCT commanders and Commanding General 2d Logistical Command," January 21, 1951, Ridgway MSS, Box 21.

52. Ibid.

53. Richard Slotkin, *Gunfighter Nation: The Myth of the Frontier in Twentieth-Century America* (New York: HarperPerennial, 1993), 22.

54. Beishline to Ridgway, October 13, 1951, Ridgway MSS, Box 20; TKW, 110–111; Blair, *Forgotten War*, 751, 752.

55. "Memo for Corps, Division, Separate Brigade or RCT commanders and Commanding General 2d Logistical Command," January 21, 1951, Ridgway MSS, Box 21. Interestingly, this last passage was removed from the version of this document reprinted in TKW.

CHAPTER 11

Problems of Supreme Command

You are having a tough time, with our interrupted negotiations, a growing battle, and I suppose many other difficulties which I am not aware
of. You seem to take it all calmly, which is very impressive to the general
public.[1]

—George C. Marshall to Matthew B. Ridgway

RIDGWAY, MACARTHUR, AND THE SOCIAL
CONSTRUCTION OF HEROISM

The art of government is the organization of idolatry.[2]

—George Bernard Shaw

President Truman's decision to substitute Ridgway for MacArthur as theater
commander came as a complete surprise to both generals, although Truman
had carefully planned it to be otherwise. Ridgway found out about his promotion by accident when a war correspondent asked him whether he was
due for congratulations. Army Secretary Frank Pace later officially informed
Ridgway of his new orders while the two men were standing outside in a
hailstorm. Nor did the Joint Chiefs consult him on the choice of a field
commander, imposing a Collins favorite, General James Van Fleet, whom

Ridgway almost certainly would not have chosen on his own. Ridgway flew off to Tokyo the next day to confer with MacArthur.[3]

Ridgway's report of their meeting suggests that MacArthur had become crazy and paranoid; MacArthur's mental state dissolved any doubts Ridgway may have had about the wisdom of Truman's decision. In his diary, Ridgway reported that MacArthur was "monumentally egotistical." MacArthur blamed his dismissal on the president's supposed mental and physical illness. Truman "won't last more than six months," MacArthur insisted.[4]

In the wake of General MacArthur's firing, the American public was inundated with media images of two very different heroes: the older general who was being treated to a huge hero's welcome and the younger general whose face had started to make the magazine covers when he began to recapture lost territory in South Korea. Many of the news and magazine stories made direct comparisons between the two, with reporters scrambling for information about Ridgway, who was nowhere near the media god that MacArthur was.

Soon MacArthur was waving to crowds of hundreds of thousands in Hawaii, Chicago, New York, and Washington. According to his biographer D. Clayton James, the fervor of the reception had two basic causes: gratitude for an old warrior and "pent-up exasperation . . . over the nation's course in foreign affairs and the uncertain and frightening era of the atomic bomb and the Cold War." In specific terms, many of those cheering for MacArthur were cheering against the perceived impotence of Truman and the stalemated Korean War. Years later, Ridgway compared MacArthur to the ambitious General George McClellan, who was defeated in his race for the presidency against Lincoln because he was "confusing his popularity as a symbol of patriotism in a Nation at war with his duty as a general on active service."[5]

Ridgway had no illusions of such acclaim—he knew his job was to maintain an increasingly unpopular American position in Korea without publicly squabbling with his commander-in-chief, Harry Truman. The many interviews and photographs that filtered back to the United States from Korea made a deep impression on media leaders. When Ridgway won his fourth star, the editors of the *New York Times* praised his qualities and contrasted them implicitly with MacArthur's. Ridgway's new star, they wrote, "is not a star in the Napoleonic sense. General Ridgway, the possessor of thirty-odd decorations, is as far from being a man on horseback as any soldier could be. He is an intelligent student of the military arts and sciences, a man of superb courage who, whether the operation is a parachute jump or an attack on hostile lines, orders no one to go where he will not go himself." How did Ridgway manage to get such a glowing review so early on in his command? According to the reporters and photographers who covered him in Korea during those months, Ridgway had a lucky combination of features that cloaked him, in the words of *Life* reporter James Michener, in "a legend vastly complimentary, and almost wholly true."[6]

It was true, for example, that he was photogenic, deeply religious, all-American, and was married to a young, beautiful woman. He was one hundred percent Army, individualistic enough to be a family man, yet tough enough to stage Operation RIPPER. The many pictures of Ridgway in popular magazines show a tall man with a craggy, handsome, face and piercing eyes, a ready-made Hollywood war hero. He was known for setting a high physical standard for himself and demanding the same of everyone else, a trait that apparently appealed to Americans anxious about whether the new postwar affluence would feminize its men. In a 1951 cover story in *Life* about Ridgway's takeover in Tokyo, photos show Ridgway in rapid stride and, typically, separate from the group; "General Sets Grueling Pace," reads the caption. Ridgway's charisma combined directness with decisiveness. Ridgway associate Walter Winton said, "The force that emanated from him was awesome. It reminded me of Superman. You had the impression he could knock over a building with a single blow, or stare a hole through a wall if he wanted to."[7]

At Eighth Army, Ridgway had had a no-nonsense approach to dealing with the press that won journalists over, though when he became Supreme Commander he instituted a much stricter press policy, which hurt his relations with the media. To photographers, especially, he seemed to be a favorite subject, partly because of his knack for giving them good "photo ops." The journalists emphasized stories about his personal feeling for the troops.

In February 1951, for example, he was on a tour of the front and noticed a Marine corporal with a heavy radio on his back stumbling along with an untied shoelace. The general slid down a snowy embankment and tied the soldier's shoe, garnering great publicity from the war correspondents. Because the incident received such wide play, however, many journalists accused Ridgway of deliberate showmanship. This was a very touchy subject, since grandstanding had been a major criticism of MacArthur.[8]

Ridgway had a good press agent in Korea—James T. Quirk, who frequently deployed such stories for his boss's greater glory. Ridgway, perhaps sensitive to the theatrics of MacArthur and of (Patton disciple) Walton Walker, strenuously denied that the shoe-tying incident was staged. Though admitting that "showmanship can be a valuable attribute," he insisted that the important thing for a commander "is to be yourself. If you're a showman, be one. If not, then don't. You can't fool your comrades."[9]

Like MacArthur, Ridgway was enough of a showman to establish a trademark uniform: a grenade hanging from one strap of his parachute harness while on the other he wore a paratrooper's first-aid kit that contained a morphine syringe. The dashing uniform set him apart and also built solidarity with combat troops, thereby displaying his democratic sentiments to both GI and the folks at home. The *Life* photo series entitled "General Matt and General Mud" shows Ridgway and the 1st Marine Division engulfed in Korea's spring muck. According to *Life*, some of the GIs who called him "wrong-way Ridgway" when he first took command and ordered them on the offensive, later dubbed him "Leo Durocher," after the much admired and famously combative manager of the New York Giants.[10]

Ridgway always maintained that the grenade he carried was not for show but for getting out of a tight spot in combat, if necessary. Such combat readiness led troops to identify with him. But journalists loved the show, and it helped make Ridgway a hero to the public. *Time* called him the "Airborne Grenadier," *Newsweek* the "Pineapple King." But his own troops revealed the potency of the grenades; they called Ridgway "old iron tits"—a patriotic reference to the trusty old battleship *Constitution*, but also an indication of affection for the general, an appreciation of his nurturing concern for them. Along with stern paternal direction, Ridgway provided an armored substitute for mom and apple pie.[11]

Some writers picked up on the striking difference in personal style between the jaunty MacArthur and the combat-minded Ridgway. Sociologist Morris Janowitz observed that, unlike the heroic individualist MacArthur, "Ridgway epitomized the fighter spirit and sought to keep it alive for organizational ends, rather than for personal honor."[12] Janowitz's formulation suggests some of the striking conflicts within the Ridgway legend, such as the loneliness of command and the singularity of Ridgway as a commander. He had to be superior to everyone else in the theater. The ideology of a liberal democratic society also required that Ridgway simultaneously maintain singularity and solidarity with the rank-and-file soldier, that he symbolize both Napoleon and Kilroy. Representations of Ridgway also illustrate the contradictions of a military style of corporate liberalism that valued both hierarchy and individualism, bold heroism and good management, capitalism, and the maintenence of a large government-subsidized and coordinated defense complex.

The hierarchical principles embodied by American military virtues are well represented in a *Life* portrait of Ridgway, sitting alone on the ground behind a stone fence in an area obviously decimated by battle. The caption reads: "As artillery shells burst against the hills perilously close to the front, completely alone as he contemplates the next move of his advancing Eighth Army." Ridgway is looking down, an exemplar of humility and self-sacrifice for all soldiers. At the same time, we also see his lonliness in his ultimate responsibility for the outcome of the battle and for the lives of his men.[13]

Ridgway used his demeanor to set standards for and to distinguish himself from other soldiers. Early on, *Newsweek* referred to Ridgway as "ramrod erect." Clay Blair writes that "his posture was ramrod straight. Even while sitting down, he did not slouch or cross his legs." Michener refers to his "stiff leadership."[14]

Yet Ridgway's singularity had to be combined with an appeal to his commonality with the average GI. In part this depended on Ridgway's separation from his family, a separation shared with all other troops. On the day before Christmas 1950, the front page of the *New York Times* carried a picture of Ridgway packing his bags to leave for Korea, while his wife looks on. The image of Ridgway fighting for the family back home was a fundamental component of his heroic stature while he commanded Eighth Army. After he left combat for the Supreme Command, his wife, Penny, and his son, Matthew Jr., joined him in Tokyo.[15]

Ridgway's family was constantly portrayed in the media as an exemplar of the families that American troops often believed they were fighting to defend. One example is a shot taken in Washington, where Ridgway stopped between tours as Far East Commander and Supreme Allied Commander, Europe. The caption reads: "The Ridgways in Washington: Mary [Penny's given name], Matt and Matthew Jr. Between a gloomy past and a dangerous future." Though the family itself looks happy enough, it is Matt's job to defend his family through the dangerous future posed by Cold War, as, by implication, it is the job of all his subordinates.[16]

Installed in Tokyo, Ridgway was praised for his intellectual prowess, as well as his military bearing, though sometimes reports of his intellectualism were exaggerated. Though Ridgway continued his customary avid reading of biography, travel, sports, and military books, he was later asked about a rumor suggesting that he liked Proust. When asked about this, he laughed and replied, "I thought it was a typographical error and looked up Proust in the encyclopedia to make sure. I've never read a word of Proust."[17]

Among the most competent and important of his subordinates was his wife, Penny, glamorously displayed in the papers. She too bridged the gap between the unsavory warlike duties of the tough "Spartan" and the more civilized domestic sphere. As "the first American lady of Japan"—a role she had to fulfill on Ridgway's small salary of $984 per month before taxes, plus a $2700 government stipend for entertainment, she tried to be a role model for American and Japanese women. Penny's poise and intelligence helped her husband immensely in his diplomatic and ceremonial duties. Her activities enhanced his image and emphasized the political and social sides of his duties as Supreme Commander. She assumed the status of the wife of a head of state—a singular, yet well-defined, woman's role.

Mrs. Ridgway appeared at ship launchings, factories, and university groups and arranged numerous social events for the Supreme Commander, as when Japanese carolers entertained the Ridgways on Christmas Day. She also helped with the important political task of showing U.S. support for troops of U.S. allies, for example, taking Mrs. Alben Barkley, wife of the vice president of the United States, to visit wounded Ethiopian soldiers. She also appeared frequently in the role of mother to young Matty, who often stole the show in the Ridgway's travels over the next eighteen months. Even

Queen Elizabeth II later asked Penny "How is Matty? I feel as if I know him. I have seen his picture so many times."[18]

Family and religious images also mediated between concepts of Ridgway as a tough, heroic commander and Ridgway as a champion of civilization in the midst of savage warfare: "Like many another tough soldier, Ridgway is both devout and sensitive." He is portrayed as a devout Bible reader, an Episcopal vestryman, capable of both intense anger and sentiment: "Once when a photographer in Korea surprised him with a carefully mounted portrait of his wife and young Matt Jr., the general broke into tears." Bishops on the Methodist Board of Missions praised him for his godliness and decorum in the administration of the occupied Japan. One described Ridgway as a "friendly, inwardly tranquil democratic man" who is "carrying on with consummate skill and wisdom." Such descriptions of Ridgway's nonmilitary heroic qualities allowed him to mediate between the battlefield and the living room of the average American.[19]

The Civil War for Northerners and World War II were depicted after the fact by some historians, by the public, and by the media as epics in which, after severe initial setbacks, truth, justice, and the American Way emerged victorious. Generals such as Grant, MacArthur, and Eisenhower became heroes and identified with the nation as the heroes of such epics. Their welcomes were large, and they have endured as heroes outside professional circles. Veterans of limited wars have rarely been celebrated. Korea is frequently termed the "forgotten war," and Ridgway has been largely forgotten by people under the age of sixty. Association with the stalemate of a war that had become extremely unpopular, the stalled truce talks, and the ugly prisoner-of-war mutiny at Koje-Do, which occurred right before Ridgway's return home, probably muted his memory as a popular hero. In the 1950s, however, Ridgway was prominent and well received, portrayed in the press as a man who could stand the lonely burdens of leadership of both an army and a family. Ridgway's reputation as a warrior, within circles of military professionals, remained high.

RIDGWAY AND THE KOREAN TRUCE TALKS

One of Ridgway's first tasks as theater commander was to implement the limited war strategy that MacArthur had tried to thwart, though on several occasions he had his own doubts about the policy and would ask the Joint Chiefs of Staff to loosen some restrictions on the conduct of the air war. He wrote General Van Fleet that he took responsibility for decisions about any offensive actions that might widen the conflict. Despite his doubts about what would eventually be called limited war strategy, Ridgway made the prevention of World War III a prime directive for operations in his theater, admonishing his subordinates that "instructions from higher authority reflect the intense determination of our people, and of all the free peoples of the world, to prevent this catastrophe, if that can be done without appeasement, or sacrifice of principle."[20]

One of the most important of Ridgway's heavy responsibilities, besides the running of the war, was the Korean truce talks. The talks commenced in July 1951 and lasted until July 27, 1953, long after Ridgway had left the Far East. Any historian of the truce talks must ask why they took so long to conclude and whether Ridgway was in any way responsible for delaying the agreement, as some observers have suggested. Ridgway's generally sympathetic biographer, Clay Blair, for example, has charged that Ridgway, like MacArthur, had become a "third party" who complicated the negotiations. Historian Rosemary Foot has suggested that Ridgway lacked diplomatic professionalism, developing "a personal sense of outrage" toward the communist negotiators that stiffened his resistance to concessions and made him all too ready to issue ultimata.[21]

These charges lead to other, broader questions about the military profession. If Ridgway was one of the first generation of senior officers with broad politico-military experience, why did that experience fail him in this assignment? Was failure implicit in the ideological assumptions inherent in military professionalism? The authorities in Washington entrusted one of the most sensitive and difficult diplomatic negotiations in modern history to military officers in no-man's land. Might not professional diplomats in a neutral capital have ended the fighting more expeditiously? The soldier got the job mostly because the State Department feared the political fallout from any sort of diplomatic recognition of the People's Republic of China. Negotiations between military officers would avoid direct recognition of the People's Republic as well as any linkage of the recognition issue to a Korea truce. U.S. Assistant Secretary of State for Far Eastern Affairs Dean Rusk told the Joint Chiefs that the use of military officers would keep the talks technical and "avoid the introduction of extraneous and political subjects." This supposed depoliticization of the talks would also hopefully speed them to a conclusion. Moreover, UN legal advisor Abraham Feller had ruled that the UN command did not have to consult with the Security Council during the talks so long as they remained "military" in nature. Military diplomacy thus avoided the possibility of awkward exchanges with the Soviet, British, or French UN delegates in New York.[22]

Ridgway himself had little doubt of his ability to render professional judgments that were scientific, objective, neutral, and in the public interest—another key component of corporatism. Buffeted by press leaks in December 1951 alleging that the UN command had done nothing about massive atrocities against UN prisoners of war, Ridgway declared that his decisions, "which presume to be no more than those resulting from an earnest effort to analyze all available facts and opinions, and to decide in the light of my best judgment uninfluenced by any political or personal motives, are little affected, if at all, by the changing currents of comment in the public press, whether of approval or disapprobation." Such truculence and insulation, rooted in a belief that he could divine neutral and objective solutions to what were in fact complex problems of ethics and politics, did him no good in the delicate diplomatic situation he entered with the commencement of the truce talks.[23]

Ridgway broadcast the initial invitation to talks on a Danish hospital ship on June 30, 1951, and the communists responded on July 1, with a proposal for talks at the old Korean royal capital of Kaesong on July 10 and 15, along with a suggestion that the communists would agree "to suspend military activities."[24] It was then that Ridgway made one of the fateful decisions of the war. Instead of embracing an immediate end to the fighting, he advised his superiors that an immediate truce "might gravely prejudice the safety and security of United Nations forces," and he notified them that, unless instructed otherwise, he would reject it. Ridgway offered strong military reasons for his decision—he feared that a halt in the fighting would give the communists the opportunity to build up their forces free of harrassment by UN troops, which might change the hard-won balance of military power on the peninsula. In the area in which he had established himself as authoritative, namely, troop morale, he also feared that a ceasefire might give troops a false sense that the war was almost over, blunting the offensive spirit he had worked so hard to create in Eighth Army. He could not have known that the negotiations would last as long as they did, but the decision proved a fateful one for many men on both sides who became casualties.[25]

Ridgway was, himself, sensitive to his lack of diplomatic skill, and he had requested two experienced hands, Ambassador to Korea, John J. Muccio, and the Ambassador to Japan, William J. Sebald, to act as his political advisors. This reasonable step was urgently countermanded by Joint Chiefs of Staff, presumably at the instance of the State Department, because the presence of the ambassadors "would invite [the] impression that [the] talks are to go beyond a military basis." Washington, in other words, was perfectly happy to continue the fighting to avoid the domestically troublesome issue of the recognition of China, and Ridgway had to content himself with advice from lower-ranking diplomats.[26] It also meant that the Joint Chiefs would have to micromanage the negotiations to prevent serious blunders on Ridgway's part, such as a proposed statement attacking Soviet imperialism in Mongolia in an effort to "detach China" as an ally of the U.S.S.R.—even though the gist was accepted policy. "Manchuria and Sinkiang are next," Ridgway would have warned, had not the Joint Chiefs suppressed the statement, which, they said, would at a minimum have "undesirable domestic and international repercussions" and at a maximum could lead to the breakdown of the truce talks before they started. It would not be the last Ridgway statement that the Joint Chiefs would have to modify.[27]

The Joint Chiefs of Staff sent Ridgway deceptively simple instructions on the basic American goals in the negotiation. The Joint Chiefs proposed to set up a military armistice commission with equal representation from both sides. The commission would police a twenty-mile demilitarized zone based on the current line of demarcation between the two sides and would inspect units to make certain that they had not been reinforced beyond existing levels. Ridgway was also to negotiate an exchange of prisoners of war.[28]

By July 1, Supreme Commander Ridgway had personally chosen a vice-admiral, C. Turner Joy, for the job of chief negotiator, and with Joy had chosen the other members of the U.S. delegation to the truce talks: Major General Henry I. (Hank) Hodes, a longtime Ridgway associate, Air Force Major General Laurence C. Craigie, the colorful Rear Admiral Arleigh A. Burke, and Major General Paik Sun Yup, Republic of Korea Army (ROKA), the Korean commander whom Ridgway esteemed most. According to RAND analyst Herbert Goldhamer, who worked at a high level for the delegation, Joy was widely viewed as a "somewhat bungling, oldish, and indecisive person," disdained if not disrespected by the more junior Burke. Burke thought the Joint Chiefs had sent him to Korea to counteract Joy's weakness.[29]

For an instant, at the start of the negotiations, Ridgway took a patient and understanding approach. He warned his negotiators to expect and endure long, propagandistic speeches from the communist negotiators, as well as possible misunderstandings from mistranslations. He also stressed the importance of offering the Chinese and North Koreans a "golden bridge" over which they might withdraw from previously held positions "without unacceptable loss of face."[30]

The first meeting of the truce negotiators is generally considered to have been a disaster, wherein, according to Admiral Joy's account, the communists allegedly tried to humiliate the UN negotiators by making them sit in shortened kiddie chairs, while the communists looked down at them from high chairs, facing south—supposedly, according to "oriental custom," the direction in which the victor faces. According to historian Rosemary Foot, the attempt of the communists to gain a propaganda victory by making it appear as if the UN was suing for peace "was to prove costly in terms of the relations between the two delegations."[31]

There were, however, more serious matters discussed at the meeting than seating, such as the scope of the negotiations and the agenda. As official historian Walter Hermes noted, the communist delegation was composed of members who had considerable political experience, as well as military experience. The opposition of "technical military" matters to "political matters," which the Americans often insisted on maintaining, made little sense to anyone with a Leninist perspective that drew no distinction between the technical and the political.

The parties wrangled over the agenda until July 26, mostly on the basis of UN rejection of communist demands that the UN retreat to the 38°

former border between North and South Korea, as well as Allied insistence on halting the fighting, based mostly on the positions of the troops at the time. After the initial meeting, the negotiators also concluded an agreement on the neutrality of the zone around Kaesong, the former royal capital of Korea, where the negotiations were taking place.[32]

Ridgway firmly believed that as commander he had the responsibility to prevent press coverage that might undermine the offensive spirit of his troops or might lead to the sort of pressure for demobilization that had led to GI demonstrations at the end of World War II. Once again his sort of corporatism—the management of different social forces to maximize a "neutral" public interest in military security—showed itself in his efforts to manage the press. Just before the truce talks started, he wrote Van Fleet of his concern that news of the talks would undermine the effectiveness of the Army. Ridgway recalled the end of World War II, when he had seen "members wearing the uniform of the United States haranguing crowds like any Communist" and ordered Van Fleet to take "every step within the bounds of our authority to completely eliminate the type of thinking which resorts to such expressions." In a war zone, Ridgway harbored no democratic illusions. "If this be 'thought control,'" he continued, "then I am for it."[33]

For Ridgway, the truce talks were a duty imposed by higher authority and a frustrating obstacle to the conduct of a war he had been winning, which may explain in part his lack of diplomatic professionalism and his quickness to anger over communist actions that may or may not have been designed to provoke him. Time after time, Washington had to cool him down. On August 4, for example, a fully armed Chinese infantry company marched through the Kaesong neutral zone leading to a boycott of the talks by the UN. Ridgway wanted to issue a statement on the radio that was so denunciatory that the Joint Chiefs had to tone it down, fearing that it might end the talks for good. When the communists finally did apologize for the violation, Ridgway complained that the Japanese translation of the apology was "insolent and peremptory in tenor" even though the English and Chinese versions were acceptable. Despite his previous caution to the delegation members about the possibility of accidental misunderstanding in the complicated process of multiple translations, in this case he was convinced that the enemy had tried deliberately to give the impression that they were "dictating to their vanquished UN enemies."[34]

Ridgway was, perhaps, looking for an excuse to end the talks. At 1 A.M. that morning, his patience completely worn away, he sent the Joint Chiefs a long diatribe on the talks, declaring that they were "military" and "the language of diplomacy is inappropriate and ineffective." To treat the communists as civilized was "to deride one's own dignity." The UN delegation should be instructed to "employ such languages and methods as these treacherous savages cannot fail to understand, and understanding, respect."[35] This is obviously not the language of conciliation that one expects from a peace negotiator and suggests that Ridgway would have been happier fighting a mobile war without the burden of a truce line. Like Ridgway's explanation of "Why We Are Here," it is a declaration of savage war.[36]

In his blast of frustration to the Joint Chiefs of Staff, Ridgway converted the enemy armies into Indians who must be completely defeated in the name of progress—the ancient frontier myth of the "Old Army" that Ridgway grew up with. Ironically, in defense of "Line Kansas" and "Line Wyoming," Ridgway wanted to tell the communists to "get out of Dodge." His managers, the Joint Chiefs, however, were, in mythic terms, constrained by "civilization" (or more specifically by public opinion at home and in Allied nations) to continue the negotiations that Ridgway saw as a sham.

In reality, treachery could appear on both sides. Communist charges of a subsequent killing of a young Chinese soldier in the Kaesong neutral zone turned out to be the work of Republic of Korea partisans, who were probably trying to sabotage the talks. When the talks did reconvene on August 10, the two sides merely restated their position. After the communists repeated their demands for an armistice line at the 38th parallel, both sides cooperated by maintaining a remarkable two hours and eleven minutes of complete silence, marred only by General Nam Il nervously tapping his cigarette lighter on the table.[37]

When Joy finally broke the silence and suggested moving on to another agenda item, the communists refused. Ridgway abruptly ordered the delegation to break off the talks within seventy-two hours of the communists, only to be immediately countermanded by the Joint Chiefs.[38]

Incidents continued to plague the neutral zone. As early as August 3, Ridgway had sought authority to change the location of the talks. The communists suspended talks on 23 August, claiming that UN planes had napalmed a village inside the neutral zone, which, after subsequent investigation, the UN claimed was faked. Privately, however, Admiral Joy conceded in his diary that the strafing was the work of Republic of Korea partisans. Dean Rusk was concerned lest President Rhee publicly claim credit for disrupting the talks with these attacks.[39]

After another neutral zone incident on September 11, in which the UN had to apologize for a plane that admittedly had strafed a village in the neutral zone, Ridgway asked to terminate the neutrality of the zone—a huge step toward complete breakoff of the talks. He continued to grow farther apart from his superiors in Washington, especially with his insistence on categorically refusing to return to Kaesong.[40]

On September 21, when Nam Il offered unconditional resumption of the talks, Ridgway proposed a response that threatened a permanent cutoff if he did not agree to a new site. The Joint Chiefs cut this part out once again, curtly informing the UN commander that the changed message was "intended to avoid the public implication or impression that there is any intransigence on our side regarding resumption of the negotiations. Lieutenant

General Charles L. Bolté assured Livingston Merchant, the acting assistant secretary of state for Far Eastern affairs, that "this was a reproof that general Ridgway would understand" and that he would "moderate the tone acceptably."[41]

Ridgway did not change his tone much. He shifted from bombast to stubborn argument in his correspondence with the JCS. He even drew some sympathy from them on the matter of changing the site. Bradley and (commissioned naval officer) Admiral William M. Fechteler considered one argument that Ridgway made against the Kaesong site—that it would ensure the safety of the negotiators—"bad PR" if publicized.[42]

In addition to the site issue, Ridgway maintained his opposition to progress on defining an armistice line, viewing the negotiations as worthless. Never wavering from his determination to change the truce site—an issue that Counselor to the Secretary of State Charles Bohlen termed "artificial," Ridgway continued to try to force a break in the talks. He had proposed a truce line that would have required the communists, but not the UN, to withdraw, claiming that "any concession made to the Communists upon the resumption of subsequent discussions will be equivalent to making a series of blackmail payments." "Blackmail never ends with the first payment," especially in dealing with communists, Ridgway continued.[43]

The blackmail metaphor contradicted Ridgway's assessment of the military situation. Due to tactical advantages and the coming winter, he wrote, "time is on our side"; and he considered the advantage strong enough to advise Washington, despite the earlier rebuke, that he would not return to Kaesong "except by direct order." Ridgway's refusal to compromise—and particularly his proposal for a truce line requiring communist, but not UN withdrawals—seemed particularly unwise to General Bradley, who noted that "reciprocity means a lot to the Communists." Though Bradley recognized that "when you are so close to those sons-of-bitches you have different views," he also thought that Ridgway had better learn that "you can kick these fellows and still be polite to them."[44]

With memories of a manic MacArthur fresh in their minds, the Joint Chiefs decided to send Bradley and Bohlen to Tokyo to bring the new Supreme Commander into line. Bradley and Bohlen found that Ridgway and Joy felt that they had made "steady concessions to the Communists on procedural matters" and had "possibly created an appearance of weakness which the military situation did not justify." Considering how difficult it is from the historical record to find any significant concessions made to the communists in this period, and considering that Bradley and Bohlen disagreed with Ridgway's position, one can only attribute the difference to ideology—a frontier mentality on the part of Ridgway and Joy. Perhaps Bradley and Bohlen failed to dissuade Ridgway from his views because he still had hopes for a more decisive victory, which he recognized would be virtually impossible once a truce line was agreed to and the front reverted to positional warfare.[45]

Ridgway proved to be right on the site issue, in the sense that the communists were willing to concede it to get the talks going again. After some stickiness over the size and shape of the new neutral zone, and an apology by Ridgway for yet another UN air force plane that had strayed inside it, killing a twelve-year-old and wounding a two-year-old, talks started up again at Panmunjom—a site far more comfortable for the UN negotiators, as it was located on a river along the line of contact, and not under the control of either side. At the suggestion of Nam Il, who had originally gotten the idea from Admiral Joy, subdelegate meetings were held to draw a demarcation line. Ridgway was faced with the enormous communist concession of a demilitarized zone that was four miles on either side of the line of contact, with some modifications. He continued to resist, claiming that the line he had offered earlier was the UN's "final offer." Bohlen and Bradley, he claimed, had agreed to such a stance when they were in Tokyo. The Joint Chiefs quickly pointed out that the communist proposal met the U.S. minimum objective of security for Line Kansas and even exceeded it by offering security for the outposts of Line Wyoming. They sympathized with Ridgway's reluctance to give up any ground purchased with UN blood, but they felt the deal was a fair one.[46]

Ridgway also insisted on getting control of Kaesong, the former royal capital, in order to impress "Asian public opinion." When Ridgway failed to agree to the current line of contact if the communists would agree to come to terms on the other points within a short deadline, Bradley told the Joint Chiefs, "I am damned if I understand why they refuse to put that forward." While an annoyed Joint Chiefs debated going to the president to force Ridgway to comply, the commander made a last ditch attempt to thwart an agreement that he feared might lead to a de facto ceasefire. "We have everything to lose" by concessions, he argued, and need "more steel and less silk" in our negotiating positions. He asked for authority to take final, inflexible positions, claiming that flexibility "inevitably induces an aggressive attitude in the Communists."[47]

On November 17, the delegation finally presented the cease-fire line proposal and deadline, which was duly accepted by the communists. Staff officers worked out a suitable line by November 27. The de facto ceasefire that Ridgway so feared and fought became a reality once the armistice line was initialed. Two weeks before, Ridgway had ordered Van Fleet to mount an "active defense." While this was mostly rhetoric designed to keep up morale, the order called for Van Fleet to seize the most favorable terrain along the existing defensive line, and, if the operation required no more than one division, to exploit "favorable opportunities" for inflicting casualties on the enemy.[48]

The day after the truce line was initialed, Ridgway's attempts to keep Eighth Army fighting were countermanded in effect by orders from below. Eighth Army Commander Van Fleet ordered his corps commanders to restrict their operations to "counterattacks to regain key terrain lost to enemy assault" and to make "every effort" to "prevent unecessary casualties."[49]

With the truce line agreed to, two main issues remained for the truce negotiators—it would take nineteen more months before they would be resolved. One issue was limitations on the expansion and renewal of military forces and infrastructure and the means for verifying compliance with those limitations. The other was exchange and repatriation of prisoners of war.

Neither issue looked like a candidate for quick progress. After his experience with the Baruch Plan, Ridgway never expected that the communists would agree to inspection. On December 4, however, Ridgway reported a surprising concession—the communists had agreed in their proposals to inspection behind-the-lines by a commission of neutral nations—not precisely the UN proposal, but closer than anyone had expected. Ridgway continued to fear communist treachery. He pressed for the rejection of the proposal on the rather specious ground that acceptance would introduce unspecified "political matters" into the negotiation.[50]

President Truman tended to agree with Ridgway. When the Joint Chiefs presented Truman with a proposal that Ridgway opposed, insisting on rotation of personnel, but that would concede rehabilitation of everything but airfields, the president told them that he thought that the United States was making too many concessions. Secretary Lovett and acting Secretary of State James E. Webb persuaded the president to accept the proposal, but only with considerable difficulty. Lovett argued that the United States was not in good shape militarily, and that the British were bankrupt. He favored a joint declaration by the UN that China would face a general war if they broke the armistice. Ridgway was unimpressed with the threat and thought that the Chinese might well call the Americans' bluff, forcing use of the atomic bomb.[51]

After the communists conceded on inspections, the negotiations made considerable progress, and by February agreement was quickly reached on rotation and other technical matters of armistice enforcement. A new bottleneck emerged, however, as the communists insisted that the U.S.S.R. be included as one of the neutrals on the commission.[52]

Ridgway took this proposal as an almost personal insult—even though the United States had agreed to allow communist nations like Poland and Czechoslovakia to join the inspection commission. By mid-March, officers in both Tokyo and Washington felt that the UN should offer a "package deal" trading agreement on the prisoner-of-war and U.S.S.R. issues for a UN concession allowing rehabilitation of airfields. This idea went completely contrary to Ridgway's strategy—a stance without concession or compromise: "Our final positions must be stated and if not accepted" then "we must be

prepared to continue their iteration indefinitely until either our patience or
that of the communists is exhausted." Ridgway had little interest in striking
a deal. He stuck to the argument that the best negotiating tactic was not to
negotiate but to "stand inflexibly on stated minimum positions." Compromise could only bring "humiliation derogatory to our national dignity."[53]

He then vetoed a proposal by Admiral Joy for presentation of a complete
armistice agreement, accompanied by an ultimatum. Ridgway feared it would
force a break in the talks, which would exceed his instructions. Nonetheless,
he argued that the UN should publicly repudiate the proposed Soviet membership on the inspection commission. The State Department, however,
having agreed to allow Soviet satellites on the commission could not see why
Soviet membership was any worse, so long as the Soviets were not designated
as "neutral." Fortunately, cooler heads than Ridgway's prevailed, and on
March 15 the Joint Chiefs instructed Ridgway to resolve as many minor
issues as possible, segregate prisoners of war who said they would violently
resist repatriation, and offer to meet with the communist senior commander
(either Kim Il Sung or Peng Teh Hueh) to discuss an armistice package.[54]

Ridgway disliked the Joint Chiefs' proposal. He thought that the meeting
between field commanders before the signing of the armistice would be a
farce because the communist commander would not have authority to negotiate, and he thought that the proposal should have a time limit. Why
Ridgway thought it was worse to have leaks of classified information to Soviet communist inspectors behind his lines than to Polish or Czech communists is inexplicable, except that he was resisting the entire idea of
agreement. Ridgway's most telling and accurate objection to the plan was
that it was unlikely to be acceptable because it required two concessions from
the communists, regarding prisoners of war and Soviet commission membership, and only one concession from the Americans, namely, acquiescence
to airfield reconstruction.[55]

Once again, Ridgway's negotiating style was not to negotiate and to be
completely convinced of the justice of his own position—far better qualities
for a warrior than for a diplomat. Perhaps he knew that more compromise
was in the offing when he grumbled the following to the press on March
12:

> The average American's objectives, his national characteristics—
> one of his greatest is impatience for meeting a reached decision.
> To do something it must be accomplished in a minimum of time,
> usually by the most direct approach. Not the Oriental, not the
> Slav at all. There is a timelessness about his objective which
> makes it difficult just to deal with him. He is willing to change
> his tactics innumerable times completely reversing his approach,
> biding his time, which wouldn't make much difference as I see it
> from Communist China's point of view if she has to sit there

months, six months, nine months, one year, if she could ultimately be sure of the destruction of our forces.[56]

Ridgway detested critics who blamed him for the lack of progress in the
talks. He blew up once again, when *Newsweek*, on March 31, questioned the
competence of the UN truce negotiators and reported moves to strengthen
the team with professional negotiators. Though this was an obvious possibility, Ridgway believed that it was the result of a leak and should be inves-
tigated "with urgency." He urged the Joint Chiefs to have an official
spokesman affirm their confidence in the negotiators and "discredit" the
official concerned.[57]

By the time the so-called package proposal was ready for presentation at
the end of April, however, Ridgway had some hopes for it. His more conciliatory attitude may have been influenced by a wish for a success at the
truce talks before he left for his new post as commander of NATO. When
finally presented to the communists, however, the proposal was "like a peb-
ble dropped into the ocean," according to official historian Walter Hermes.
Blundering by the UN on the emotionally charged prisoner-of-war issue
had humiliated communist pride and national dignity, as much as communist
intransigence had wounded Ridgway's sense of patriotism.[58]

When the agenda item on prisoners of war first came up, both Ridgway
and the communists had probably expected it to be a relatively simple one
of making logistical arrangements for the exchange of the approximately
12,000 UN prisoners for 130,000 communist prisoners held by UN forces.
This was to be done without regard to the prisoners' wishes, as dictated by
the Geneva Convention of 1949. At the time that the issue arose on the
agenda, Ridgway seems to have had the early return of UN prisoners as his
primary goal, with little interest in whether Chinese and Korean prisoners
were forced to repatriate to the other side, though the Army psychological
warfare bureau and the Joint Intelligence Committee had stressed the propaganda value of voluntary repatriation.[59]

Their desire was increased by leaks to the press about allegations of atrocities against UN prisoners of war by North Korean and Chinese captors.
News of atrocities against American prisoners of war was particularly ago-
nizing to the American people. On November 14, as the truce line was being
drawn, Ridgway's Judge Advocate General, Colonel James Hanley, released
figures purporting to show that 5,500–6,000 prisoners had been murdered.

In two statements to the press, Hanley failed to provide any details to
show how these statistics were derived. Hanley's allegations "have shocked
America," General Collins wrote to Ridgway, while requesting clarification.
I. F. Stone, citing numerous newspaper sources, charged that the figures
were used to increase hatred for the enemy at a time when peace seemed
close at hand and when the will to fight at home and on the front was
waning.[60]

After first endorsing Hanley's statement, Ridgway compounded the problem in a November 20 statement in which he said that Hanley had exaggerated, that it was "possible" that 6,000 had been killed, but there were only 365 proven cases of atrocities against servicemen, a figure based on reports to General MacArthur of atrocities by the North Koreans earlier in the war, atrocities stopped by the Chinese. Back in New York, journalists discovered that Ridgway had reported 8,000 UN prisoners of war killed in a report submitted to the UN on December 12, two days before Hanley's statement. Understandably, Ridgway took a bludgeoning from the press. *Time* called the snafu a "Four-Star Blunder," which caused "cruel anxiety" to the prisoners' relatives. The incident must have strengthened the resolve of Ridgway and the Joint Chiefs to get their men home.[61]

The proposed all-for-all exchange was first breached by the new chief negotiator, Admiral Ruthven E. Libby, in January 1952, but did not become hardened U.S. policy until ordered by President Truman a month later. Some senior State Department officals had suggested that voluntary repatriation was "not a good stumbling block" and that the United States should consult with its allies before taking such a stance; the Joint Chiefs and Lovett for a time opposed voluntary repatriation; Acheson sensed Truman's deep commitment to the issue and pushed it through the govenment.[62]

The ambivalences within the government on the issue of voluntary repatriation are striking. At first, the Joint Chiefs and Secretary Lovett seemed to follow the lead of the Army's psychological warfare chief, General Robert McClure, who pointed out the considerable long-term propaganda advantages of insisting on voluntary repatriation when the issue first came up in late August 1951. Acheson, who in World War II had opposed forcible repatriation, had reversed himself during negotiations for the Geneva convention of 1949, and initially called for exchange of all prisoners of war without regard to their preferences (except for impressed South Koreans and collaborators with the UN). Acheson's objections led the Joint Chiefs to agree on a policy of one-to-one exchange followed by repatriation of all remaining communist prisoners.[63]

Republican senators leaped on the voluntary repatriation issue and President Truman, who, as William Stueck points out, felt guilty for presiding over the involuntary repatriation of Soviet prisoners after World War II (many of them were executed or severely punished after repatriation), characteristically dug in his heels, believing he had a moral responsibility to protect the communist prisoners of war. Once the decision was made by Truman, Acheson, who had played both sides of the issue since 1945, swung into line behind the president.[64]

In his memoirs, Acheson takes credit for the policy on voluntary repatriation; he certainly did everything he could to reinforce Truman's prejudices on the issue by keeping the dissenting opinions of other State and Defense Department officials from reaching the president. The voluntary repatriation decision, which may have prolonged the fighting for twenty months, was in part a product of Truman's anger against the communists, in part an attempt to win propaganda points, and in part a result of fear that an armistice would jeopardize Truman's military rearmament program. Acheson, moreover, hoped that military advantages might accrue by giving communist soldiers an incentive to defect.[65]

After Truman solidified his hard line, prospects for peace got both better and worse, because the communists did not realize how nonnegotiable the stance was. Otherwise, compromise was steady and successful on all other parts of the agreements. The communists, for a while, even seemed to be willing to compromise on the voluntary repatriation issue, asking for estimates on how many prisoners would be involved. Here the UN Command fouled up badly, when Ridgway's chief of staff, Lt. General Doyle O. Hickey, gave the communists a vague estimate of 16,000 prisoners who would resist repatriation, an estimate that was conveyed to the communists.[66]

Preparatory to the package proposal, which was to be offered after the settlement of as many outstanding issues as possible, General Van Fleet was ordered on April 8 to begin the screening and segregating of prisoners to discover who wished to return home and who would forceably resist repatriation. Ridgway believed that this would be tacitly accepted by the other side.[67]

No one was as shocked as the communist delegates when the results came out: 74,000—almost half the prisoners—said they would forcibly resist repatriation to North Korea or the People's Republic of China. Forty-four thousand prisoners resisted screening—a prelude to the bitter conflicts that would soon rock the prisoner-of-war camps.[68]

Most probably the communists assumed that the UN had intentionally generated these figures to deliberately mislead them. Moreover, it was difficult for the communists, subsequent writers, and even some UN allies to buy the UN line that the prisoners were uncoerced. Indeed, the UN camps had consistently indoctrinated prisoners with anticommunism and had encouraged Nationalist Chinese prisoners to politicize and terrorize the compounds, just as the communist secret agents who had been infiltrating Koje-Do since December engaged in countercoercion.[69]

Though Ridgway began his tour with a stunning military feat on the peninsula, his tour ended with the embarrassment of the incompleted truce talks and yet another explosion in the prisoner-of-war camps at Koje Do, where communist prisoners rioted and took American Brigadier General Francis Dodd hostage just as Ridgway was turning command over to General Mark W. Clark. In diplomacy, Ridgway had allowed himself to be overtaken by anger, though he remained calm in the stormiest of battles. Although he had had plenty of experience in military diplomacy, his previous duties had required very little flexibility or negotiating skill. By the early 1950s, American diplomacy was militarized to an unprecedented degree. In Europe, the major foreign policy initiative was carried forward by NATO Commander General Dwight D. Eisenhower. In the East, Ridgway was entrusted with the conduct of the truce talks. With the possible exception of the UN military staff committee, where he had little responsibility for policy, Ridgway had never before been involved in negotiations of such delicacy and complexity. In Nicaragua, General McCoy had been a virtual proconsul; in Latin America during and after World War II, Ridgway was dealing with countries that were not at war with the United States. Rather than increase cleverness and flexiblity to bring the negotiations to a successful conclusion, Ridgway acted like the great infantryman he was and urged his superiors never to surrender or concede. The jump to being a great diplomat, was, as he himself admitted, too much for him.[70]

It is impossible to fully explain his motives for trying to slow the conclusion of an armistice. Certainly his general strategic ideals—keeping the initiative, maintaining maximum mobility, and attacking whenever feasible to kill as many of the enemy as possible—were not in accord with a truce. Ridgway feared that truce talks would destroy the morale of the army he had worked so hard to create. Under such circumstances, how could he fail to resist the loss of military initiative that a fixed cease-fire line would imply? Yet Allied and domestic political pressures made the order to negotiate direct and unavoidable. Ridgway reached ideological closure in this situation by trying to vent his anger against the communists and resisting negotiation as much as he had resisted the idea of withdrawal from the peninsula.

NOTES

1. Marshall to Ridgway, September 11, 1951, Ridgway MSS, Box 18.

2. Quoted in Eric Bentley, *A Century of Hero Worship: A Study of the Idea of Heroism in Carlyle and Nieztsche* (Boston: Beacon, 1957), 1.

3. TKW, 158; Joint Chiefs of Staff to Ridgway, April 12, 1951, CCS 383.21, Korea Section 45, RG 218, National Archives. Ridgway inherited many posts from MacArthur, including Commander of United Nations forces in Korea; Supreme Commander, Allied Powers (SCAP), in charge of the U.S. occupation of Japan; and U.S. Commander-in-Chief, Far East Theater (CINCFE), with ultimate authority over all U.S. forces from the Aleutians to Formosa. These multiple commands required Ridgway to combine military experience with political savoir-faire. See Joint Chiefs of Staff to Ridgway, April 16, 1951, CCS 383.21, Korea Section, RG 218, National Archives, giving Ridgway all commands and authority formerly enjoyed by MacArthur.

4. Diary entry, April 12, 1951, *Ridgway MSS, Box 20*; Joseph C. Goulden, *Korea: The Untold Story of the War* (New York: Times Books, 1982), 495; Michael Schaller, *MacArthur*, 240; JB, 2:3:81.

5. D. Clayton James, *The Years of MacArthur*, Vol. 3, *Triumph and Disaster, 1945– 1964* (Boston: Houghton Mifflin, 1985), 621; Ridgway, *Korean War*, quoting Trumbull Higgins, Appendix 1, p. 261.

6. *New York Times*, editorial, May 12, 1951; *Life*, April 30, 1951.

7. *Life*, April 30, 1951; Winton quoted in Blair, *Forgotten War*, 559.

8. Blair, *Forgotten War*, 722; Murray Schumach, "The Education of Matthew Ridgway," *New York Times Magazine*, May 4, 1952.

9. Blair, *Forgotten War*, 722; Schumach, "Matthew Ridgway."

10. "General Matt and General Muck," *Life*, March 12, 1951; "G.I.s See Gen. Ridgway as Leo Durocher Double," *New York Times*, April 30, 1951. Durocher was known for his determination to win games and for the proverb "Nice guys finish last." Leo Durocher Homepage, Internet, http://www.cmgww.com/baseball/durocher/durocher.html, May 10, 1997.

11. Gertrude Samuels, "Ridgway—Three Views of a Soldier," *New York Times Magazine*, April 22, 1951, 10; *Time*, March 5, 1951; *Newsweek*, February 12, 1951; Blair, *Forgotten War*, 570. Blair, Ridgway, and Appleman all strongly emphasize the fact that he only wore one, not two, grenades. While it is plain in all Korean War photographs that the container on his left strap is not a grenade, in a frequently reprinted 1945 photo he does appear to be wearing two grenades (c.f. *Newsweek*, January 8, 1951, 32).

12. Morris Janowitz, *The American Soldier* (New York: 1960), 162.

13. *Newsweek*, January 8, 1951; *Life*, February 19, 1951, 29.

14. *Newsweek*, January 8, 1951; Michener, *Life*, April 30, 1951; Blair, *Forgotten War*, 559.

15. *New York Times*, December 24, 1950.

16. *Time* June 2, 1952.

17. Schumach, "Matthew Ridgway."

18. *Collier's*, March 8, 1952; Michener, *Life*, April 30, 1951; "Son of UN Commander Takes Over," *New York Times*, December 10, 1951; Ridgway, *Soldier*, 255.

19. Michener, *Life*, April 30, 1951; "Ridgway Praised as Churchly Man," *New York Times*, January 18, 1952.

20. Memo from Ridgway to CG, Eighth Army (Van Fleet), April 25, 1951, Ridgway MSS, Box 21. See also copy of the above, Ridgway to Van Fleet, April 19, 1951, in CCS 383.21, Korea Section 45, RG 218, National Archives.

21. Blair, *Forgotten War*, 939; Rosemary Foot, *A Substitute for Victory* (Ithaca: Cornell University Press, 1990), 59, 73.

22. Memo of conversation by director of Office of North East Asian Affairs, June 28, 1951, Ambassador's briefing, June 29, 1951, Gross to Secretary of State, June 30, 1951, *Foreign Relations* 7 (1951): 566–67, 570, 593, 605–606; Hermes, *Truce Tent*, 1992, 16.

23. Ridgway to Hull, December 6, 1951, Ridgway MSS, Box 20.

24. Ridgway to Joint Chiefs of Staff, July 1, 1951, *Foreign Relations* 7 (1951): 609.

25. Hermes, *Truce Tent*, 32; Ridgway to Joint Chiefs of Staff, July 2, 1951, *Foreign Relations* 7 (1951): 610.

26. Joint Chiefs of Staff to Ridgway, July 9, 1951, *Foreign Relations* 7 (1951): 640; Ridgway to Joint Chiefs of Staff, July 10, 1951, *Foreign Relations* 7 (1951): 648.

27. Joint Chiefs of Staff to Ridgway, July 9, 1951, *Foreign Relations* 7 (1951): 639. On the centralized supervision of the negotiations by the Joint Chiefs of Staff and the White House, see James F. Schnabel and Robert J. Watson, *The History of the Joint Chiefs of Staff: The Joint Chiefs of Staff and National Policy, Part II*, reprint (Wilmington, Del.: Michael Glazier, n.d.), 589–593.

28. Joint Chiefs of Staff to Ridgway, June 30, 1951, *Foreign Relations* 7 (1954): 598, 599.

29. Hermes, *Truce Tent*, 17. For a sardonic examination of the internal dynamics of the team, especially the bickering between Admirals Burke and Joy, see Herbert Goldhamer, *The 1951 Korean Armistice Conference: A Personal Memoir* (Santa Monica, Calif.: RAND, 1994), 6.

30. Memo for General and Staff Flag Office Members of the U.S. Delegation to the Armistice Negotiations, July 6, 1951, Van Fleet MSS, Marshall Library; see also *Foreign Relations* 7 (1951): 681.

31. Hermes, *Truce Tent*, 20–21; Foot, *Substitute for Victory*, 43; Allen E. Goodman, ed., *Negotiating While Fighting: The Diary of Admiral C. Turner Joy at the Korean Armistice Conference* (Stanford, Calif.: Hoover Institution Press, 1978) (hereafter Joy Diary), 17–18.

32. Foot, *Substitute for Victory*, 44–47; Hermes, *Truce Tent*, 29–31; Joy Diary, 22.

33. Ridgway to Van Fleet, July 4, 1951, Ridgway MSS, Box 21.

34. Foot, *Substitute for Victory*, 48, 55, 56; Joy Diary, 24.

35. Ridgway to Joint Chiefs of Staff, August 7, 1951; *Foreign Relations* 7 (1951): 787, 788.

36. Slotkin, *Gunfighter Nation*, 12.

37. Joy to Ridgway, August 8, 1951, *Foreign Relations* 7 (1951): 794; Ridgway to Joint Chiefs of Staff, *Foreign Relations* 7 (1951) :807; Joy Diary, 26, 34.

38. Ridgway to Joint Chiefs of Staff, Joint Chiefs of Staff to Ridgway, August 11, 1951, *Foreign Relations* 7 (1951): 807; Joy Diary, 26.

39. Ridgway to Joint Chiefs of Staff, September 3, 1951, *Foreign Relations* 7 (1951): 875–877, Ridgway to Joint Chiefs of Staff, August 23, 1951, *Foreign Relations* 7 (1951): 848–852; Foot, *Substitute for Victory*, 49.

40. Ridgway to Joint Chiefs of Staff, September 11, 1951, *Foreign Relations* 7 (1951): 900.

41. Ridgway to Joint Chiefs of Staff, September 21, 1951, *Foreign Relations* 7 (1951): 926; Memorandum by Merchant, September 22, 1951, 7:927; Joy Diary, 44–45.

42. Memo of State–Joint Chiefs of Staff meeting, September 25, 1951, *Foreign Relations* 7 (1951): 939, 944.

43. Bohlen to Secretary of State, October 4, 1951, *Foreign Relations* 7 (1951): 990; Ridgway to Joint Chiefs of Staff, September 23, 1951, *Foreign Relations* 7 (1951): 953.

44. Ridgway to Joint Chiefs of Staff, September 23, 1951, *Foreign Relations* 7 (1951): 953–955; State–Joint Chiefs of Staff meeting, September 26, 1951, *Foreign Relations* 7 (1951): 955–962.

45. Bohlen to Secretary of State, October 4, 1951, *Foreign Relations* 7 (1951): 990; Foot, *Substitute for Victory*, 51–52; Joy Diary 45–51.

46. Ridgway to Joint Chiefs of Staff, November 13, 1951, *Foreign Relations* 7 (1951): 1128; Joint Chiefs of Staff to Ridgway, November 14, 1951, *Foreign Relations* 7 (1951): 1131.

47. Ridgway to Joint Chiefs of Staff, November 8, 1951, *Foreign Relations* 7 (1951): 1102; State–Joint Chiefs of Staff meeting, November 12, 1951, *Foreign Relations* 7 (1951): 1122; Ridgway to Joint Chiefs of Staff, November 13, 1951, *Foreign Relations* 7 (1951): 1130.

48. Ridgway to Joint Chiefs of Staff, November 13, 1951, *Foreign Relations* 7

(1951): 1130; Joint Chiefs of Staff to Ridgway, November 14, 1951, *Foreign Relations* 7 (1951): 1131; Ridgway to Joint Chiefs of Staff, November 15, 1951 *Foreign Relations* 7 (1951): 1139; Hermes, *Truce Tent*, 119, 176–177.

49. Hermes, *Truce Tent*, 176–177. See also Schnabel and Watson, *Joint Chiefs of Staff*, 622.

50. Ridgway to Joint Chiefs of Staff, December 7, 1951, *Foreign Relations* 7 (1951): 1258.

51. Joint Chiefs of Staff to President Truman, December 7, 1951, *Foreign Relations* 7 (1951): 1278; memo of meeting for president, December 10, 1951, *Foreign Relations* 7 (1951): 1290; Ridgway to DEPTAR, January 7, 1952, *Foreign Relations* 15 (1952–54): 10, 11.

52. Hermes, *Truce Tent*, 161–163.

53. Ridgway to Joint Chiefs of Staff, March 11, 1952, *Foreign Relations* 15 (1952–54): 80; Ridgway to Joint Chiefs of Staff, December 18, 1951, *Foreign Relations* 7 (1951): 1366–1368.

54. *Foreign Relations* 15 (1952–54): 80 n.2; Hermes, *Truce Tent*, 163–165; memo, State–Joint Chiefs of Staff meeting March 12, 1952, *Foreign Relations* 15 (1952–54): 82–86; Joint Chiefs of Staff to Ridgway March 15, 1952, *Foreign Relations* 15 (1952–54), 89.

55. Ridgway to Joint Chiefs of Staff, March 17, 1952; *Foreign Relations* 15 (1952–54): 95.

56. Ridgway press conference tape transcript, March 12, 1951, Ridgway MSS, Box 17.

57. Ridgway to Joint Chiefs of Staff, April 2, 1952, CCS 383.21, Korea Section, 92, RG 218, National Archives.

58. Hermes, *Truce Tent*, 174; Schnabel and Watson, *Joint Chiefs of Staff*, 166.

59. Ridgway to Joint Chiefs of Staff, October 27, 1951, *Foreign Relations* 7 (1951): 1068. The best account of the emergence of voluntary repatriation policy is Foot, *Substitute for Victory*, 87–101.

60. I. F. Stone, *The Hidden History of the Korean War* (Boston: Little, Brown, 1952), 325, 332; Collins to Ridgway, November 16, 1951, Ridgway MSS, Box 20.

61. Stone, *Hidden History*, 326–327; *Time*, December 3, 1951.

62. Hickerson to Matthews, February 4, 1952, *Foreign Relations* 15 (1952–54): 38; memo for record, February 7, 1952, *Foreign Relations* 15 (1952–54): 42–44; Acheson to Truman, February 8, 1952, *Foreign Relations* 15 (1952–54): 44, 45.

63. Foot, *Substitute for Victory*, 88.

64. Steuck, *Korean War*, 289; Foot, *Substitute for Victory*, 89.

65. Steuck, *Korean War*, 252, 263; Dean Acheson, *Present at the Creation*, 652–653; Foot, *Substitute for Victory*, 88–90.

66. Foot, *Substitute for Victory*, 94; memorandum of conversation, February 25, 1952, *Foreign Relations* 15 (1952–54): 58, 59.

67. Ridgway to Joint Chiefs of Staff, April 4, 1952, Ridgway to G-3, April 10, 1952, *Foreign Relations* 15 (1952–54): 136, 142.

68. Ridgway to G-3, April 12, 1952, *Foreign Relations* 15 (1952–54): 144.

69. C.f. Steuck, *Korean War* 271–278; Foot, *Substitute for Victory*, 98–100, 112–113.

70. On the Koje-Do incident, see Hermes, *Truce Tent*, 233–262; Steuck, *Korean War*, 263–264; Schnabel and Watson, *Joint Chiefs of Staff*, 768–774.

CHAPTER 12

The Far East and Europe: Ridgway as a Theater Commander

RIDGWAY AND JAPANESE-AMERICAN RELATIONS

MacArthur's firing brought Ridgway to the highest level of Army command, but his promotion was a mixed blessing, which brought him a fourth star, honor, and power, as well as a myriad of political responsibilities that he was not especially well equipped to handle. In addition to the truce talks and oversight of the conduct of the Korean War, these responsibilities would include the administration and phaseout of the occupation of Japan, the rearmament of Japan, and later, when he went to NATO as Supreme Allied Commander, Europe, the rearmament of Western Europe.[1]

Ridgway would never have the kind of influence over Japanese society that MacArthur the conqueror had. Japan and the United States concluded a peace treaty soon after Ridgway took over the theater. He met frequently, however, with treaty negotiators John Foster Dulles and Yoshida Shigeru and took a strong liking to the Japanese prime minister. At the end of his term in Tokyo, an American magazine commented that Ridgway's administration had "been so evenly conducted and he is so unobtrusive it is difficult to think of him except officially."[2]

When MacArthur assumed responsibility for the postwar reconstruction of Japan, a popular Japanese biography called him "a living god." Ridgway never held so aloof. "Ridgway," wrote James Michener, "has done little but witness (and intelligently abet) the final reemergence of Japan as a sovereign power." While Ridgway stayed in the background of Japanese politics, he believed that the most important task was to incorporate Japan into the American struggle against the Soviet Union and its allies, consistent with his guiding principle of coordination and cooperation between societies and classes in order to ensure Western security. According to American journalists, both Matthew and Penny Ridgway tried hard get to know Japanese of all walks of life and to learn as much about the country as possible. "Almost immediately," according to *New York Times* reporter Murray Schumach, "Japanese politicians lured him into a trap. Always desirous of unloading unpopular decisions on the Occupation, they prevailed upon him to ban a May Day demonstration." According to Schumach, Ridgway learned fast to remain in the background so far as Japanese domestic politics was concerned.[3]

When Ridgway arrived in Tokyo in 1951, he believed there was an imminent threat of Soviet invasion and tried desperately to get Japanese officials to take the threat more seriously. Warned by the Joint Chiefs of Staff that Soviet forces in the maritime provinces were in an advanced state of readiness for war, in protest of the imminent agreement in a peace treaty, Ridgway passed the information on to Yoshida, but the Japanese Prime Minister did not seem apprehensive in the least. Two days later, General Collins wrote that "the overall situation while continuing serious has not steadily worsened as a result of Treaty negotiations."[4]

The integration of Japan into a permanent part of the American system for military containment contained three main parts. The first was to make the Japanese economy an integral part of the the U.S. military-industrial economy. When demand for industrial production skyrocketed owing to the Korean War, the United States turned to Japanese industry to supply its needs. The second was the insistence on extensive and permanent base rights for American forces as the sine qua non of any treaty returning Japanese sovereignty. This was agreed to, though the terms were so widely condemned by the Japanese public that the treaty had to be renegotiated in 1960. The third was the remilitarization of Japan, perhaps in violation of its own antiwar constitution. Rearmament was tied to the treaty but was accomplished semicovertly by the Occupation authorities.

Despite U.S. pressure, the Japanese government resisted rearmament. Though Yoshida warned that rearmament might wreck Japan's fragile economy, the United States made Japan pay the costs of the secret conversion of Japan's National Police Reserve into a force of trained soldiers equipped with armor and other sophisticated military weapons. According to Ridgway, equipping the National Police Reserve was the "most vital single present element in Japan-U.S. relations." Occupation financial czar Joseph C. Dodge insisted that Ridgway, not Yoshida, determine the level of Japan's rearmament. The Supreme Commander increased defense spending in the 1952 Japanese government budget to 30 percent of the total—more than Japan had spent to defray the entire costs of the Occupation the previous year. This budget, rammed through the Diet by Yoshida, more or less on the insistence of the Occupation authorities, allocated 65 million yen for the support of U.S. forces and a huge sum of 56 million yen for the quasi-military national police and coast guard.[5]

Ridgway also improved the U.S. business community's access to the Supreme Commander and worked to promote American business interests in Tokyo. When Trading Company executives suggested meetings to give young soldiers the American businessman's point of view about Japan, Ridgway "heartily agreed" and hoped he would repeat the suggestion to the Chamber of Commerce and the Rotary. Beginning in January 1952, he held meetings with top executives of U.S. corporations in Japan, more or less industry by industry. Mostly, he solicited their advice. A representative of the specialty store operators asked him to foster closer liaisons between the American and Japanese business communities and the U.S. military and diplomatic community. General Marquat (head of the Occupation's economic section) demurred. The government would help where appropriate, but he claimed that unlike the United Kingdom, the U.S. government tried to keep business decisions independent "of government interference and without undue reliance upon governmental authority and prestige." In other meetings, Ridgway did not share Marquat's reservations about close cooperation between business and the state. For example, he worked closely with oil executives, coordinating petroleum supplies for the war effort in Korea, and on antisabotage efforts, as he had in Latin America.[6]

RIDGWAY AND DESEGREGATION

Racial integration of the Far East Theater is one of Ridgway's most important achievements. As historian Richard Dalfiume observed, the racist belief that African Americans were cowards was held by many army officers in the early postwar period. This pseudoscientific racism began to crumble in the 1950s, opening the eyes of officers like Ridgway to the underused potential of African American personnel. As during the Civil War, military and political necessity would be the mother of a certain degree of tolerance.[7]

After World War II, a board of officers led by General Alvan C. Gillem Jr. recognized the inefficiency of World War II army racial policies and called for the elimination of "special consideration based on race" but suspended judgment on the issue of integration. The migration of African Americans to the cities of the North, however, where they could vote, made them a force to be reckoned with in presidential elections. Though African Americans had initially mistrusted President Truman because of his border state background, he tried to court their votes. Segregation was also an embarassment in the Cold War, an easy target for anyone who wanted to expose the hollowness of American promises of "freedom."

In 1948, reacting to these political pressures, Truman issued an executive order concerning racial discrimination in the armed forces. Although White House aides gave the impression that the order banned segregation, it did not. While the Navy and Air Force began to integrate, the Army did nothing. Eminent soldiers like General Omar Bradley protested the order, claiming that integration would jeopardize combat effectiveness. "The Army is not out to make any social reform. The Army will not put men of different races in the same companies. It will change that policy when the nation as a whole changes it."[8]

Proponents of segregation claimed that integration would increase the number of poorly educated and trained troops, and assumed without any evidence that inter-racial violence would mar the performance of integrated units. Segregation became increasingly inefficient, however. Segregationist officers of the late 1940s tried to argue that Negroes were "peculiarly suited" to labor battalions instead of combat units. The tendency after 1945 to replace men with high-tech machines had begun to make such labor battalions obsolete; segregation was out of synch with the new division of labor required by the army.[9]

An ideology of racism, sometimes inherited from the Confederacy, permeated arguments for the efficiency of segregation. One of the most persistent opponents of integration was Vice Chief of Staff Wade Hampton Haislip, namesake of the former Confederate general and post-Reconstruction governor of South Carolina. Another segregation advocate was the deeply bigoted Lieutenant General Edward M. Almond, a Virginian, who served as MacArthur's chief of staff and commander of X Corps in the Korea War. During World War II, Almond was assigned to command a poorly performing Negro division, and he probably blamed the division for retarding his career. Almond continued to believe, contrary to all subsequent experience of the Army, that skin color carried with it inherent differences that might undermine combat effectiveness. As late as 1972, Almond insisted that "there is no question in my mind of the inherent difference in races. This is not racism—it is common sense and understanding. Those who ignore these differences merely interfere with the combat effectiveness of battle units."[10]

To counter such attitudes in the Army, Truman appointed a commission led by liberal Atlanta attorney Charles Fahy to examine the problem of segregation. The commission found that segregation led to gross inefficiency in the Army. This commission laid the basis for integration by getting Army Secretary Frank Pace to abolish regulations prohibiting the integration of units by local commanders. Pace also deleted the racial quota that limited the number of African Americans inducted into the army to 10 pecent of all inductees.[11]

At the time, these seemed like only modest gains; yet once war in Korea came, these gains laid important groundwork for integration on the battlefield. More and more African Americans were drafted and recruited into the Army once the quota was lifted. Segregated black units in Korea were manned over their authorized strength, at the very time when white units were understaffed. Battlefield commanders began to remedy the problem by integrating units ad hoc as early as August 1950. Military journalist Brigadier General S. L. A. Marshall publicized the promising results of these experiments. African American soldiers fought better and their morale improved in integrated units. Integration also simplified administrative and logistical demands for separate facilities. Moreover, white soldiers readily accepted black soldiers on the line. The Chamberlain Board, a conservative panel of generals appointed to study integration, admitted that integration was a success and decreased racial friction, even as they called for the reimposition of segregation.[12]

Ridgway did not accept the view of some other officers that African Americans were cowards. Before the Korean War started—at a time when segregation was the norm in the Army, and was still publicly supported by boards of generals and by such top brass as Omar Bradley, the Chairman of the Joint Chiefs of Staff, and General Dwight D. Eisenhower—Ridgway told military audiences that "human courage is universally distributed. It is daily displayed by the yellow, the brown, and the black as well as by those of lighter pigments. It needs no battlefield stage to show its actors. It knows neither race, nor sex, nor age."[13]

A year after he declared his position in favor of integration, Ridgway found himself on the battlefield. For the first time, he commanded an entire army and could not go to his superiors for reinforcements. Ridgway had to squeeze every combat soldier he could from the forces available to him. In his peregrinations across Korea, he tried to stop the misuse of African American troops as laborers. On March 8, he complained to a corps commander about "highly inefficient use of U.S. military personnel" when he observed eleven African American soldiers who were loading stones into trucks with their hands. "We can use these men better as infantry," he remarked. Ridgway took other action to improve the morale of the African Americans under his command, overruling his own judge advocate general and supporting the contention of the NAACP's Thurgood Marshall that black GIs were subjected to unfair and improper court-martial procedures.[14]

Shortly after General Ridgway took command of the Far East Theater, he submitted a plan to the Pentagon to integrate his entire theater. Washington's approval was needed because several federalized national guard units were involved. Ridgway met with a favorable response when he took the matter up with Secretary of Defense George C. Marshall, when Marshall visited Ridgway in June 1951. Marshall approved the integration order a month later. With training camps and the Far East Theater integrated, the rest of the Army was certain to follow. It took three more years; but by the end of 1954, the Army was an integrated service.[15]

Ridgway's stand in favor of integration won plaudits from African American groups. The Chicago *Defender* named him to its honor role "for his order banning Jim Crow in the Pacific Command and speeding up integration of units of the Army." A few months later, the National Newspaper Publishers Association, a group of African American publishers, presented Ridgway with an award named in memory of editor John B. Russwurm. The publisher of the Michigan *Chronicle* wrote that such awards are given "in recognition of outstanding achievements in making possible a richer conception of democratic principles and for upholding the highest of American traditions." Ridgway's reply reveals his pride in the integration program and his vision of a corporatist society reaching toward a single goal of victory: "I accept this expression of trust and confidence, not for myself, but for the thousands of Americans of many racial stocks, who have proved again and again in Korea that a willingness to die, if need be, in defense of the ideals our country represents, is limited to no one group among us." The term "racial stocks" betrays the survival of an older Progressive era discourse about race, savagery and civilization. Ridgway, shrewd and adaptive to new conditions, still retained more than a residue of an earlier ideology about the savagery of non–Anglo-Saxons. The Cold War had created a more dangerous racial Other in Asia. Cold Warriors of the Ridgway stripe, who saw unity at home as paramount, had little use for continuing racial division.[16]

Though Ridgway clearly favored integration of the Army, he was not always willing to take political risks to accomplish it. When he took command at NATO in the spring of 1952, U.S. troops in the European theater were still not integrated, largely due to opposition from General Thomas T. Handy, Ridgway's deputy in charge of U.S. troops stationed there. A leading African American banker, William R. Hudgens, wrote Ridgway, asking whether integration in Europe would proceed as it had in the Far East. At first, Ridgway drafted a reply sympathetic to speedier integration. Army Secretary Frank Pace told Ridgway, however, that the prointegration letter was too hot politically: "No Southerner will read this thing except to say, 'What in the hell is Ridgway doing?' " If Ridgway sent it, Pace was "perfectly glad to let him take the heat, but we have consistently sought to protect you people [the uniformed military]. It is up to you to make up your mind." Under these circumstances, Ridgway replied with a noncommittal letter, telling Hudgens that the integration decision rested in Washington. The letter that was finally sent to Hudgens omitted a paragraph in an earlier draft, declaring Ridgway's unqualified support for integration, which would proceed "as rapidly as local conditions make desirable."[17]

GENERAL RIDGWAY GOES TO PARIS

Ridgway's predecessor as Supreme Allied Commander in Europe (SACEUR) General Dwight D. Eisenhower, was a consummate politician. Even while serving as a military officer, Eisenhower was a possible, indeed a likely successor, to President Harry S. Truman—a fact that added to his considerable personal leverage with European governments and with the news media. After Eisenhower left Paris and Ridgway had been there two months, a press officer at Supreme Allied Headquarters noted a fall off of fifty to sixty requests by correspondents for interviews or briefings each week to "a scant half-dozen a week," an indication of the younger general's lack of political power compared to Eisenhower's.[18]

President Truman appointed Ridgway as Supreme Allied Commander in Europe over General Eisenhower's objections. Eisenhower had favored General Alfred M. Gruenther and campaigned for his appointment as early as December 1951. Gruenther had been Eisenhower's chief of staff, alter ego, and world class bridge partner at NATO headquarters. He enjoyed a reputation for efficiency and political astuteness that led many Europeans to favor his appointment. Gruenther campaigned hard for the job.[19]

General Omar Bradley, Chairman of the Joint Chiefs, favored his old friend Ridgway over Gruenther, mostly because of Ridgway's experience as a field commander. Now that Eisenhower was running for the presidency as a Republican, Bradley may also have wanted to thwart his choice in retaliation for embarrassing charges by congressional Republicans about the mismanagement of ammunition supplies in Korea. But Bradley and Truman had other reasons for choosing Ridgway. Despite his reputation for bluntness, Ridgway possessed a considerable résumé of politico-military assignments. At the time, it was thought that the new SACEUR, whoever was appointed, might be promoted to five-star general because he would have to command subordinates of an equivalent rank such as British Field Marshal Bernard Montgomery. That would mean a Ridgway appointment, because Gruenther did not have the combat experience or time in grade necessary for promotion to an army rank held only by Marshall, MacArthur, Eisenhower, and Bradley.[20]

Ridgway, according to *Newsweek*, "boasted a reputation as a fighting leader that was surpassed, among Army men on active duty, only by Eisenhower and General Omar N. Bradley." A correspondent from *Le Monde* remarked that while Ridgway had an "extraordinary power" and "mesmerizes listeners, with his dagger-like eyes," he was not a very "international type" but was "army, army, jugular, jugular" in his approach. Gruenther himself, speaking after Ridgway's appointment, conceded that "General Ridgway's prestige is very great indeed. There is still a great deal of urging necessary" in dealing with the NATO governments, and "prestige is important in all of that." Ultimately Truman chose Ridgway, but announced that Gruenther would remain as chief of staff. Gruenther wrote Ridgway a cordial and friendly letter, describing the Supreme Commander's house (and personal trout pond) in a park eight miles outside Paris in the town of Marnes-La-Coquette. "Grace [Mrs. Gruenther] and I are confident that you will like your house and the grounds," he wrote. He proved a loyal chief of staff to Ridgway, for whom he often smoothed over disagreements with officials of NATO countries resulting from Ridgway's insistence on rapid expansion of forces.[21]

Though Truman reportedly favored giving Ridgway a fifth star, the promotion never materialized in the waning months of the Democratic Administration. Perhaps this was due to Republican threats to investigate Ridgway's role in the Koje-Do uprising. General Ridgway requested complete disclosure of records relating to the Koje-Do incident, noting a statement by Republican Senator Styles Bridges implying that Ridgway might be a target of such an investigation. Ridgway warned Bradley that such an inquiry would fuel communist propaganda. In the first days of the Eisenhower Administration, Senator Leverett Saltonstall suggested that five stars for Ridgway might "speed up" NATO, but he waited for Eisenhower's recommendation.[22]

On May 27, 1952, Ridgway arrived at Supreme Headquarters, Allied Powers Europe. It was a time of enormous change in European politics, as well as in the structure of the NATO organization. On May 26, the Treaty of Bonn establishing the sovereignty of West Germany was signed; and on the 27th, the Treaty of Paris, never ratified, promised the creation of a multinational European armed force, the European Defense Community (EDC). Both treaties provided a vehicle for the rearmament of West Germany, a development that many French people, as well as the Soviets, found threatening. According to Pelletier, "propagandizing to a hostile French public" about the European Defense Community was one of Ridgway's major problems. According to French scholar Pierre Mélandri, writing much later, many French thought that the EDC treaty "tended to make the old continent a veritable American protectorate" inasmuch as the European armed forces would be placed under the command of the American SACEUR.[23]

As the politics of Europe changed, so did NATO's structure. The original 1949 treaty that created the North Atlantic Treaty Organization emphasized joint military planning. It was essentially a paper organization. A year later, the Allies first appointed General Eisenhower to transform NATO into a military force.[24]

Originally a council of foreign ministers, which met relatively infrequently, made major political decisions. Just before Eisenhower's departure, the NATO foreign ministers created a civilian political structure—a council of permanent representatives and a Secretary-General who would have important power as vice chair of the council and as a neutral intermediary between the Allies. A British soldier–civil servant, General Lord Hastings

Ismay, became NATO's first Secretary-General. Where Eisenhower had had considerable political latitude, Ridgway was subject to the political guidance of the council. In theory his job was primarily that of a military technician, with few "political" functions. In practice, as the most visible representative of the Alliance, the Supreme Commander could not avoid a political role.[25]

The Allies made these structural changes at the February 1952 Lisbon Conference. But that conference proved most important for the generous promises of force levels made by member nations—about 50 divisions, 4,000 aircraft, and 704 combat vessels by 1952; 75 divisions and 6,500 aircraft by 1953; 96 divisions and 9,000 aircraft by 1954, with 35–40 divisions to be ready for combat at all times. Twelve of these divisions would come from a newly rearmed West Germany, and other components from newly admitted Greece and Turkey. These force commitments were seen as a triumph of Eisenhower's diplomacy, vastly increasing European confidence in the Alliance, but they were seen more as a deterrent statement of NATO's potential in the unlikely event that the Soviets decided to invade. The planning and infrastructural improvements were the concrete commitments—forces would continue moderate expansion but actually reach their full Lisbon levels only if the political situation dictated. By the time of Ridgway's arrival, these commitments were clearly eroding as hard-pressed postwar governments tried to reconstruct their devastated civilian sectors. By June 19, the British Chiefs, for example, had already decided that NATO plans should be geared more toward, as they put it, preparation for Cold War rather than for hot war. In practice, this meant a strategy based on nuclear rather than conventional deterrence of the sort advocated by Air Chief Marshal Sir William Slessor, who thought there "was not the remotest chance" of the Lisbon goals being achieved. Eisenhower, who as president (much to Ridgway's distaste) adapted Slessor's ideas about strategic nuclear deterrence, probably understood that Lisbon was more of a political threat to calm Soviet sabre rattling than the ironclad "i.o.u." that Ridgway thought it was.[26]

When Ridgway arrived, he believed that "it was [his] job to translate promises into deeds, to collect on these I.O.U.s" given at Lisbon—and that a neutral public interest required that NATO try to meet Soviet capabilities, regardless of the political situation. From his first briefing by the State Department, Ridgway was "fully aware that the position of [Supreme Commander in Europe] has a high political content." However, Ridgway never seemed comfortable as a military politician and tended at first to cling to a technical "military" role. When he felt that a more political appeal was needed, he inflexibly pursued his goals, complaining bitterly of the slowness of the NATO Council in making decisions. His lack of ability to compromise may have alienated some European politicians.[27]

Ridgway faced much more difficult "local conditions" at NATO than he did in the Far East Theater. Rearmament of allies remained his major concern in both theaters, but in Europe he felt he had to persuade twelve Allied governments to devote increasing sums to rearmament at a time when the civilian sector desperately needed capital resources. In addition, significant popular movements in many countries opposed the Alliance, which was perceived as an instrument of American imperialism. In Europe, Ridgway could not give orders as he had in the Far East. Before Japan's national sovereignty was restored, Ridgway had possessed almost vice-regal powers. In Europe, Ridgway had to rely on persuasion rather than power. At NATO the bureaucratic structure had been constructed by Eisenhower expressly to prevent his successor's recommendations regarding force increases from directly reaching the NATO Council—the Alliance's political leadership. Such recommendations would go no further than the council's Military Committee.[28]

Persuasion involved political skills that at first Ridgway had not recognized as relevant. Only after it was apparent that his strictly technical military approach had failed did Ridgway change his approach, by making frank public statements about the need for more NATO spending, even though the State Department had warned him that "several governments have suffered opposition attacks for having been too susceptible to U.S. influence, and these attacks do not come exclusively from Communists and fellow travellers."[29]

Ridgway was out of his depth in the complicated world of postwar European politics. Ridgway's tenure as NATO Supreme Commander and as Chief of Staff were the highest ranking jobs he held, yet his performance in both proved controversial because of his bluntness in urging governments with pressing domestic needs to rearm. He displayed his talents better by fighting on the battlefield in Korea than by political infighting in Paris, Tokyo, or Washington.

THE RIDGWAY RIOTS

Ridgway arrived in Paris during a series of demonstrations, many of them protesting Ridgway's alleged use of bacteriological warfare in Korea, a charge Ridgway firmly denied. There had already been riots over the issue in Tokyo, and Ridgway expected trouble. While Ridgway was in Washington addressing Congress, M. Jean Baylot, the Parisian *préfet de police* was also there conferring with J. Edgar Hoover. It is hard to believe that Baylot and Hoover did not discuss the impending communist demonstrations.[30]

The French government requested that Ridgway postpone his arrival, which he refused to do, despite small, but violent, demonstrations on May 23 and 24. Then the crackdown began. André Stil, the editor of *L'Humanité*, the Communist Party newspaper, was arrested on May 26, under an 1848 antiriot law. On May 28, the police confiscated *L'Humanité* because it continued to promote anti-Ridgway demonstrations. To many in a population only eight years removed from Nazi occupation, such measures by a pro-American government must have seemed ominous indeed, particularly in the context of U.S. pressure for German rearmament. The government's re-pressive policy may have fed anti-Ridgway sentiment. Ridgway himself tried to paper this over in his memoirs: "Whatever plans the Communists may have had for giving me a boisterous welcome," he wrote, "they must have abandoned them," noting that he saw only one "untoward incident" at Villejuif when one man broke through the police lines toward Ridgway's car but was quickly hustled off. He failed to mention the events of the following day. Many years later, he wrote that "all we saw was an occasional pointed wall sign 'Go Home Ridgway.'" When a journalist asked Penny Ridgway about the many "Ridgway Go Home" signs around the French countryside, she replied, "It makes us sad. We're only human."[31]

Despite Ridgway's feigned indifference toward the rioters, Maréchal Alphonse Juin wrote that Ridgway was deeply affected by the demonstrations, particularly as he had been the first American general to land in France during the June 1944 invasion of Normandy. Furthermore, though Ridgway might have been insulated from French opposition to NATO, his staff was not. George Pelletier, an officer under Ridgway at Supreme Allied Headquarters, reported that in the course of his tour of duty, his automobile windshield was plastered with two death's-head stickers with the slogan "Americans Go Home." Other American servicemen, particularly those living in working-class Paris suburbs, reported their tires slashed.[32]

The Ridgway rioters protested Ridgway's alleged involvement in waging bacteriological warfare against the Koreans and Chinese. Given the political situation in France, the mere arrival of Ridgway was inflammatory. The Parti Communiste Français (PCF) was already calling for more militancy and confrontation after the formation of a conservative government under M. Antoine Pinay, whom the Communists dubbed "the man from Vichy." U.S. backing for German rearmament and the creation of an independent West Germany, which the U.S. affirmed in treaties signed two days before, reinforced the already strong tendency on the French Left to equate Americans with Nazis. The Communist Party took the opportunity of Ridgway's arrival to make him the center of protest against U.S. influence in France.[33]

On May 28, demonstrators clashed with police in small groups all over Paris. The May 28 riots resulted in the death of an Algerian worker, Bélaïde Hocine, when police opened fire on marchers near the Stalingrad métro station in a working-class quarter of Paris. Over seven hundred demonstrators were arrested, including the Secretary-General of the PCF, Jaques Duclos, and police raids on Communist Party offices. Scores of demonstrators and police were wounded in the mélée.[34]

In the days before the riot, extreme anti-Communists, such as Interior Minister Charles Brune, accused Duclos and the Party of trying to launch a civil war and wanted an excuse to outlaw the Communist Party. A few days after the arrest of Duclos, the Communists launched an unsuccessful general strike calling for his release. Duclos, who was charged with attempting to overthrow the French Republic, remained in prison from May until July. As time went on, the case against him lost credibility. For example, the police had claimed that some dead pigeons found in Duclos's car were carrier pigeons, used for sending secret messages in an uprising. An autopsy proved the pigeons to be a species more suitable for cuisine than for conspiracy.[35]

The treatment of General Ridgway in the French press prior to his arrival reflected two completely incompatible views. Ridgway encouraged the friendly Center-Right view. For example, he took a well-publicized trip to the village where he first landed during World War II, on June 6, the 8th anniversary of the Normandy invasion. The Mayor of Ste. Mère Église presented him with the key to the city. Le Figaro, a Center-Right daily, repeatedly ran positive stories about the Supreme Commander, including pictures of Ridgway and his family. Figaro stressed Ridgway's role in the liberation of France in 1944 and his status as a respectable and upstanding family man. L'Aurore, a paper further to the Right, ran a full-page spread of very complimentary pictures of Ridgway on the day after his arrival.[36]

In an editorial entitled "Hate and Lies," Figaro warned that the bacteriological warfare allegations were a "Machiavellian" attempt "to portray the Americans as bellicose and cynically cruel, to single them out for hatred under the cover of a false humanitarian movement." Figaro applauded the arrest of L'Humanité editor André Stil, claiming he was making a public appeal to engage in "murder." The editors of L'Aurore exclaimed that "these Communist demonstrations against the arrival of Ridgway, ordered and paid for by a foreign power who haven't renounced invading us are intolerable, and we are waiting for the government to do its duty."[37]

The Communist press called for demonstrations throughout the month of May and, for its part, concentrated on the germ warfare charges, which Ridgway and the bourgeois press dismissed as totally false. They did not care so much about Ridgway's personality or family life as about his responsibility for what they considered war crimes. The Communists also denounced Ridgway as a symbol of American power. Their anti-Americanism was often grounded in more-specific concerns about French politics. In the Communist press, Ridgway was continually referred to as "General Microbe" or "General Plague." "Who will prevent the French people from expressing their distaste at the criminal who ordered aviators to bomb Korean cities and villages with bombs full of plague and cholera; a general in charge of troops who burned women, children and old people alive, a confidante of Truman who comes to France to spread the same criminal plans to plunge the world into blood and fire." But the Communists were quick to add that Ridgway was "the protector of [conservative French Prime Minister Antoine] Pinay and his confederates who sacrifice our country to their profit and their class interests" and was "the great commander of the new army of German revanchards."[38]

The Communist writer Courtade, writing one month earlier, described Ridgway as "the man of napalm as well as germ war . . . a conspiratorial creature of [General George C.] Marshall, who belongs to [Ambassador W. Averell] Harriman/Wall Street." One cartoon from the Communist daily *Ce Soir* appealed to French nationalism to encourage opposition to Ridgway; the cartoon showed Ridgway standing on the Eiffel Tower, looking north at Montmartre. In an allusion to the division of Korea and Germany (and perhaps the division of France during the Occupation), the caption reads: "49th Parallel . . . North France, South France, Done!" Another cartoon showed Ridgway with his feet up on the desk of a French official, resembling Defense Minister René Pleven; in this cartoon, Ridgway is made to quip, "Don't Worry! We will not tolerate foreign agents."[39]

The charge that the United States used biological warfare against China originated in a February 1952 news conference conducted by Chinese Premier Zhou Enlai. Allegedly, U.S. planes dropped bombs full of contaminated insects and rodents, aiming to cause an epidemic. In the months between the original charge and Ridgway's arrival in Paris, the Communist press printed more and more details about the Chinese allegations and urged their validity. The non-Communist left French press debated the merits of the Chinese charges, while the U.S. government vehemently denied them.[40]

The Communist Party sometimes felt it more persuasive to attack the U.S. biological warfare program without debating the question of its use against China. A French Communist Party broadside of May 1952 skirted the complicated question of whether the U.S. actually used such weapons in China. Instead the leaflet condemned American production of biological weapons and the failure of the United States to ratify the Geneva convention banning their use.[41]

Historians have not been able completely to substantiate U.S. denials of germ warfare charges. Even before the international campaign against biological warfare, the Chinese maintained that the United States had pardoned Japanese scientists who conducted cruel biological warfare experiments on prisoners during World War II. In return, the Americans received the cooperation of Japanese scientists in setting up a program for laboratory experimentation in biological warfare. According to Mark Ryan, the most careful student of the question of the use of biological weapons in the Korean War, Chinese allegations about cooperation between the Japanese scientists and the Americans appear to have been essentially correct. It is far less likely that the United States ever actually deployed biological weapons agents against China or Korea; however, the historical record remains unclear. Ryan judiciously concluded that "considered as a whole . . . these documents tend to refute charges that the United States employed BW [biological warfare] in Korea or China. On the other hand, the documents declassified so far do not conclusively exclude such a possibility, and some documents on their face at least raise suspicions in this regard," suspicions that cannot be entirely allayed until the federal government opens the entire documentary record. John Toland, who interviewed Chinese miltary historians and officers for a recent book, suggests that the Chinese sincerely believed that the United States waged biological warfare. Ryan reached the same conclusion. Though it seems probable that the United States did not wage biological warfare, the Communist charges were probably not an intentional fabrication, as Ridgway maintained at the time, but more likely the kind of wild, but sincerely believed, rumor that circulates even among government officials in war, similar to the rumors of Japanese saboteurs that led to the round-up of thousands of American citizens in the first days of World War II.[42]

AUGMENTING NATO FORCE LEVELS

Expanding NATO forces interested Ridgway much more than the riots or germ warfare. Under his command, NATO forces never reached anything approaching the levels set for 1952 at Lisbon. Nonetheless, by the time he left, Ridgway had helped construct a force that he claimed would deter, though not defeat, a Soviet advance.[43]

Ridgway worked fourteen hours a day, seven days a week, learning the ins and outs of his new job. His senior staff worked equally hard. In his first months on the job, the new Supreme Commander conferred with Allied diplomats and soldiers and visited military installations in Italy, Germany, and Scandanavia. One of the more important meetings was with Vincent Auriol, the moderate Socialist President of France. This was on the first day of the threatened, but failed, general strike. A pro-American crowd in front of the Elysée Palace acclaimed the general as he entered to visit. According to Auriol, the two immediately struck up a friendship. Auriol emphasized France's commitment to collective security and called for greater propaganda efforts by the West. As for the protests of the Communist Party, the president explained to him that "there wasn't any real communism in France, but only malcontents. This is due, above all to the egoism of the industrialists and also the clumsiness of the Allies who leave Russia with a monopoly on peace propaganda." Auriol mentioned specifically that he would appeal again on Sunday to industrialists to improve the lot of workers, which he hoped "would take the edge off a great deal of Communist propaganda." Ridgway encouraged Auriol to work things out with the industrialists, yet another instance where he sought a negotiated harmony between classes to obtain a consensus for expanded military efforts. Auriol also advised Ridgway not to hold a separate press conference to deny the germ warfare charges, suggesting that a specific denial would be a recognition of the Communist charges. Instead, Ridgway should wait "for a suitable occasion" for such a speech.[44]

By July 1952, after a month of intensive work, Ridgway began to arrive at an analysis of the military situation in Europe. Publicly he stressed confidence—that "a good start has been made and the framework is strong," while insisting on "perseverance" to meet NATO's objective to "resist aggressive force." Privately, he was pessimistic, writing General Omar Bradley, "If war should come without major improvement in the power ratio, no amount of recrimination could absolve the governments concerned for disaster to these gallant covering forces should this be the result of such failure. We deal here with no theory, but with cold-blooded realities, capable of implementation by cold-blooded implacable enemies presently possessed of greatly, perhaps overwhelmingly superior combat strength." The cold-blooded reality, though, was that some military planners and many statesmen thought the risk of war was low—not worth upsetting the fragile recovery of their civilian economies.[45]

Though Ridgway publicly expressed confidence in NATO unity, these professions did not reflect Ridgway's true opinion of the strength of the alliance. "Language difficulties in all echelons of Command and Staff, serious inadequacies in numbers of staff officers with even basic staff training, national distrusts, and political pressures of many kinds—in fact all the weaknesses inherent in any coalition—are present and will operate to lower the combat effectiveness of our field forces, if forced to fight within the next eighteen months ON THE SOIL OF SOME OF THEIR OWN MEMBERS [caps original] against a homogeneous uni-national force flushed with initial successes which are likely to be theirs." In the succeeding months, he continued to be much preoccupied with the problems of coalition warfare.[46]

Ridgway himself may have caused some of those problems. Whereas Eisenhower had allowed British officers fairly free access to American documents, Ridgway clamped down. There was a perception that he had a "shadow cabinet" of American officers who froze out staff officers from other countries. Some of the American officers surrounding Ridgway were quite sensitive to this problem, especially as Brigadier General John R. Beishline, who ran Ridgway's personal staff, often insisted that the American Special Assistants to the Supreme Commander's Chief of Staff handle problems that should normally have gone to the international staff.[47]

Ridgway's difficulties with diplomacy persuaded him to alter his concept of civilian-military relations. "The problems here are myriad and more complex than any I have ever encountered," he wrote to General Mark Clark, the commander who replaced him in the Far East. "Not only do they have their roots in the governmental institutions of member nations," he continued, "but those roots draw upward into the problems themselves all the age-old international distrusts, suspicions and aspirations, including, of course, all the inter-service jealousies and personality factors."[48]

Besides the usual difficulties with coalitions, Ridgway thought the fundamental problems of his command included the political instability of certain members, the limited "economic capabilities, themselves inaccurately determined, of certain members," "unsound command organization" owing to inadequate logistics, and a bureaucracy (the NATO Council) incapable of quick decisions in peacetime. In line with his belief that social differences within capitalist society had to be harmonized in order to fight the Cold War, he wrote that "underlying all the foregoing faults is human selfishness, individual, group, service and national. Until and unless this fault is attacked, there will be no substantial correction of these deficiencies." Despite the "fundamental" nature of these problems, his solution was a "public information campaign," a bit reminiscent of Woodrow Wilson's ill-fated attempts at public diplomacy, in that Ridgway was just as certain as Wilson had been in 1919 that what he wanted was required by the public interest, determined by an allegedly neutral technical elite, but was being obstructed by their political leaders. The campaign suceeded mostly in irritating the leaders of NATO countries whose goodwill was essential to the success of his mission.[49]

By the end of August 1952, the *New York Times* reported that Ridgway "no longer believe[d] that he can discharge the 'military' side" without reference to political and economic issues. In order to learn his new job, Ridgway apparently tried to conserve time by directing political problems to other organs of NATO, including budgetary issues, which some politicians thought could only be resolved by applying the prestige of the Supreme Commander. As the scope of military activity expanded to affect more and more of society, Ridgway had to bend his ideas about the limitations of the military sphere in order to do his very political job, even as he continued to pay lip service to the idea that policy could be separated from military technique.[50]

Ridgway's increasing concern for such political issues showed in a press conference in which he openly declared that the Soviet threat had not "abated" but that NATO strength was "seriously inadequate in certain vital categories." The Supreme Commander attacked NATO governments for failing to meet the Lisbon goals, despite the fact that that they had the "capability" to do so, and for failing to institute a twenty-four-month period for conscription. The conscription issue, a particularly hot political potato, was set for discussion at a meeting of the European Defense Community the next day. Where Eisenhower was famous for his warm smile and friendly, reassuring manner, Ridgway was obviously distant. The *New York Times* branded his replies to questions as "evasive" and described him as "attentive, formally polite and icy cold." Even outside press conferences, the *Times* reported that Allied officers found Ridgway to be "curt on matters of importance, especially when his interest was not aroused." "He has," wrote the reporter, "subordinated the human side."[51]

Criticism in the press did not induce Ridgway to modify his approach, which caused further embarrassments for the program of rearmament. At a Pilgrim Club dinner, Prime Minister Winston S. Churchill toasted General

Ridgway by pledging Britain to do as much as possible to rearm "short of going bankrupt." As Britain was nearly bankrupt at the time, Churchill promised very little.

Even the old prime minister thought the civilian economy would have to take priority. Worse, from Ridgway's perspective, Churchill dismissed Ridgway's warnings about Soviet military superiority. Churchill stated publicly that war was unlikely. As the main voice opposing British complacency in the face of the German threat in the 1930s, no one could accuse him of "appeasement." His comparative dovishness was a considerable setback to Ridgway's effort to gain public support for a more drastic rearmament program. The public rift with Churchill demonstrates how little Ridgway understood about the political and economic pressures that limited the enthusiasm of European statesmen for rearmament.[52]

RIDGWAY'S POLITICAL HEADACHES

By continuing to concentrate on NATO's technical problems, Ridgway remained out of touch with political reality. He did not seem to appreciate that the lame duck status of the Truman Administration that appointed him had reduced his own influence. Though friendly with Truman, Ridgway probably voted for Eisenhower. Gruenther assured Eisenhower that "SHAPE is all excited over the forthcoming elections. It is very difficult to get the necessary concentration with this distraction so prominent. Parties planned. I can assure you that you will carry this precinct by a score of 383 to O."[53]

It is not clear that Ridgway understood the extent to which Eisenhower's election would undermine his own position at NATO, though he might have anticipated and welcomed the possibility of an appointment as Army chief of staff. It is clear that with Eisenhower's election, Ridgway lost some power to Gruenther who had his own direct line of communication to the new president. When René Pleven wanted the president-elect to stop in Indochina in the course of his trip to Korea, he asked Gruenther, not Ridgway.[54]

In addition, the clear implication of Eisenhower's trip to Korea was that he was determined to end the Korean War. Partly as a result of this declining tension, the North Atlantic Council, at its December 17, 1952, meeting, cut by 45 percent NATO's military construction program. The decision came as a bitter disappointment to Ridgway, though some of the money was restored the following spring.[55]

As Eisenhower's inauguration neared, Ridgway's tone became more conciliatory toward the Europeans. Though he predicted that the reluctance to spend more money on NATO might result in large numbers of casualties in the event of war with the U.S.S.R., he "displayed a high degree of confidence," declaring himself "enormously encouraged by the progress made since the beginning" in creating a cohesive defense force."[56]

Ridgway's defeat in the North Atlantic Treaty Organization Council and the increasing prominence of Gruenther, whose special relationship to the president was well known, raised questions in the press as early as January about Ridgway's continuation as Supreme Allied Commander in Europe. Bradley further told Ridgway that when columnist Constantine Brown wrote that Ridgway was "dissatisfied and wanted to quit," the rumors were not emanating from President Eisenhower. Bradley reassured Ridgway that "certainly those of us who know you put no stock in such stories." But Brown had recently visited Paris, carrying a letter of introduction to Ridgway. If they had an interview, it is conceivable that Ridgway himself, or his staff, in an attempt to get more support from Washington for Ridgway's budgetary demands, may have been a source of such rumors.[57]

Ultimately the impetus for replacing Ridgway as Supreme Commander came from Eisenhower who discussed the "anti-Ridgway campaign" with Bradley on March 23. Secretary of Defense Charles E. Wilson had not decided to replace Ridgway as late as March 1953, when he wrote the president, "I have assumed that it is not desirable at this time to move either Ridgway or Clark." Nonetheless, the rumors were so persistent that on February 1, 1953, Ridgway issued a press statement that unequivocally denied published rumors that he was 'fed up' with his present assignment, or that for any reason he was contemplating asking for relief from his duties." Secretary of State John Foster Dulles had publicly to renew his confidence in the SACEUR.[58]

Still, the rumors continued. In a one-to-one meeting with the Supreme Commander, French Defense Minister René Pleven orally translated an article from Le Monde about the status of Ridgway's command. The Le Monde reporter obviously had sources within Supreme Headquarters and suggested that the "greater part of the news items concerning General Ridgway's possible departure had their origin" in Britain, reflecting British disagreement with the American's strategic ideas. Ridgway wanted to build NATO forces to the level that they could halt a Red Army drive at the Rhine and then begin offensive operations. The British, according to Le Monde, wanted smaller forces of higher quality and doubted that NATO could, or should, plan to hold the Rhine line. The report in Le Monde was consistent with Field Marshall Bernard Montgomery's position, as Ridgway later reported it to Bradley just before his departure in June, 1953, and Montgomery could conceivably have been the source. The year before, a senior American NATO officer had asked the Joint Chiefs to order the Supreme Commander to muzzle Montgomery, who "could hardly have gone farther off the deep end." Ridgway, however, did not know Montgomery advocated an alternative strategy at the time of his conversation with Pleven. Indeed, Ridgway's apparent astonishment at Montgomery's criticism of NATO strategy in June, despite the public report in February, shows that Ridgway was startlingly insulated from the British. The Le Monde article also correctly speculated that Ridgway would be moved to the position of Army Chief of Staff when the term of the incumbent, General J. Lawton Collins, expired in July 1953.[59]

If the rumors were true, it is ironic that the primary opposition to Ridgway should have been British. Despite his conflicts with them during the war, his memoirs are replete with Anglophilia. The high points of his tour of duty were his several meetings with Queen Elizabeth II, as well as his attending her coronation in May 1953 in Westminster Abbey, and his meetings with Prime Minister Winston Churchill.[60]

Ridgway spent much of his final period as Supreme Commander in evaluating NATO's military program. He tried to raise as much alarm as possible, but the death of Stalin in March 1953 had substantially reduced East–West tensions. Neither President Eisenhower nor European statesmen were seeking to increase defense spending at such a time. Nevertheless, Ridgway continued with his blunt assertions of the priority of military spending. Military men, he wrote, "are also ever conscious of the impelling human need for raising the standard of living," but he conceded that "many NATO governments, with the best of will, may find the concurrent maintaining of living standards and support of defense budgets on the present scale, beyond their politico-economic capabilities." In the end, he argued that security needs must have priority. "They must contemplate in reaching their decisions, what would happen to their nations' living standards under Soviet defeat and occupation or rule by governments in the Soviet pattern."[61]

Despite such appeals, Ridgway never came close to meeting the Lisbon goals for 1952. He told Congress that NATO forces remained far short of what they should be—about 20 percent, or ten divisions short of the Lisbon goal for 1952. Other problems included building stocks of ammunition and other supplies, developing aircraft control and warning systems, maintenance and training for a modern airforce, logistics and infrastructure.[62]

One additional major difficulty was German rearmament. In his report to the House, Ridgway noted that no defense could be forward-based without German participation. The only way to do this seemed to be the Pleven Plan for an integrated European Defense Community, which would include German soldiers, but under international control. Ridgway's concern for German rearmament shows how far he was prepared to go for the security goals that he considered a priority. He apparently advocated early freedom for war criminals, in order to court support of the German right for rearmament under American or European auspices. His stance was contrary to U.S. policy at the time. Despite the resistance to rearmament, Ridgway noted with satisfaction that "the meager forces that existed in 1950 have been more than doubled in number." The "limited, but indispensable progress in the development of logistical and support capability," also continued, despite "acute" deficencies. Nontheless, he believed that the growth of forces, particularly in the face of a perceived growth of Soviet strength, was "unsatisfactory." To the NATO Standing Group, he was more strident than with Congress. While acknowledging that "all but the military aspects" of security were beyond his purview, Ridgway insisted that a rapid force buildup was necessary because "a full scale Soviet attack within the near future would find Allied Command Europe critically weak to accomplish its present mission."[63]

Ridgway claimed that there was an objective, technical need for rearmament and that if the public only understood it, their choice would be clear. Unlike more politically sophisticated officers, such as Marshall and Eisenhower, in making such assessments, Ridgway completely discounted politics as irrelevant to military goals. He wrote: "If they saw the peril, their reaction would be positive, immediate and adequate. I believe the time is overdue for giving them these facts."[64]

Ridgway's progress in convincing NATO countries to establish forces on a level with the agreed-on Lisbon goals was limited at best. Nonetheless, under his tenure, his hard work significantly improved NATO's logistical support, infrastructure, and airpower capabilities. Troop strength also rose, though not to the Lisbon levels. Ridgway also helped sort out some sticky command problems, such as the split between the British and the Americans in the Mediterranean and the appointment of the French Marshall Juin as commander-in-chief for the central front. Far from satisfied, the president believed Ridgway had been impolitic. The Communists's anti-Ridgway campaign was also a factor. Eisenhower was determined to make Gruenther Supreme Allied Commander in Europe and offered Ridgway the job of Army Chief of Staff. With the expiration of General J. Lawton Collins's term as Army Chief of Staff, "the opportunity arose to kill three birds with one stone," General Bradley later wrote. "With his prestige, background and energy, Ridgway would be an inspiring Chief of Staff. If he got overzealous, as he tended to, Eisenhower would be right there to restrain him," Bradley continued. Thus, Ridgway was kicked upstairs to the highest uniformed position in the Army.[65]

NOTES

1. Memo of conversation between Ridgway and Pace, April 14, 1951, Ridgway MSS, Box 20.

2. *U.S. News and World Report*, April 20, 1951; "Maintaining Powers of Supreme Commander Allied Powers Pending Ratification," Ridgway memo, April 22, 1951, Ridgway MSS, Box 20; *Newsweek*, May 5, 1952.

3. "Living god" Yamazuke Kazuyoshi quoted in James, *Years of MacArthur*, 3:4, also called "the Yankee Shogun," *U.S. News and World Report*, April 20, 1951; James Michener, "A Tough Man for a Tough Job," *Life*, September 12, 1952; Murray Schumach, "The Education of Matthew Ridgway," *New York Times*, May 4, 1952; Ridgway, *Soldier*, 225.

4. JB, 2:4:5; Collins to Ridgway, May 9, 1951, and May 10, 1951, quoted May 11, 1951, Ridgway MSS, Box 20. See also memo of conversation between Ridgway, Dulles, and Sebald, April 22, 1951, Ridgway MSS, Box 20.

5. *New York Times*, January 27, 1951; Marquat to Ridgway, November 19, 1951, Ridgway MSS, Box 20; Howard B. Schonberger, *Aftermath of War: America and the Remaking of Japan, 1945–1952* (Kent, Ohio: Kent State University Press, 1989), 268.

6. Ridgway meeting with representatives of Remington Rand, Ford, and International General Electric, January 23, 1952, Ridgway Papers, Box 20; meeting with executives from Caltex, Standard Vacuum, Tidewater Associates, and the Union Oil Co., January 30, 1952, Ridgway MSS, Box 20.

7. Richard M. Dalfiume, *Desegregation of the Armed Forces* (Columbia: University of Missouri, 1969), 189.

8. Ibid.; Jack Foner, *Blacks and the Military in American History* (New York: Praeger, 1974), 183.

9. Morris J. MacGregor, *Integration of the Armed Forces, 1940–1965* (Washington, D.C.: U.S. Army Center of Military History, 1981), 428, 617.

10. Almond to Center of Military History, April 1, 1972, Center of Military History files, also quoted in MacGregor, *Integration of Armed Forces*, 440, 441.

11. Dalfiume, *Desegregation of Armed Forces*, 201, 202.

12. Macgregor, *Integration of Armed Forces*, 434; Dalfiume, *Desegregation of Armed Forces*, 206, 207.

13. Matthew B. Ridgway, "The Role of the Army in the Next War," Address to the Armed Forces Staff College, February 15, 1950, Ridgway MSS, Box 15.

14. TKW, 101; Ridgway to CG, IX Corps, March 8, 1951, Ridgway MSS, Box 17; conference, Ridgway and Allen, March 14, 1951, Ridgway MSS, Box 20.

15. MacGregor, *Integration of Armed Forces*, 444; Dalfiume, *Desegregation of Armed Forces*, 210, 220; Foner, 191, 192; Ridgway, TKW, 193.

16. *Defender*, January 5, 1952; Louis E. Martin to Ridgway, March 24, 1952; Ridgway to Martin, April 19, 1952, Ridgway MSS, Box 18.

17. William R. Hudgens, President, Carver Federal Savings and Loan, to Ridgway, July 22, 1952; Handy to Ridgway, n.d., suggesting that "minimum publicity" be given to integration efforts; Memo for General Beishline, August 6, 1952, for comments on the Hudgens letter made by Secretary Pace in the presence of himself and General Taylor; unused draft of letter from Ridgway to Hudgens, July 31, 1952; Ridgway to Hudgens, August 7, 1952, Ridgway MSS, Box 23.

18. George Eugene Pelletier, "The Ridgway Regime at SHAPE [Supreme Allied Headquarters]," master's thesis, Georgetown University, 1955, p. 18. Mr. Pelletier was an officer assigned to the public information section of the Supreme Allied Headquarters when General Ridgway was Supreme Commander. His thesis is well documented and includes many useful personal observations.

19. Beishline to Ridgway, n.d. (early December 1951); Beishline to Ridgway, March 29, 1952, Ridgway MSS, Box 18; *New York Times*, April 28, 1952, see also author's interview with General Andrew J. Goodpaster, June 24, 1994. Copy available at the Columbia University Oral History Research Office. General Goodpaster was Special Assistant to the Chief of Staff, Supreme Allied Headquarters, during Ridgway's tenure as Supreme Allied Commander in Europe. His long and distinguished career later included service as military aide to Presidents Eisenhower and Kennedy, and as Supreme Commander, NATO.

20. George Eugene Pelletier, "Ridgway: Trying to Make Good on the Promises," in R. Jordan, ed., *Generals in International Politics: NATO's Supreme Allied Commander, Europe* (Lexington: University Press of Kentucky, 1987), 38; *New York Times*, April 10, 1952.

21. *Newsweek* May 5, 1952; *Le Monde*, May 23, 1952; Gruenther to Ridgway, May 2, 1952, Eisenhower Library, Alfred M. Gruenther MSS, Box 15; Goodpaster interview.

22. *Newsweek* May 5, 1952; *Le Monde* May 23, 1952; Gruenther to Ridgway, May 2, 1952, Eisenhower Library, Alfred M. Gruenther MSS, Box 15.

23. Pelletier, "Ridgway," 69; Pierre Mélandri, *L'alliance Atlantique* (Paris: Gallimard/Juillard, 1979), 92.

24. Robert S. Jordan, *Political Leadership in NATO: A Study in International Diplomacy* (Boulder: Westview Press, 1979), 6–14.

25. Ibid., 6–14, 271; see also Lord Ismay, *NATO: The First Five Years, 1949–1954* (Brussels, n.d.); Ridgway, *Soldier*, 240.

26. Stephen E. Ambrose and Morris Honick, "Eisenhower: Rekindling the Spirit of the West," in Jordan, ed., *Generals in International Politics: NATO's Supreme Allied Commander, Europe* (Lexington: University Press of Kentucky), 28; Assistant Secretary of Defense for International Security Affairs (Nash) to the Deputy Secretary of Defense (Foster), February 23, 1952, *Foreign Relations* 5 (1952–54): 46; Resolution by North Atlantic Council, February 23, 1952, *Foreign Relations* 5 (1952–54): 220–224; DDE Papers, 13:1027 n.1; COS (52) meetings, 90–119, June 24, 1952, and July 22, 1952 (Appendix), DEFE 4/55, PRO.

27. Ridgway, *Soldier*, 240; Bonbright to Acheson, May 21, 1952, *Foreign Relations* 5 (1952–54): 298 n.1.

28. See Goodpaster interview.

29. Memo by the Deputy Assistant Secretary of State for European Affairs (Bonbright) to Secretary of State (Acheson), May 21, 1952, *Foreign Relations* 5 (1952–54): 298. On the briefing of Ridgway "along the lines" of this document, see n. 2.

30. On the effect of the Ridgway Riot on French politics, see Michel Pignet, *Au coeur de l'activism communist des années de Guerre Froide: La manifestation Ridgway* (Paris: L'Harmattan, 1992) and Pierre Milza "La guerre froide à Paris—'Ridgway La Peste' " *L'Histoire* 25 (Juillet–Août 1980): 39–50; Ridgway, address to Congress, reprinted *New York Times*, May 23, 1952; Baylot returned from Washington May 19, 1952 (*L'Aurore* May 19, 1952); *Le Monde*, May 3, 1952 reported that on May 1 there was a bloody demonstration in Tokyo with 7 people killed, 1,400 wounded, and 153 arrests. The demonstators set fire to many autos belonging to Americans and broke the windows of Ridgway's headquarters before the Japanese police and American MPs gained control over the crowd.

31. Ridgway, *Soldier*, 235; *Liberation*, May 28, 1952; Milza, "La guerre froide à Paris—Ridgway la Peste," *L'Histoire* 25 (Juillet–Août): 38–47; "A Salute to Mary Princess Anthony Ridgway," July 1979, Ridgway MSS, Box 34E; Helen Worden Erskine, "Pretty Penny Ridgway," *Collier's*, May 16, 1953.

32. Ridgway, *Soldier*, 235; Maréchal Juin, *Memoires* (Paris: Fayard, 1960), 2:236; Pelletier, "Ridgway," 84; Goodpaster interview.

33. Milza, 39–40.

34. Ibid., 44–46.

35. Ibid.

36. Pictures of Ridgway and family ran in *Le Figaro*, May 3 and 4 and May 14, 1952; *L'Aurore*, May 28, 1952.

37. *Le Figaro*, May 9, 1952; regarding Stil, see *Le Figaro*, May 26, 1952; *L'Aurore*, May 23, 1952.

38. *L'Humanité*, May 28, 1952, p. 1. This issue was suppressed at the time by the police.

39. *L'Humanité*, April 29, 1952; "49th Parallel," *Ce Soir*, May 25 and 26, 1952; "Don't Worry!" *Ce Soir*, June 3, 1952.

40. See *Le Figaro*, April 18 and May 20, 1952; *Le Monde*, 2-part series on biological warfare in China, May 16 and 17, 1952; Milza, "La guerre froide," 46.

41. See Parti Communiste Française leaflet in dossier entitled "Ridgway, guerre bacteriologique" in Archives National, Paris F^7 15.374.

42. Mark A. Ryan, *Chinese Attitudes Towards Nuclear Weapons: China and the United States During the Korean War* (Armonk, N.Y.: M. E. Sharpe, 1989), 89, 95, 104; Toland, *In Mortal Combat*, 595.

43. Ridgway, *Soldier*, 241.

44. *New York Times*, July 26, 1952; Vincent Auriol, *Journal du Septennat*, ed. Dominique Boch, (Paris: Armand Colin, 1978), entry for June 3, 1952, 7:1042; Memo by Lt. Col. Vernon Walters of meeting between Ridgway and Auriol, June 3, 1952, Ridgway MSS, Box 24. Auriol also advised Ridgway not to hold a separate press conference to deny the germ warfare charges, suggesting that a specific denial would be a recognition of the Communist charges. Instead, Ridgway should wait "for a suitable occasion" for such a speech.

45. Memo by Ridgway, "Some major points to cover in my talks with the press in all NATO countries," July 8, 1952. Ridgway MSS, Box 24; Ridgway to Bradley, July 19, 1952, Ridgway MSS, Box 24.

46. Ridgway to Bradley, July 19, 1952, Ridgway MSS, Box 24. To the post–Cold War reader, the characterization of the Red Army and Warsaw Pact forces as a "homogenous uni-national force" seems ill-informed.

47. Goodpaster interview.

48. Ridgway to General Mark Clark, July 30, 1952, Ridgway MSS, Box 23.

49. Ridgway, "Notes on Fundamental Problems," August 6, 1952, Ridgway MSS, Box 24. See also Goodpaster interview.

50. *New York Times*, August 12, 1952. I have relied heavily here on articles in the *Times* by Benjamin Welles. According to former Supreme Allied Headquarters officer Pelletier, Welles's inside contacts in Supreme Allied Headquarters were excellent and his stories were dead on. Welles was the son of Sumner Welles, an old friend of General Ridgway; he may well have had access to the general himself. See Pelletier, "Ridgway," 13.

51. *New York Times*, August 12, 1952.

52. Ibid., August 25, 1952, October 15, 1952.

53. Gruenther to Eisenhower, November 1, 1952, Alfred M. Gruenther MSS, Eisenhower Correspondence Series, Box 1, Eisenhower Library.

54. Memo of conversation between Pleven and Gruenther, November 15, 1952, Eisenhower Presidential MSS, Ann Whitman File, Administration Series, Box 16, Gruenther Files, Eisenhower Library.

55. *New York Times*, December 18, 1952; Matthew B. Ridgway, "How Europe's Defenses Look to Me," *Saturday Evening Post*, October 10, 1953, p. 142.

56. *New York Times*, January 6, 1953.

57. Bradley to Ridgway, January 2, 1953. Brown, armed with a personal introduction from Senator Harry Cain, an old friend of the Supreme Commander went to Paris to see Ridgway. (Cain to Ridgway, September 29, 1952, Ridgway MSS Box 23).

58. See memorandum to the president, March 24, 1953, Eisenhower Presidential MSS, Ann Whitman File, Administration Series, Box 30, Eisenhower Library, enclosing an advance copy of an article from *U.S. News and World Report*, March 27, 1953, entitled "Ridgway: Target of Communists. They would like to force him out of Europe," which attributed criticism of Ridgway to the Communist Party; Wilson to Eisenhower, March 19, 1953, Eisenhower Presidential MSS, Ann Whitman File, Administration Series, Box 16, Gruenther Files, Eisenhower Library; Supreme Allied Headquarters press release, February 1, 1953, Ridgway MSS, Box 25.

59. Ridgway, "Memo for record of a 50 minute talk alone with Pleven at his office this date at my [Ridgway's] request," February 20, 1953, Ridgway MSS, Box 24. On muzzling Montgomery, see Vice Admiral Davis to Bradley, June 5, 1952, Chairman's File (1952), 092.2 North Atlantic Treaty, RG 218, National Archives; Ridgway to Bradley, June 18, 1953, Ridgway MSS, Box 24. Ridgway vigorously protested Montgomery's position in the June meeting, fearing that the British strategy would lead to plans for the temporary abandonment of most of the European continent, a strategy that Ridgway believed would break up the Alliance.

60. Ridgway, *Soldier*, 249–257.

61. Matthew B. Ridgway, "How Europe's Defenses Look to Me," *Saturday Evening Post*, October 10, 1953, p. 143.

62. Statement for National Security Subcommittee of House Committee on Foreign Affairs, 4th Draft, April 4, 1953, Ridgway MSS, Box 24.

63. Frank M. Buscher, *The U.S. War Crimes Trials in Germany, 1946–1955* (New York: Greenwood Press, 1989), 79; Second Annual Report, Supreme Allied Commander, Europe, May 30, 1953, Ridgway MSS, Box 24.

64. Ibid.; see also letter from Ridgway to NATO Standing Group in appendix to this document. On the contrast with Marshall and Eisenhower, see Goodpaster interview.

65. General Omar N. Bradley and Clay Blair, *A General's Life* (New York: Simon and Schuster, 1983), 659.

CHAPTER 13

Chief of Staff: Ridgway and the New Look, 1953–1956

The vexations and frustrations I encountered in Europe, though they were many and great, were in no way comparable to the vexations, the frustrations, the sheer travail of spirit which were my final lot in my two year tour as Chief of Staff.[1]

—Matthew B. Ridgway

General Ridgway was ready to return home when President Dwight D. Eisenhower offered him a choice between remaining at NATO or assuming the most prestigious post in the U.S. Army—Chief of Staff. Ridgway had spent only three of the preceding ten years in the United States. A return to America would give him the opportunity to make social contacts and find a lucrative postretirement job.

Since World War II, Ridgway had been groomed to be Army Chief of Staff, partly through the efforts of General Omar N. Bradley, with a blend of political, military, operational, and staff assignments perhaps unequaled by any other Army officer. Korea had made Ridgway a hero. Perhaps his name was not as famous as Eisenhower's or MacArthur's, but in 1953 Ridgway was a household word. Having been born into the Army and having made it his life, he could not turn down the Army's highest honor.[2]

As Chief of Staff, Ridgway, who was famous in Korea for the importance he attached to morale, presided over the largest army that Americans had maintained in peacetime to that date. Yet this army's morale was in tatters, owing to circumstances beyond Ridgway's control. The best he could do was to try to build for the future by starting new high-tech programs and slowly building congressional support for them. However, Army morale was to get worse before it got better. Among the reasons for poor morale were budget cuts, Senator Joseph McCarthy's attacks upon the Army, and a growing perception among Army officers that the public no longer respected them. Historian A. J. Bacevich has noted that the most popular images of the Army at the time included the goldbricking Beetle Bailey, and Sgt. Bilko, a TV sitcom about a corrupt, but very funny, noncommissioned officer.[3]

Sworn in as Chief of Staff in August 1953, Ridgway would lead an army in crisis and transition. Just before he took office, on July 26, 1953, an armistice ended the open warfare in Korea. Like Pershing and Eisenhower before him, Ridgway faced the traditional problems of a peacetime Army chief competing for a share of the federal budget, compounded by the unpopularity of the stalemate warfare of the last two years of the Korean War. Since World War II, the competition between the services for funds had reached unprecedented levels.

Bureaucratic budgetary rivalry was only part of Ridgway's problem. He also faced the demands of an unprecedented revolution in military technology, the conclusion by the Department of State of a worldwide network of military alliances, and periodic pressure to intervene abroad. As General Maxwell D. Taylor put it, the Army was about to enter a period of "Babylonian Captivity," in which its programs were opposed by the administration. Ridgway noted that the "arbitrary" reduction of the Army during his term made it an unhappy assignment, though he commanded the then-largest peacetime American army in history. Eisenhower met with Ridgway and the other chiefs individually when each arrived in Washington and explained his ideas on strategy, so Ridgway probably knew from the very beginning that the Army budget was under fire. He also had plenty of opportunity to discuss matters with the other chiefs when they spent a month, often together, touring military installations.[4]

From his initial speech at his swearing-in ceremony, Ridgway made it clear that he intended to be an independent-minded chief of staff. Ridgway understood the contradictions inherent in his relationship with civilian officials. Professional officers, he asserted, should give "fearless and forthright expressions of honest, objective professional opinion up to the moment when they, themselves, the civilian commanders, announced those decisions. Thereafter they could expect completely loyal and diligent execution of those decisions. However . . . civilian authorities must give their military services the same unqualified loyalty they received."[5]

Ridgway's belief in "honest objective professional opinion" did not fit

Eisenhower's ideas of how the Joint Chiefs of Staff should operate. The president expected the chiefs to examine the "bigger picture" and reach a unified position on his New Look defense policy. The New Look, wrote Eisenhower, required a "new outlook" on the part of the chiefs; he wanted them to abandon service rivalries. But service rivalries and ideological differences remained. Ridgway confided his discomfort with consensus to Bradley, who was sympathetic, but said nothing to the president.[6]

Another source of annoyance to Ridgway was his relationship with Secretary of Defense Charles E. Wilson. Ridgway's anger toward him remained undiminished even twenty years later, when Ridgway commented that Wilson "was intolerant and prejudiced and wouldn't listen and knew nothing about a military establishment."[7]

The harshness of Ridgway's animosity toward the secretary of state had class roots. Wilson was a self-made man who had worked himself to the top of General Motors from the bottom. His brusqueness was legendary. He is most famous for his confirmation hearing statement, "What was good for our country was good for General Motors and vice versa." While instructing his deputies to communicate with generals, he used phrases like "tell the men," as if they were workers on an assembly line. Ridgway, who had run entire countries and theaters of war with a restrained gentility, was repulsed by what he perceived as Wilson's backslapping babbitry. Ridgway claimed that Wilson never listened to a word he said and that he demanded Ridgway's instant presence at what Ridgway called "long and frequently fruitless sessions," which upset his working schedule. General Barksdale Hamlett, a member of the General Staff, who worked closely with Ridgway at the time, gave his appraisal of their relationship: "Wilson was out to get Ridgway; there is no doubt about it."[8]

THE NEW LOOK

Upon taking office, Eisenhower began a complete review of defense policy, hoping to reduce spending in the wake of the Korean War. In the end, he compromised between fiscal conservatives, who wanted a minimal peacetime defense budget, and military professionals, who wanted to maintain larger armed forces. Eisenhower hoped that his defense policy, which Defense Department public relations flacks dubbed the "New Look," would balance "minimum requirements in the costly instruments of war and the health of our economy." Fiscally, the New Look tried to limit defense spending to an amount sustainable by the economy "over the long pull," a phrase co-opted from NSC-68, the Truman security blueprint. Maintaining low taxes and balancing the federal budget remained a top priority. Strategically, the program relied largely on atomic weapons and airpower for deterrence and "massive retaliation." Such retaliation might not be a direct response to Soviet actions. The United States would respond "at a time and place of our own choosing" and in a way that would emphasize its peculiar military, economic, and geopolitical strengths. Though "massive retaliation" has often been thought to mean a nuclear strike, Eisenhower also emphasized other options as well, such as military action by American-backed allies.[9]

To implement his new strategy, Eisenhower's budget expanded Air Force capability, from 114 to 137 wings, but slowed their construction in order to save money. The program reduced Army manpower from approximately 1.5 million in fiscal year 1954 to approximately one million by fiscal year 1956, eliminating two combat divisions and 77,000 civilian jobs. Each division lost 1,300 men. Most of the positions eliminated were support, clerical, and food service jobs.[10]

The basic strategic concept of the New Look was already long in place by the time Ridgway became Army Chief of Staff. President-elect Eisenhower and his principal advisors, including Admiral Arthur Radford, agreed upon the basic outlines of the New Look as early as December 1952, as they returned from Korea aboard the cruiser *Helena*. As early as May 1953, Eisenhower ordered Project Solarium, a secret reevaluation of security policy alternatives that fleshed out more details of the New Look approach. National security policy debate on the permissible level of defense spending had already occurred, and the Bureau of the Budget ordered defense reductions pursuant to a management review as early as March 21, 1953.[11]

Eisenhower briefed the new service chiefs on his general ideas about national security when they arrived in Washington in July 1953. The incoming Chiefs of Staff never collectively pondered the New Look program until they met on board the yacht *Sequoia*, which put to sea on August 6. Radford chose the yacht meeting as a means to force the chiefs (who had not yet officially taken office) to agree on a defense strategy. The yacht would remain at sea, he later wrote in his memoirs, until they reached consensus. After two days of difficult discussion, the dissenting chiefs finally agreed to a paper that evolved into the New Look. Radford remarked, with a tinge of sarcasm, that he had "never been sure why agreement was reached on Saturday when Friday had been so difficult" but suspected that "Matt Ridgway, wanting to get home to his young bride for the weekend, began to see traces of merit in certain things he had opposed the day before."[12]

Both Radford and the president knew that Ridgway had agreed to the *Sequoia* plan with the utmost reluctance. Radford tried to give the original copy of the New Look paper bearing the chiefs' signatures back to Eisenhower, "but he would not take it. He said it was too hot to handle," possibly because he already knew that Ridgway might publicly repudiate the agreement.[13]

Treasury Secretary George Humphrey described the *Sequoia* report as "the most important thing that has happened since January 20" (when Eisenhower took office). The *Sequoia* plan called for a huge redeployment of troops back to the continental United States, with an increase in mobility so that forces could be dispatched wherever they were needed in the event of war. Forward bases abroad would be retained for nuclear retaliation, or perhaps for a first strike. Continental defense would become the first priority.[14]

Admiral Radford argued that Ridgway had acquiesced in the New Look program and in Army budget cuts. Though it is true that Ridgway signed the *Sequoia* agreement, he criticized it at the first National Security Council meeting after the *Sequoia* conference. Ridgway repeatedly challenged the *Sequoia* report, stressing the unofficial nature of the paper and the "terrifying" effects of U.S. troop withdrawal upon NATO. He also warned about the disastrous political and moral effects of preventive war. Eventually, such redeployment plans were dropped, in part because of Ridgway's protest. It is true that the Army Chief of Staff did not renew his objections at the October 7th meeting where NSC-162/1, the New Look policy paper, was polished, perhaps because he still hoped for a 43-billion-dollar defense budget, a figure reduced by the National Security Council on October 13, 1953. By the time of the final vote on October 29, which made the New Look "basic national security policy," Ridgway sent Vice Chief of Staff Bolté as a substitute. Ridgway's absence may not have indicated acquiescence, as Radford later claimed, because, as historian Saki Dockrill has pointed out, many issues, including the redeployment of Army troops abroad, were not finally settled at that meeting.[15]

When Ridgway published his memoirs in 1956, he protested efforts by civilian authorities to "compel adherance to some politico-military 'party line' against the honestly expressed view of responsible officers." The pressure exerted on him aboard the *Sequoia*, along with his perception of Secretary Wilson as an ill-mannered parvenu, undoubtedly increased the bitterness of his charges.[16]

Ridgway did not fight New Look policies consistently in this period. On December 9, Ridgway made no statement at a Joint Chiefs of Staff meeting, at which it was agreed, to make cuts of 20 percent in Army strength, though Secretary of the Army Robert Stevens did protest the cuts to the National Security Council on December 20, possibly at Ridgway's behest. Admiral Radford asserted that Ridgway's silence at the December 9 Joint Chiefs of Staff meeting signified assent, but the former leader of the Revolt of the Admirals might have realized that an old infantryman like Ridgway was planning an ambush. The document generated by the meeting contained several potent escape clauses, including provisos that the chiefs' agreement to the stated force levels would only hold if there were no changes in international threats and tensions and if German and Japanese rearmament reached sufficient levels. As threat estimates can be somewhat subjective, this was tantamount to Ridgway's promising to agree unless he changed his mind.[17]

On the same day that Secretary of Defense Charles E. Wilson announced that new technologies would enable his department to cut its budget, United Press International reported that Ridgway told an audience in Cleveland that weakening of ground forces would be "a grievous blow to freedom." Ridgway criticized those who believed that new untested technology could substitute for men. By December 2, 1953, the *Washington Post* openly reported that "Army Chiefs" felt they could not meet their worldwide commitments with the proposed 10 percent cut in forces for fiscal year 1955.[18]

The Army Chief of Staff continued to object to the New Look plan. On December 22, 1954, he told the president that he was "deeply troubled" as to the security of U.S. forces overseas owing to the lack of any reenforcements. In response, Eisenhower seemed to indicate that his strategy was to delay enemy forces with tactical nuclear weapons while the U.S. mobilized.[19]

A few weeks later, Ridgway protested Eisenhower's strategy before the House Defense Appropriations Subcommittee by damning the New Look with faint praise: "The Army believes that the programmed distribution of strength and forces for the fis[c]al year 1955 is the best attainable within the authorized end strength of 1,164,000 personnel." He implied that budgetary limitations prevented better results. His testimony criticized the assumption of the New Look, namely, that machines could modify and replace men: "Because of the increasing complexity of land warfare and the resultant greater battlefield demands, the individual soldier, far from receding in importance, is emerging ever more clearly as the ultimate key to victory." Then he made a classic statement of the primary importance of humans as opposed to machines in warfare: "No machine can replace the intangible qualities of the human spirit nor the adaptability of the human mind. Man is the master of weapons and not their servant. He is the indispensable element necessary to achieve victory and will remain so in the forseeable future."[20]

His position amounts to a repudiation of the technological fix of "more bang for the buck" sought by proponents of the New Look. These criticisms are subtle, but it is not hard to agree with Congressman Errett P. Scrivner (R-Kans.) that "sometimes the inference [from Ridgway's testimony on the needs of the Army] seems to be that it is being completely wrecked." Indeed, the questions led Congressman Gerald R. Ford (R-Mich.) to inquire whether Ridgway was claiming that the 1955 Army budget would lead to disaster, but Ridgway stopped short of such an openly hostile claim.[21]

In the Senate, Ridgway was more coy, telling a Southern Democratic senator that the Army appropriation was a "sound" program, but refusing to say it was a "sufficient" program. Then he declined to give his personal opinion of the budget unless the committee went into secret session, so he could keep his strongest criticism of the administration private.[22]

In November 1954, Ridgway, at the request of the president, presented his alternative defense policy to the National Security Council. While he agreed with the New Look paper, NSC-162/2's general analysis of the world strategic situation, his objectives for military security differed substantially from then-current policy.[23]

Most notably, Ridgway argued that national security policy must recognize that "in the execution of our national policies we must not sacrifice either essential national security interest or our fundamental moral principles regardless of dollar costs," a stand justified on the grounds that "national fiscal bankruptcy would be far preferable to national spiritual bankruptcy." Ridgway minimized the damage to the economy that New Look proponents foresaw as a consequence of excessive defense spending. In the event of damage to the civilian economy by overspending, Ridgway declared, American "virility, ingenuity, industry and faith" would soon rebuild the economy, so long as the United States remained unconquered. To some critics, this leap of faith seemed fanciful.[24]

If part of Ridgway's proposed national security policy appealed to lofty morality, his long-range objectives were down to earth. Most strikingly, Ridgway called for a policy that encouraged a split between China and the U.S.S.R.—a partial abandonment of the doctrine of monolithic communism. Ridgway's proposed China policy may not have been so alien to the administration as commonly supposed. Drew Pearson reported in 1953 that Richard Nixon got into trouble with his right wing confrères when he suggested to President Nehru of India that the United States would recognize Communist China if it acted a little more reasonably. But playing the "China card" was only one item of Ridgway's agenda for the reform of American foreign policy. He also called for the United States to abandon support for "colonialism," while suggesting that the Monroe Doctrine allowed United States intervention to prevent communist governments from taking power in the Western Hemisphere. Such a construction of the Monroe Doctrine implies continued intervention, as had occurred in Guatemala just a few months before Ridgway wrote his paper.[25]

Discussion, but no action, ensued after Ridgway presented his paper to the National Security Council. After the presentation, Ridgway was asked to leave the room. Secretaries Wilson and Humphrey perceived Ridgway's paper as a cynical attempt to get more money for the Army. The president, perhaps recalling his own days as Army Chief of Staff, displayed an unexpected sympathy for his successor. He defended Ridgway's call for balanced forces as sincere and not "merely a 'parochial' Army viewpoint," though, said the president, "the United States could not afford to prepare to fight all kinds of wars and still preserve its free economy and basic institutions." When Secretary Humphrey remarked, with some justification, that Ridgway had little or no regard for the "maintenance of the economy," the president remarked forgivingly that "this did somewhat less than justice to General Ridgway's views." Eisenhower's remark to Humphrey indicated a regard for Ridgway's sincerity, not a repudiation of the New Look. Indeed, while Ridgway's ruthless bureaucratic infighting often irritated the president, Eisenhower understood at some level that the army chief of staff was genuinely perplexed about how to back the Administration's expanding Cold War goals with declining Army strength.[26]

In February 1955, Eisenhower met a group of Republican senators who were preparing to respond to Ridgway's statement to a Senate committee. The Army Chief had said that cuts in the Army would jeopardize to a degree the security of the United States. Contrary to his statement at the December 3, 1954 National Security Council meeting, the president told the senators that he thought Ridgway was merely advocating his own narrow service interest without seeing the equation between security and the economy that Eisenhower made the basis of his policy. The president indicated to Senator Knowland that he had bent over backward to see that Ridgway's views were seriously considered. Eisenhower's generosity toward Ridgway's views at the December National Security Council meeting was merely an example of bending over backward.[27]

When Ridgway argued for building a capacity to fight nonnuclear Korea-type wars, the president attacked him for trying to fight a nuclear war with conventional weapons. After the destruction of perhaps fifteen U.S. cities in a nuclear attack, Eisenhower said, "Anyone who thinks we are going to immediately ship out of this country division after division is just talking through his hat. It couldn't be done and if I tried to do it, you would want to impeach me." But Ridgway was arguing against reducing the standing army precisely because he believed the United States needed to reinforce troops in combat in Europe or Asia without having to create new divisions or drain away reserve units needed to keep civil order. Each saw the other's position as impractical. Eisenhower exclaimed: "He's talking theory—I'm trying to talk sound sense. He did the same thing at SHAPE [Supreme Allied Headquarters]. I was there before Ridgway went over and he tried to ruin it with the same sort of talk. We have to have a sound base here at home."[28]

By the end of January, Ridgway had decided to reveal his objections to the New Look in testimony before Congress, and he turned to General of the Army George C. Marshall for advice. He sent Marshall a copy of his proposed statement, which Marshall urged him to tone down. As written, the statement invited "an intense showdown fight on the Hill. If that is what you want, then I guess the statement is okay." Despite Marshall's warning that "you are leading with your right," Ridgway did not greatly modify his statement, telling the House Defense Appropriations Subcommittee that the budget "provided substantially less than what I regarded was the minimum." For the first time he made a charge that would become famous—that the force levels chosen resulted from a "directed verdict" from unspecified higher authority. This time he claimed, probably with a touch of irony, "There is not the slightest criticism implied in this."[29]

Ridgway did criticize airpower enthusiasts in bluntly racialist terms: "Personally, I have the gravest of doubts that you will break the will to resist of a people like the Slav and the Oriental by destruction rained on their metropolitan centers and fixed industrial installations from the sky. We have had one example in recent years, and that was Germany, where her cities were reduced to piles of rubble. We did not get a capitulation."[30]

At the May 1955 Senate Hearings, Ridgway pulled few punches. He stated bluntly that Army cuts would cause concern among NATO allies. He also testified that atomic war, contrary to the theory of "more bang for the buck," would require more, not fewer, men.[31]

This testimony led Eisenhower to decide not to reappoint Ridgway. Before Ridgway left, he had prepared a final report to Wilson incorporating his criticisms of the Department. To insure he would get a public hearing, Ridgway cleared the report for publication through the regular channels. Despite the clearance, Secretary Wilson personally classified the report "Confidential." His action dismayed the Army General Staff, where some lower-ranking officers leaked his final report to Wilson to the *New York Times*. The *Times* trumpeted the retired general's dissent in large headlines over page one, column one.[32]

One major theme of Ridgway's final report was his contention that, in an age of "nuclear plenty," when the U.S. and the U.S.S.R. have enough weapons for mutual destruction, that "common appreciation of the consequences of unlimited nuclear war may well result in general unwillingness to employ these weapons in recognition of the mutual disaster which would follow wherein the peoples, property and institutions of much of the world would vanish." Ridgway believed the Soviets would not fight a general war unless it would materially improve their "power position."[33]

Ridgway never believed that the U.S.S.R. was eager to use nuclear weapons. The Soviets would still threaten limited wars, a threat which left the United States peculiarly vulnerable because of its worldwide treaty alliances. "No one knows when these ominous sight drafts may be presented for payment. No one can tell at this time the form or scope of performance these commitments may require of the United States. But they obviously may involve action by U.S. military forces in many different types of climate and terrain, such as the mountains of Greece and Korea or the jungles of Indochina." Ridgway stressed the limits of American power, arguing that U.S. forces were too weak and too concentrated on airpower to meet America's worldwide military commitments.

Instead, Ridgway called for military containment around the Soviet perimeter, which required "an immediately available mobile joint military force of hard hitting character in which the versatility of the whole is emphasized and the preponderance of any one part is deemphasized." The remainder of the memo argued the importance of morality in defining American defense options. Implicitly, this moral evaluation questioned the New Look stress on nuclear bombing.[34]

The *Times* article did not reveal the full dimensions of Ridgway's assault on the New Look, which came six months after he retired, with the serialized publication of his memoirs in the *Saturday Evening Post* on January 21, 1956. The memoirs, Ridgway's most overt attack on Eisenhower's defense policy, were timed to coincide with the president's 1956 budget message. The furor created by Ridgway's memoirs was fed by the published remarks of Secretary of State John Foster Dulles, who rashly boasted that he had brought America back from "the brink of war" several times. Americans worried about Dulles rattling a sabre that Ridgway characterized as rusty. In part one of the memoirs, entitled "Conflict in the Pentagon," Ridgway began by establishing his authority, stressing his heroic, military, and intellectual credentials. He alluded to his father, an army colonel, and to his boyhood on Army posts.[35]

"Professional soldiers are sentimental men, for all the harsh realities of their calling. In their wallets and in their memories they carry bits of philosophy, fragments of poetry, quotations from the Scriptures, which in times of stress and danger, speak to them with great meaning." Pictures also added to the symbolic authority that the magazine sought to attribute to the august general. On the first page, he is shown sitting in the library of his home in Pittsburgh, surrounded by his books and medals, holding a large book, leather bound like a bible, entitled "XVIII Airborne Corps." His feet straddle a white bear rug, which the avid hunter probably shot himself. The caption sums up both his authority and his primary political message: "From experience, I have learned one lesson—that in the world today there can be no peace that is not based on strength."[36]

Then, the general developed the peace-through-strength theme, from his immediate post–World War II experience in demobilization, as a politico-military negotiator at the United Nations, and in Louis Johnson's penny-pinching Pentagon at the beginning of the Korean War. His argument was buttressed by pictures of him in combat in World War II and with MacArthur in Korea. Smiling photos of Ridgway with Eisenhower and Secretary Wilson were also included, though the accompanying article attacked Wilson personally, as well as the New Look policy.

In the center of the last page of the article, the magazine placed a picture portraying the Ridgways as an ideal suburban family, with Matthew bearing his son on his shoulders and Penny beside him, shaking hands with the dog, a symbol of faithfulness, standing in front of the trees of their home. This image brings Ridgway—the hero on a pedestal portrayed in the preceding pages with other heroes like Eisenhower and MacArthur—to the level of the civilian reader. Military containment, the pictures imply, is the necessary precondition to family life.[37]

In the articles, Ridgway argued that tactical nuclear weapons were insufficient to substitute for army manpower and that Eisenhower expected the chiefs to follow a "party line," a metaphor implying that Administration decision making imitated totalitarian practices. Most sensationally, the general protested President Eisenhower's statement in his 1954 State of the Union message that his budget was based on a new military program "unanimously recommended" by the Joint Chiefs of Staff, when, in fact, Ridgway had dissented. The charge attracted media attention because it implied that Eisenhower, an untouchable hero, might play politics. Ridgway also complained that Secretary of Defense Wilson ignored his opinions. In subsequent installments, Ridgway listed several specific grievances. Secretary Wilson, he charged, tried to order him to skeletonize divisions on the front line in Europe and the Far East. Such reductions proved disastrous in the Korean War. He refused to skeletonize the divisions unless he received a direct written order to do so, thereby placing responsibility for the order on Wilson. The secretary backed down. Ridgway also protested attempts to cut subsidies and perks for dependents of troops overseas like the commissary and post exchange store, and the reduction of the retirement age for officers from sixty-four to sixty as money-saving measures. Ridgway, whose leadership technique always stressed the importance of meeting the daily material needs of the GI, believed such reductions would demoralize the American army and make it much harder to retain personnel. Early retirement, Ridgway believed, hurt men whose skills and "mature judgement" were of great value to the army and who had gone out of their way to serve the country in two wars. He ridiculed Wilson's decisions: "Either the secretary was a man whose mental processes operated on a level of genius so high I could not grasp his meaning or that considerations beyond the ken of soldier's logic were influencing his reasoning."[38]

Defense Department civilians made decisions on the basis of "political expediency," Ridgway charged. He wondered, in a tone that sounded more threatening than probably intended, how long civilian control would endure if civilians continued to pressure military men for political reasons, citing political interference by the Nazi Party as a major reason for the weakness of the Wehrmacht after the Normandy invasion.[39]

The *Saturday Evening Post* placed ads in the *New York Times*, which played on American anxiety over military security, by showing, for example, Ridgway in uniform with the slogan "Keep the Army out of Politics." The ad copy read: "Why atomic warfare hasn't lessened the need for the foot soldier . . . and why putting all our eggs in one basket could lead to disaster."[40]

When reporters asked Eisenhower about Ridgway's allegations, he denied applying improper political pressure on the chiefs and referred reporters to the Pentagon on the issue of General Ridgway's agreement with the New Look program. The president dismissed the rest of Ridgway's charges as "narrowly based" military advice. Secretary Wilson, for his part, agreed that Ridgway had opposed Army cuts and denied charges that Ridgway was made to follow a "party line," blaming Ridgway himself for not getting the other chiefs to back more Army funds, a suggestion aimed at bolstering the idea that Ridgway was representing narrow Army interests.[41]

The *Saturday Evening Post* series provoked editorial comment in nearly every paper in America from the *New York Times* to the Marshall, Texas, *News-Messenger*. Liberal papers tended to be supportive of the general's dissent. The *Washington Post*, which had previously supported the New Look, was "inclined to agree" with Ridgway that an all-atomic strategy was more likely to "turn brushfire wars into atomic wars" and that Congress needed to know the "honest feelings" of officers who disagree with adminstration policy. The *Washington Post* also denounced Wilson for improperly classifying Ridgway's final report. The newspaper criticized the pleas for political detachment of security policy that appeared in the second installment. The newspaper's editorial argued that "when General Ridgway contends . . . that civilian secretaries should base their decisions solely on the security interests of the U.S., he treads on spongy ground. Are the security interests merely what the military men say they are? General Ridgway's formula is one, not for civilian control, but for military domination."[42]

Hanson Baldwin, writing in the *New York Times*, agreed with Ridgway about the necessity of building a limited war capability in order to deter nuclear war. Baldwin argued that massive retaliation was outdated in an age of "atomic plenty." He cautioned, however, against exaggeration, noting that the "U.S. is neither weak, nor powerless."[43]

Other liberal papers gave more unqualified support to the Army general's position. The *Atlanta Constitution* labeled the New Look "ridiculous," and the *St. Louis Post-Dispatch* agreed with Ridgway, quoting Senator Stuart Symington as charging that "the security of the nation is being thrown into the marketplace to be traded for political considerations."[44]

Within the Army, the articles were thought a great success. The new Army Chief of Staff, Maxwell Taylor, secretly urged other retired generals to take up the pen on behalf of the Army, while in public he defended the Administration against Ridgway's charge that the chiefs were subject to political pressure. Taylor pointed out that the army was at its highest peacetime strength in history. However, while he pretended to support the administration against Ridgway, he continued to pitch limited war strategy, thus agreeing with his predecessor where it really mattered.[45]

General Gavin, who would soon resign in protest of administration defense policy, wrote Ridgway that the magazine articles "helped us gather momentum." Pro-Army congressmen such as Democrats Daniel Flood of Pennsylvania and Robert L. F. Sikes of Florida, the chair of the House Subcommittee on Army Appropriations congratulated Ridgway on the articles. Sikes immediately invited Ridgway to testify before his committee, an affair thought, at the time, to have had a potential for scandal similar to the Army-McCarthy hearings.[46]

Harsher criticism of Ridgway came from the margins of political discourse. Writing under the pseudonym "Mad," a reader complained in the Eau Claire, Wisconsin, *Leader* that Ridgway was the member of an elite officer corps that opposed any reduction in the armed forces because such a reduction might adversely affect their interests or those of their subordinates.[47]

A woman from Guthrie Center, Iowa, wrote Ridgway with a bold challenge to Ridgway's articles from a populist and pacifist point of view. Replying to Ridgway's characterization of the American soldier as "the finest product of our civilization," she noted that "if any soldier as such is the finest product of civilization, then woe to mankind." She added that her son, recently discharged from the Army, found Ridgway's statement "a hoot." After offering a revisionist interpretation of the origins of World War II, blaming the Versailles Treaty, Britain, and the West for the start of World War II, she recommended that Ridgway read a Quaker tract on war.[48]

On the far Right, the press split into militarist and isolationist camps. The conservative *Indianapolis Star* suggested that Eisenhower was correct to impose budgetary restraints but argued that excessive federal spending for nonmilitary purposes prevented funding an adequate defense program. The federal budget, argued the *Star* "is increasingly taking on the aspect of a Soviet Five Year plan." The *New York Sunday News* chewed Ridgway out for his moral reservations about the use of nuclear weapons. Such reservations, the *News* noted, are encouraged by communist propagandists. Like the Christians fighting the Moslems at Tours in 732, the *News* said, the United States must use every weapon at its disposal.[49]

In contrast, the more traditional midwestern conservative Chicago *Tribune* complained that the real problem with the army was internationalism. In an inversion of Ridgway's argument that the expansion of overseas commitments required building an army capable of meeting those commitments, the *Tribune* declared that "internationalists" had overcommitted the United States to military alliances around the world. The United States could not afford an army which could meet all those commitments.[50]

Finally, there were the proadministration papers that defended Eisenhower and the New Look. The *Washington Star*, for example, in an editorial entitled "A Soldier Goes Astray," lambasted Ridgway for invading the domain of politics. A later editorial complained that Ridgway smeared Secretary Wilson by charging that Wilson acted out of pure partisanship.[51]

More commonly, newspapers argued that the public should trust in Eisenhower's military expertise rather than in Ridgway's. A good example is the South Bend, Indiana, *Tribune*, which, after mentioning that defense expenditures were already at a record high, urged support for the president. "General Ridgway has a great record as a professional militarist, but in this instance it is not a matching of a general's judgment against that of a civilian President lacking military experience. President Eisenhower is also an experienced militarist."[52]

The pro-Eisenhower press also argued, like the *Chicago Sun-Times*, that the Democrats should not use the defense budget for political ammunition, that the charges were old hat, and that the strength of the economy needed to be preserved against excessive spending.[53]

Democratic presidential candidates joined in criticism of Eisenhower's military policy. Stuart Symington said that the security of the nation "was being thrown into the marketplace to be traded." Adlai Stevenson characterized Dulles's statements about massive retaliation in *Life* magazine and Ridgway's allegations of politicized defense budget cutting as "two ominous and frightening statements." Averell Harriman denounced the president for not taking responsibility for his previous statement that the New Look had unanimous Joint Chiefs of Staff approval. Finally, Senator Estes Kefauver (D-Tenn.) called for a complete review of defense policy based on Ridgway's charges.[54]

In 1956, the Democrats' attacks on the adminstration as a result of the Ridgway-Dulles controversy were, as James Reston observed at the time, blunted by continuing peace and prosperity, as well as Republican cooptation of many Democratic programs. Though Ridgway himself was not a Democrat and maintained only tenuous contact with Democratic politicians in this period, Ridgway and the Democrats shared a willingness at the ideological level to use state power to produce what the military felt it needed.

RIDGWAY, EISENHOWER, AND THE IDEOLOGIES OF THE NEW LOOK

Behind the lobbying for and against the New Look is an ideological conflict between Ridgway and Eisenhower. President Eisenhower saw the ideal American society as "a system that recognizes and protects the rights of the individual and that ascribes to the individual a dignity accruing to him because of his creation in the image of a supreme being and which rests upon the conviction that only through a system of free enterprise can this type of democracy be preserved."[55]

Eisenhower considered the growth of the civilian economy to be a military asset. For example, he told Senator Styles Bridges that "if I had all the money I wanted right now I wouldn't use that money to keep 300,000 men in the Army. I would use it for other purposes. Why, even from the question of the defense of the United States I would much rather put that money into new highways and roads so that we could get around this country in a hurry in case of attack." Security forces had to be adequate, but expenditures should be the minimum necessary. "It is, of course, obvious that defensive forces in America are maintained to defend a way of life," he wrote Secretary Wilson. "They must be adequate for this purpose but must not become such an intolerable burden as to occasion loss of civilian morale or individual initiative on which, in a free country, depends the dynamic industrial effort which is the continuing foundation of our nation's security." Eisenhower added that excessive defense spending might eventually damage America's economic growth and force the economy into "regimented controls."[56]

Both Eisenhower and Ridgway claimed to accept a model of the state that attempted to balance an assumed conflict between individual rights and the rights of society. But Eisenhower's primary concern was minimizing excessive state interference in what he called "free enterprise." He considered the threat of statism as important as the threat of communism.

Individualism posed more of a problem for Ridgway because he believed that military security should have a first lien on the resources of American society. Ridgway said he did not want a garrison state, but warned that Soviet capabilities posed a threat more important than financial prudence. "The Nation's fiscal solvency is, of course of fundamental consequence but, I submit, it is secondary in importance to that degree of military strength which will insure, beyond any reasonable doubt, military victory in any future war," he observed. He worried that Americans were too "soft" to meet the Soviet challenge, a challenge he perceived as a threat to every aspect of the American identity."[57]

The consequence of Ridgway's strong stand before Congress at the May 1955 Senate Hearings was that the president did not reappoint him to the Joint Chiefs of Staff when his term expired. Ridgway always maintained that he was not forced to retire, he had always planned to retire at age sixty after one term as chief of staff. This may be true, though there is evidence, albeit from Admiral Radford, a source hostile to Ridgway, that Eisenhower had decided not to invite Ridgway to remain on the Joint Chiefs. Radford, who was privy to Eisenhower's thoughts on the matter, traces the president's decision not to reappoint Ridgway to the latter's Senate Defense Appropriations Subcommittee testimony of March 1955, when Ridgway made his differences with the administration unmistakable and clear. On that occasion, Ridgway "disturbed the President and the Secretary of Defense. He certainly disturbed me." Radford "was not happy" that Ridgway had to go "but . . . considered that there was no other choice." He also believed that the Army Chief of Staff himself preferred to retire. Eisenhower made every effort to honor Ridgway upon his retirement. He was decorated with an additional cluster of the Distinguished Service Cross and promoted to the permanent rank of general.[58]

Ridgway spent March and April 1955 job hunting for a position that would enable him to retire and support Penny and his young son, Matty. His first impulse was to join the Kaiser Company as manager of their Argentine auto manufacturing subsidiary. Ridgway spoke fluent Spanish and had excellent contacts with the Argentine military. He consulted many people about the venture, including, surprisingly, Secretary of Defense Wilson, who had been the president of General Motors, and Nelson A. Rockefeller, well known for his business interests in Latin America, who advised him not to take on the deal unless he became involved in Kaiser's Brazilian operations as well, possibly to insure that Ridgway would command sufficient resources to insure efficient production.[59]

Ultimately, the appeal of a stable home in the United States, after a lifetime of moving all over the world, led Ridgway and his family to choose Pittsburgh over Buenos Aires. The general accepted a job as Director of the Mellon Industrial Research Institute, a position offered to him by General Richard S. Mellon, a member of the prominent Pittsburgh banking and steel family. His tenure there was controversial—he got into a "schism" with the research director, Paul Flory, who wanted to steer the institute more toward pure science and away from applied research. Chairman Paul Mellon reportedly had to force Ridgway to retire a year early in 1960.[60]

NOTES

1. *Saturday Evening Post*, January 21, 1956, 46.

2. Ridgway, *Soldier*, 259.

3. A. J. Bacevich, *The Pentomic Era: The U.S. Army Between Korea and Vietnam* (Washington, D.C.: National Defense University Press, 1986), 20.

4. Ridgway, *Soldier*, 266; Taylor, *Uncertain Trumpet* 108; JB, 2:4:35, 36; Admiral Arthur Radford, *From Pearl Harbor to Vietnam* (Stanford, Calif.: Hoover Institution Press, 1980), 27; Ridgway, *Soldier*, 267.

5. Ridgway, *Soldier*, 270.

6. JB, 2:4:35, 36.

7. Bruce Geelhoed, *Charles E. Wilson and the Controversy at the Pentagon, 1953–1957* (Detroit, Mich.: Wayne State University Press, 1979), 18; JB, 2:4:28.

8. Ibid., 46; Eisenhower, "State of the Union Message," *Washington Post*, 8, January 1954; *Soldier*, 272, 283; Hamlett quoted in Bacevich, *Pentomic Era*, 34; see also Bacevich, *Pentomic Era*, 11, 12.

9. There is a relatively large literature on the New Look. The most recent and thorough study is Saki Dockrill, *Eisenhower's New Look National Security Policy, 1953–61* (New York: St. Martin's Press, 1996), 15–115. This account also draws on Daun Van Ee, "From the New Look to Flexible Response," in Kenneth J. Hagan and William R. Roberts, eds., *Against All Enemies: Interpretations of American Military History from Colonial Times to the Present* (Westport, Conn.: Greenwood, 1986), 321–340. Bacevich, *Pentomic Era*, chap. 2. Some other useful accounts include: Richard Aliano, *American Defense Policy from Eisenhower to Kennedy* (Athens: Ohio University Press 1975); Richard K. Betts, *Soldiers, Statesmen and Cold War Crises* (Cambridge: Harvard University Press, 1977); H. W. Brands, "The Age of Vulnerability," *American Historical Review* 94 (October 1989): 963–989; Brian R. Duchin, "The New Look: President Eisenhower and the Political Economy of National Security," Ph.D. diss., University of Texas, Austin, 1987; John Lewis Gaddis, *Strategies of Containment* (New York: Oxford University Press, 1982); Douglas Kinnard, *President Eisenhower and Strategy Management* (Lexington: University Press of Kentucky, 1977); Iwan W. Morgan, *Eisenhower v. the Spenders* (New York: St. Martin's Press, 1990); Glen Snyder, "The 'New Look' of 1953," in W. Schilling, ed., *Strategy, Politics and Defense*

Budgets (New York: Columbia University Press, 1962); Samuel Huntington, *The Common Defense* (New York: Columbia University Press, 1961).

10. House Appropriations Subcommittee *Hearings on Army Appropriations for FY 1955*, 83d Cong., 2d sess., 1954, pp. 2, 9, 58.

11. Stephen E. Ambrose, *Eisenhower: The President* (New York: Simon & Schuster, 1984), 33, 43; Glen Snyder "The New Look," 394. On Project Solarium see Gaddis, *Strategies of Containment*, 145–155. See also Brands "Age of Vulnerability," (1989): 963–989.

12. Radford, *Pearl Harbor to Vietnam*, 321.

13. Ibid.

14. National Security Council meeting, August 27, 1953, FR 1952–1954, 2:444; Radford, *Pearl Harbor to Vietnam*, 327–329.

15. Radford, *Pearl Harbor to Vietnam*, 447, 448, 454; Memcon, October 7, 1953, FR 1952–1954, 5:527; Dockrill, *Eisenhower's New Look*, 42.

16. Ridgway, *Soldier*, 270.

17. Van Ee, "From the New Look to Flexible Response" 326.

18. Radford, *Pearl Harbor to Vietnam*, 325, 326; *New York Times*, November 11, 1953.

19. Ann Whitman Diary Series, Box 3, December 22, 1954, folder, December 1954 (2). Eisenhower Papers, Eisenhower Library.

20. House Army Appropriations Subcommittee, *Hearings for FY 1955*, 83d Cong., 2d Sess., 1954, pp. 45, 49.

21. House Army Appropriations Subcommittee, *Hearings for FY 1955*, 83d Cong., 2d Sess., 1954, pp. 55, 73.

22. Senate Defense Appropriations Subcommittee, *Hearings for FY 1955*, March 15, 1954, p. 43.

23. Ridgway to presidential National Security Advisor regarding review of basic national security policy (NSC 162/2 and NSC 5422/2), November 22, 1954, Ridgway MSS, Box 30.

24. Ibid.

25. Ibid.; *Washington Post*, December 23, 1953.

26. Ridgway to presidential National Security Advisor regarding: review of basic national security policy (NSC-162/2 and NSC-5422/2), November 22, 1954, Ridgway MSS Box 30; Mark S. Gallicchio, "The Best Defense Is a Good Offense: The Evolution of American Strategy in East Asia, 1953–1960," in Warren I. Cohen and Akira Iriye, eds., *The Great Powers in East Asia, 1953–60* (New York: Columbia University Press, 1990), 63–85, 64.

27. National Security Council, minutes of 227th meeting, December 3, 1954, FR 1952–1954, 2:804, 805; Ferrell, *Hagerty Diary*, 182.

28. Ferrell, *Hagerty Diary*, 182. See also Bacevich, *Pentomic Army*, 31.

29. Marshall to Ridgway, January 28, 1954, George C. Marshall MSS, Marshall Foundation Library, Lexington, Virginia; U.S. Congress, House, *Subcommittee on Defense Appropriations Hearings*, 84th Cong., 1st sess., February 7, 1955, pp. 44, 78.

30. U.S. Congress, Senate, Defense Appropriations Subcommittee, *Defense Appropriations Hearings for FY 1956*, April 4–June 6, 1955, p. 105.

31. Ibid., pp. 215, 223–225.

32. *New York Times*, July 15, 1955.

33. Ridgway to Wilson, June 27, 1955, reprinted in Ridgway, *Soldier*, Appendix 1, pp. 323, 324.

34. Ibid., 326–332.

35. *Saturday Evening Post*, January 21, 1956, pp. 17, 18. On Dulles and "brinksmanship," see *Life*, January 16, 1956.

36. *Saturday Evening Post*, January 21, 1956, pp. 17, 18.

37. Ibid., p. 48.

38. *Saturday Evening Post*, January 28, 1956, p. 74.

39. Ibid.

40. *New York Times*, January 24, 1956.

41. *Saturday Evening Post*, January 21, 1956, p. 46; *Washington Post*, January 8, 1954, *New York Times*, January 19, 1956, *Pittsburgh Press*, January 19, 1956.

42. *Washington Post*, January 19, 1956, January 28, 1956.

43. *New York Times*, January 22, 1956.

44. *Atlanta Constitution*, February 11, 1956, *St. Louis Post-Dispatch*, January 18, 1956.

45. *New York Times*, January 27, 1956; see also Drew Pearson, *Washington Post*, February 5, 1956.

46. Gavin to Ridgway, February 19, 1956, Flood to Ridgway, January 17, 1956, Ridgway MSS, Box 41; *New York Times*, January 18, 1956.

47. Eau Clair *Leader*, n.d., Ridgway MSS, Box 48.

48. Mrs. G. Sherman Held to Ridgway, February 23, 1956, Ridgway MSS, Box 41.

49. *Indianapolis Star*, January 20, 1956, *New York Sunday News*, January 29, 1956, Ridgway MSS, Box 48.

50. *Chicago Tribune*, January 29, 1956.

51. *Washington Star*, January 18, 1956, Ridgway MSS, Box 48.

52. South Bend *Tribune*, January 20, 1956, Ridgway MSS, Box 48.

53. *Chicago Sun-Times*, January 20, 1956, Ridgway MSS, Box 48; *New York Times*, January 18, 1956.

54. *New York Times*, January 17, 18, 21, and 24, 1956.

55. Richard H. Immerman, "Confessions of an Eisenhower Revisionist," *Diplomatic History* 14 (Summer 1990): 319, 325, 328.

56. Ferrell, *Hagerty Diary*, 182; Eisenhower to Wilson, January 5, 1955, Ann Whitman File, DDE Diary, Box 9, Presidential Papers, Eisenhower Library.

57. Speech to English High School Association, Boston, Massachusetts, May 3, 1954, Ridgway MSS Box 36B; Ridgway to Secretary of Defense Neil McElroy, February 6, 1958, Ridgway MSS, Box 31.

58. Ridgway, *Soldier*, 260. Ridgway wrote Lawrence Korb on October 12, 1986, insisting that he had resigned voluntarily (Ridgway MSS, Box 34J; Radford, *Pearl Harbor to Vietnam*, 330; *New York Times*, June 29, 1955.

59. Rockefeller meeting, memo by Ridgway, April 28, 1955; Wilson meeting memo by Ridgway, May 12, 1955, Ridgway MSS, Box 30.

60. Burton Hersh, *The Mellon Family: A Fortune in History* (New York: Morrow, 1978), 528–529.

CHAPTER 14

1954: McCarthy and Dienbienphu

If any year of Ridgway's life in peacetime could be compared to the rigors of battle, it was 1954. In addition to fighting the battle of the budget, Ridgway had to fight for the Army in the battle of the Army versus McCarthy and against American intervention in the Battle of Dienbienphu in Indochina. Just as he had framed World War II, according to some, as his personal struggle against the Wehrmacht, so too these struggles in Washington became personalized to some degree.

RIDGWAY VERSUS MCCARTHY

The only political figure who exasperated Ridgway more than Secretary Wilson was probably Senator Joseph McCarthy (R-Wisc.), who launched an inquisitorial investigation of the Army's internal security late in 1953. McCarthy attacked the Army for promoting a dentist, Dr. Irving Peress, from captain to major, despite his refusal to swear that he was not a Communist. Lieutenant General W. A. "Pinky" Burress had informed Vice Chief of Staff Charles L. Bolté about the case as early as November 6, 1953, hoping to speed Peress's discharge and anticipating that the affair might cause trouble from McCarthy. Indeed, McCarthy soon tried to use the case to substantiate sensational charges that Army security procedures were lax. He implied that the Army might be a nest of Communists. The climax of the Peress case was the testimony of Peress's commanding officer, Brigadier General Ralph Zwicker. The day of Zwicker's testimony, McCarthy felt ill. He had been knocked unconscious in an auto accident the night before when a drunk driver rammed the taxi he and his wife were riding in. He was in a bad mood, with a big lump on his head, and had just found out that his wife's ankle had been broken in the accident. When the hearing started, the senator berated Zwicker during his testimony, publicly questioning the war hero's intelligence and loyalty. McCarthy implied that Zwicker, a decorated hero of D-day, was "unfit to wear the uniform" and made abusive statements like, "Either your honesty or your intelligence; I can't help impugning one or the other." Ironically, it may have been Zwicker who tipped McCarthy off to the Peress case, according to an interview that McCarthy counsel Roy Cohn later gave historian David Oshinsky. That evening Zwicker called Burress, his commanding officer, and threatened to resign. Burress in turn called Ridgway, who forwarded Zwicker's complaints to Secretary of the Army Robert Stevens.[1]

Ridgway was a frustrated spectator, who could do little to intervene politically against the senator. Ridgway's main efforts were to defend Stevens and to prevent the release of material regarding the Peress case prior to McCarthy's censure by the Senate. Stevens, after he heard about Zwicker's testimony, banned all Army officers from testifying before the McCarthy committee and volunteered to face McCarthy himself. After Stevens announced he would testify, he spoke with Vice President Richard Nixon, Senator Everett Dirksen, and others who advised him that McCarthy was likely to "tear him to pieces" on the stand and that he should avoid testifying at all costs.[2]

Shortly after his conversations with Nixon and Dirksen, Stevens lunched with McCarthy and his colleague, Senator Karl Mundt. This was the famous "Chicken Luncheon." At the luncheon, Stevens caved in to McCarthy by agreeing to honor subpoenas for documents and for Army personnel to testify before the McCarthy committee. In return, Stevens claimed that the senators had agreed not to bully committee witnesses, though it is doubtful that he actually obtained such agreement. The agreement was not part of the written memo of understanding of the meeting, and historian David Oshinsky, who portrays Stevens as rather weak-kneed, is skeptical as to whether such a bargain was struck. But on February 25, 1953, the day after the Chicken Luncheon, Ridgway defended Stevens in an address to his senior officers and told them that he had been assured that officers who testified would receive more respectful treatment. Though this does not confirm that Stevens got a promise from McCarthy and Mundt, Ridgway was in a position to know, as Stevens brought McCarthy to his office immediately following the luncheon.[3]

Eisenhower, outraged at the treatment of old subordinate Zwicker and

Stevens's political ineffectiveness, immediately repudiated Stevens's agreement at the Chicken Luncheon. At the same time, Eisenhower publically reasserted his confidence in Stevens and tried to strike a new agreement with McCarthy, through the good offices of Senator Everett Dirksen, that "Army officers, if called, would be treated with proper respect." McCarthy refused, however, and Stevens, under the supervision of White House Press Secretary James Hagerty, announced at a press conference that he would not permit the abuse of Army officers on the stand.[4]

Eisenhower then issued a surprisingly mild statement on the affair, calling for "justice and fair play" in opposing communism. Though he specifically defended Zwicker, the president deliberately omitted any explicit criticism of McCarthy. Privately, he fumed at the Wisconsin Republican. Eisenhower biographer Stephen Ambrose suggests that Eisenhower avoided a direct denunciation of McCarthy at the time and "decided to let events run their course," perhaps as a strategic plan to let McCarthy hang himself, though he was also concerned that McCarthy would publicize the case against atomic scientist J. Robert Oppenheimer, whose top secret clearance was being withheld pending investigation at the same time as the Army-McCarthy brouhaha.[5]

Eisenhower's failure to act against McCarthy greatly angered Ridgway, already furious at Ike for failing to defend General Marshall when McCarthy smeared him in the 1952 presidential campaign. Still, he was shrewd enough not to do his own talking. In an interview with Theodore White, he called in a mutual friend, General Anthony J. D. Biddle Jr., a skilled soldier-diplomat, who openly criticized Eisenhower for failing to attack McCarthy. Ridgway told White: "We're like men with our hands tied behind our back. McCarthy's only choice is whether to kick us in the groin or kick us in the face," though he also ordered streamlined procedures for mustering Communists out of the Army.[6]

Ridgway protested when, during the Army-McCarthy hearings, Eisenhower ordered Wilson to disclose the names of all military personnel having a connection with the Peress case. Ridgway thought that disclosure would destroy Army discipline by creating an atmosphere in which already dispirited officers felt they were subject to oversight by an unfair and disrespectful Senate committee. Eisenhower found Ridgway's views to be "extreme."[7]

Ultimately, the Army faced off against McCarthy in televised hearings in April–May 1954. These hearings examined charges that the Army had tried to cover up the Peress case and the Army's countercharges that McCarthy aide Roy Cohn had used McCarthy's influence to obtain favorable treatment from the Army for Private G. David Schine, a former member of the senator's staff. Though Ridgway seems to have had a hand in pressing the investigation of Schine's abuses, he remained curiously silent about the Peress case and about the hearings in his memoirs, written little more than a year after the Army-McCarthy hearings, perhaps because he did not want to alienate potential allies in his struggle against the New Look. Twenty years later, Ridgway continued to loathe McCarthy, denouncing "the worst elements in the country" who joined McCarthy in "his cry against the Army for harboring Communists."[8]

RIDGWAY AND DIENBIENPHU

Though he became a famous Vietnam war opponent while in retirement, Ridgway began his acquaintance with America's Indochina policy in 1952 as Commander-in-Chief, Far East, when he met with the king of Cambodia, Norodom Sihanouk, and the Cambodian prime minister, Huy Xanthoul. A few months later, Ridgway was in Paris as Supreme Allied Commander in Europe, discussing the transfer of planes to Indochina with the French military. By the following spring, it was clear to the Joint Chiefs, and probably to Ridgway as well, that the French were not making a strong military effort in Indochina, that the generals they sent there were, in the words of General J. Lawton Collins, "second-raters." Moreover by April 1953, it had become clear to the Joint Chiefs that the Indochina war, which the United States was funding primarily to maximize its influence in Paris on other matters, such as the European Defense Community, might increasingly conflict with France's obligation to provide forces to NATO. By the time Ridgway arrived in Washington to take over from Collins as Army Chief of Staff, he fully understood that the French lacked the "leadership, spirit, organization and intangibles" necessary to win the war. In the first meeting of the State Department with the Joint Chiefs after he was sworn in as Chief of Staff, Ridgway expressed great reluctance over the allocation of some $385 million to aid the French effort.[9]

Ridgway's opposition to American intervention in Indochina was closely connected to his difficulties about the budget and the "New Look" defense strategy. These limitations on the Army's ability to honor the worldwide political commitments that the Truman and Eisenhower administrations had made for American forces made Ridgway acutely aware of strategic choices— one reason that, as Robert Buzzanco has pointed out, "Europe-firsters" outside the military favored intervention in Indochina in order to grease relations with the French and keep pro-American governments in power, whereas military "Europe-firsters" believed that intervention would deprive NATO of necessary military resources.[10]

One aspect of Ridgway's opposition to intervention is the degree to which he was aware of Western military supremacy in the third world, a decline that Ridgway perceived as having a racial aspect. Military necessity and post-Nazi questioning of racist ideology had already led Ridgway to support integration of the armed forces. But the racial dimension of the limited war doctrine itself is often overlooked today. Maxwell D. Taylor's "Reflexions [sic] on the War in Korea" was one of the foundational documents of limited war strategy. When Ridgway received his advance copy from Taylor, he commented that it was "most thought provoking" and circulated copies to Secretary Stevens and all major commanders. In one of the report's major sections, "The Significance of Oriental Manpower," Taylor declared that the experience of the Korean War had made obsolete past racial stereotypes about what he called "Oriental manpower": "We have learned to respect the Oriental soldier as brave, hardy, disciplined, and eminently teachable. To discover that the millions of Asia can be made into formidable soldiers is not a comforting thought." Paradoxically, in challenging the Scylla of supposed Asian inferiority, Taylor falls into the Charybdis of "yellow peril" ideology. Moreover, Taylor questioned the usefulness of superior American technology in Korea, pointing out that the machines designed for waging a general war in Europe proved of limited use in Korean terrain, where the UN forces were successfully opposed by well-trained infantry "primitively armed with equipment much of which we would have consigned to museums." Taylor and Ridgway understood, as the French could not, that a small band of Europeans with a gatling gun could no longer affect the course of history in Asia. The old racial order—whose words, like *oriental*, were still used—had come tumbling down.[11]

When Ridgway arrived in Washington to become Army Chief of Staff, he already doubted the ability of the French to win the war and did his utmost to prevent direct U.S. intervention in Indochina. As in the budget debate, his primary adversary was the Chairman of the Joint Chiefs of Staff, Admiral Arthur Radford. Radford, a gung-ho naval aviator, wanted to use American planes to bomb the Vietminh forces surrounding the fortress of Dienbienphu. One plan, Operation VULTURE, favored at one point by Air Force Chief of Staff Nathan Twining, called for detonating three small atomic bombs outside Dienbienphu. Radford wanted to demonstrate his belief that airpower alone could defeat an insurgency. His opportunity came with the visit of French general Paul Ély, who arrived in Washington in March 1954 with instructions to pressure the Americans to support French efforts at a negotiated settlement. As the French military situation deteriorated, Ély had to importune the Americans for additional aid to the besieged garrison at Dienbienphu. Radford probably overstepped his authority on the last day of Ély's visit, March 25, 1954, leading the Frenchman to believe that the United States would save Dienbienphu with air strikes upon request of the French government. In order to gather support for such air strikes, Radford put the matter to a vote of the Joint Chiefs five days later. Much to his surprise, they all voted against a bombing raid in support of the French.[12]

Ridgway led the opposition, arguing that Radford had overstepped his bounds. Radford's course "would be to involve the JCS [Joint Chiefs of Staff] inevitably in politics." Ridgway resurrected this traditional paradigm of civil-military relations to limit Joint Chiefs action he disagreed with, while bending the rules when it came to the budget. Nonetheless, Ridgway gave his view that "United States capability for effective intervention in the Dienbienphu operation was altogether disproportionate to the liability it would incur." American intervention "would greatly increase the risk of general war." He also believed that militarily, the battle of Dienbienphu, which involved less than 5 per cent of French forces in Indochina, "would not in itself decisively affect the military situation there," though Ély had indicated that the importance of the battle lay in its effects on the political situation in metropolitan France.[13]

A week later, Ridgway provided his opinion of the necessary military force required to prevent "the passing of the countries of southeast Asia to the Communist orbit." The arguments over the "New Look" budget of the preceding months affected the debate over Indochina, but not in the way one might suppose. Ridgway argued that intervention with airpower would be ineffective; only a decisive defeat of China in a general war would accomplish American objectives of defeating the Vietminh. Indeed, staff studies, spurred by Ély's visit, of the possibility of an amphibious landing to seize major Vietnamese cities and defeat the Vietminh suggested that such action would require full mobilization and would leave "the general posture of the U.S. Army at its worst since World War II." At the same time, an invasion ran a grave risk of war with China, as any feasible plan for invasion of the North would have required seizure of Hainan Island, which was Chinese territory. Even intervention limited to Vietnam "would constitute a dangerous strategic diversion of limited United States military capabilities, and would commit our armed forces in a non-decisive theater to the attainment of non-decisive local objectives. The greater the United States military forces so employed, the greater would be the advantage to the true sources of Communist military power—Communist China and the USSR." Despite his hawkish tone, Ridgway did not really argue for war with China. He wanted instead to demonstrate the absurdity of a military solution to Cold War confrontation in Asia. If war were the solution, it would be general, not limited, war. After all, his other objection to intervention in Indochina was "the greatly increased risk of general war" that such intervention would cause. He believed that the United States had the power to conquer China. However, such a victory would be pyrrhic, creating a power vacuum that might then either be filled by "Russia" or by the United States "face to face with Russia along a seven thousand mile frontier."[14]

At the beginning of the Korean War, Ridgway met with Eisenhower and pointed out the failure of the Truman administration to clearly state its objectives in Korea, briefing him on a plan for developing panels of experts to define such objectives. The military could only do its job, the two generals agreed, if the political leadership explained precisely what their job involved. Ridgway knew from his past conversations with Eisenhower during the Korean War that a frank evaluation of the military situation and a request for clearly defined objectives would carry weight with the president, and he framed his memo accordingly. He argued that the confrontation over Indochina contained the prospect of a major war with China, not a limited war with the Vietminh. A war limited to Indochina, he believed, was doomed at best to a Korea-like stalemate. Ridgway believed that the United States could ill afford to underestimate the military force necessary to obtain its political objectives.[15]

Ridgway's arguments convinced not only the other chiefs, but also influenced the U.S. Congress and the British. Most important, his arguments influenced the president. By the end of April, Eisenhower had firmly decided against intervention. Scholars disagree about the depth of Eisenhower's opposition. David Anderson argues that Eisenhower seriously considered intervention "but chose to define very specific criteria" as an escape from unsustainable commitments.[16] At the April 29 National Security Council meeting, Eisenhower's language reflected the influence of Ridgway's memorandum:

> The president answered that before he could bring himself to make such a decision [for war in Indochina], he would want to ask himself and all his wisest advisors whether the right decision was not rather to launch a world war. If our allies were going to fall away in any case, it might be better for the United States to leap over the smaller obstacles and hit the biggest one with all the power we had. Otherwise we seemed to be merely playing the enemy's game—getting ourselves involved in brushfire wars in Burma, Afghanistan, and God knows where.[17]

Eisenhower, reflecting the concerns that Ridgway had raised, then declared that he was "frightened to death at the prospect of American divisions scattered all over the world. It was obvious that we should have to go to general mobilization if we followed his [Ridgway's] course."[18]

Ridgway set about to follow up the success of his earlier memo, gathering further evidence that intervention in almost any form in Indochina was impractical. Army studies and position papers opposed airfield improvement and training missions to the area, which he believed a waste of precious resources. Casting aside his earlier reservations about the chiefs getting involved in politics, he told Acting Defense Secretary Robert Anderson in the presence of Army Secretary Robert Stevens that he felt "conscience bound" to express his opinion on Indochina and proceeded to brief Anderson on his objections.[19]

Even an effort based on airpower needed substantial ground troop commitments. Ridgway argued that a shore-based air force was essential to any effort to project airpower to the interior. Such bases would require "constant local security at their every location and for their every activity. The Army will have to provide these forces and their total will be very large." Intervention in Indochina presented all the same problems "which confronted U.S. forces in previous campaigns in the South and Southwest Pacific and Eastern Asia, with the additional grave complication of a large native population, in thousands of villages, most of which are about evenly divided between friendly and hostile."[20]

Later that afternoon, Ridgway informed Secretary Stevens that he had already spoken to General Wilton (Jerry) Persons and Lieutenant Colonel Robert L. Schultz, both members of the White House staff, about personally briefing the president. Stevens agreed and directed that a summary of the briefing, the substance of which Ridgway had already given Anderson, be written up and formally conveyed over Stevens's signature as the official views of the Army.[21]

Ridgway also ordered a team to go to Indochina on May 31 and report on the logistical situation there. The team returned on July 31 and confirmed in detail Ridgway's point of view in May. Ridgway noted that he believed that "the analysis which the Army made and presented to higher authority played a considerable, perhaps a decisive, part in persuading our government not to embark on that tragic adventure." Thus, the memoirs seem to confuse the later Army report with Ridgway's earlier briefing of Eisenhower requested in the May 17 memorandum. Melanie Billings-Yun, citing the Pentagon Papers, suggested that the report came after Eisenhower's decision. She asserted that Ridgway had not told the president about the logistical difficulties of intervention until July, after the decision not to intervene had already been made. This contradicted Ridgway's memoirs, which stated that logistics had been the key topic in his May conversation with the president. Ridgway's recollection is corroborated by a story in *U.S. News and World Report* in June 1954 that Ridgway had already briefed Ike on the logistical difficulty of intervention. According to the news magazine, "A ground soldier's picture of what war in Indo-china would mean for the U.S. has influenced a White House decision to stop, look and listen before getting into that fight."[22]

Ridgway's strategic arguments against military intervention in Asia combined his conservative Christian outlook with practical politics. Ridgway assumed that victory in an Asian war required the elimination of the military power of the People's Republic of China, so naturally such intervention might move the United States "dangerously toward acceptance of the doctrine of 'preventive war.' " "Nothing could more tragically demonstrate our complete and utter moral bankruptcy," he wrote. Moreover, such a step would transform America into an empire based on conquest, into a society that Ridgway believed was liable to decay like all such empires.[23]

NOTES

1. Burress to Bolté, November 6, 1953, Bolté to Burress, December 5, 1953; Weible to Moorman, March 3, 1954, encl. Caffey to Chief of Staff; and Burress to Ridgway, February 19, 1954, COS (54), 201 Peress (March 3, 1954), RG 319, National Archives; David Oshinsky, *A Conspiracy So Immense* (New York: Free Press, 1983), 366–378.

2. Oshinsky, *A Conspiracy So Immense: The World of Joe McCarthy* (New York: Free Press, 1983), 378–380, 383.

3. Ibid., 383, 385–386.

4. Ibid., 387–388; see also statement by the president, March 3, 1954, COS (54), 201 Peress, RG 319, National Archives.

5. Ambrose, *Eisenhower*, 2: 165, 166.

6. Theodore H. White, *In Search of History* (New York: Warner, 1978), 492; Weible to Ridgway, July 13, 1954, COS, 201 Peress (May 3, 1954), RG 319, National Archives.

7. Eisenhower memo of record, May 11, 1954, Eisenhower Presidential MSS, Ann Whitman File, Adminstration Series, Box 39.

8. JB, 2:4:44, 45; memo for record (Moorman), March 15, 1954, COS, 201 Schine, David (March 15, 54), RG 319, National Archives.

9. Minister at Saigon (Heath) to Department of State, January 31, 1952, *Foreign Relations* 13 (1952–54): 250–255; Heath to Department of State, August 5, 1952, *Foreign Relations* 13 (1952–1954): 241; Heath to Department of State, September 20, 1952, *Foreign Relations* 13 (1952–1954): 255; State–Joint Chiefs of Staff meeting, April 24, 1953, *Foreign Relations* 13 (1952–1954): 496–503; State–Joint Chiefs of Staff meeting, July 17, 1953, *Foreign Relations* 13 (1952–1954): 687; State–Joint Chiefs of Staff meeting, September 4, 1953, *Foreign Relations* 13 (1952–54): 756.

10. Robert Buzzanco, *Masters of War: Military Dissent and Politics in the Vietnam Era* (New York, Cambridge University Press, 1996), 26. Buzzanco's book is by far the best account of opposition from within the military to the committment of arms and men to Indochina. On the 1950s, see pp. 29–53 of Buzzanco's book.

11. Moorman to Secretary of the Army, March 12, 1954; Ridgway to Taylor, draft, n.d.; Taylor to Ridgway, February 4, 1954; and Maxwell D. Taylor, "Reflexions on the War in Korea (Period of Stabilization)," COS, 1954, 091 (Korea) RG 319, National Archives.

12. David L. Anderson, *Trapped by Success: The Eisenhower Administration and the Vietnam War, 1953–61* (New York: Columbia University Press, 1991), 26, 27; Melanie Billings-Yun, *Decision Against War: Eisenhower and Dienbienphu* (New York: Columbia University Press, 1988), 33, 34; Lloyd C. Gardner, *Approaching Vietnam: From World War II Through Dienbienphu* (New York: Norton, 1988), 208–210; Joint Chiefs of Staff to Secretary of Defense Wilson, March 31, 1954. *Foreign Relations* 13 (1952–1954): 1198.

13. Memo for Joint Chiefs of Staff from Army Chief of Staff Ridgway, April 2, 1954, *Foreign Relations* 13 (1952–54): 1220.

14. Ibid., April 6, 1954, *Foreign Relations* 13 (1952–54): 1269; Ridgway, *Soldier*, 278–280; Ridgway to Secretary of the Army, April 24, 1954, folder, "Memo for U.S.

Army Chief of Staff on Vietnam from Gavin (G-3)"; Gavin, unpublished autobiography, 178–180, Gavin MSS, U.S. Army Military History Institute.

15. Memo for Joint Chiefs of Staff from Army Chief of Staff Ridgway, April 6, 1954, *Foreign Relations* 13 (1952–54): 1269; cover notation on Eisenhower briefing, Ridgway to Chief of Staff (Collins), October 12, 1950, Ridgway MSS, Box 16; Ridgway to Stevens, April 24, 1954, COS 1954 092 Indochina (April 24, 1954). In 1955, Ridgway also opposed intervention to protect Quemoy and Matsu, which he believed possessed no military value (Ridgway, *Soldier*, 278).

16. Anderson, *Trapped by Success*, 38.

17. Memorandum of discussion at the 194th meeting of the National Security Council, April 29, 1954, *Foreign Relations* 13 (1952–1954): 1441.

18. Ibid.

19. Buzzanco, *Masters of War*, 49. See also memo for the Chiefs of Staff regarding airfields in Indochina, May 1, 1954, Moorman to Assistant Chief of Staff, G-3, May 11, 1954, COS 1954 091 Indochina (May 11, 1954); memorandum for record, May 17, 1954, Ridgway MSS, Box 34g.

20. Memorandum for record, May 17, 1954, Ridgway MSS, Box 34g.

21. Memorandum for record, May 17, 1954, Ridgway MSS, Box 34g.

22. Billings-Yun and I agree that the influence of Ridgway's earlier memoranda in the days after the Ély mission did have a perceptible impact on the president's decision (Billings-Yun, *Decision Against War*, 57). See also "What Ridgway Told Ike—War in Indo-China Would Be Tougher Than Korea," *U.S. News & World Report*, July 25, 1954.

23. Ridgway, *Soldier*, 280.

CHAPTER 15

Ridgway in "Retirement"

At age sixty, Ridgway devoted himself to his new job at the Mellon Institute, making enough money to retire comfortably, giving speeches, working with Harold Martin on his memoirs, and thinking about American military policy. He worked at the Institute from his 1955 retirement from the Army until 1960.

Ten years after Ridgway's departure from the Joint Chiefs of Staff, in 1965 and 1966, President Johnson radically escalated the war in Indochina. Ridgway became one of several retired senior military officers who were opposed to the war and who wrote a moderate, but clear, attack on Johnson's policies entitled "Pull Out, All Out or Stand Fast" in the April 5, 1966 issue of *Look* magazine. Ridgway was most alarmed about the open-ended nature of the commitment to Vietnam, which, he feared, would deplete U.S. resources for a comparatively insignificant objective. His argument was much the same as in 1954.[1]

Ridgway argued that victory in Vietnam was impossible, and he ridiculed the "domino" theory—the idea that the "fall" of South Vietnam would lead to communist domination of all of Southeast Asia. However, he also rejected the option of withdrawal, believing that the abandonment of the Vietnamese anticommunists was also a shameful and politically undesirable course. He reiterated General James Gavin's suggestion of a withdrawal to defense enclaves, followed by political negotiations, so long as any agreement with the communists was accompanied by "ironclad guarantees." He also expressed similar views to Senator J. William Fulbright (D-Ark.) Chair of the Senate Foreign Relations Committee, who had requested his testimony in the wake of the publication of the *Look* article.[2]

By the end of 1967, Ridgway joined a group of distinguished former officials and academics at the Bermuda Conference on the Vietnam War sponsored by the Carnegie Endowment for International Peace. The endowment's vice president at that time was Charles E. Bolté Jr., whose father had served Ridgway as Army vice chief of staff when Ridgway was chief. The elder Bolté had been Ridgway's close confidante and "alter ego" at the Pentagon.[3]

The conferees took a position quite similar to Ridgway's a year earlier—they did not advocate withdrawal, but they wanted to prevent the widening of the war. They called for negotiation with the National Liberation Front, an end to the bombing of North Vietnam, a tactical shift to the defensive, and greater South Vietnamese responsibility for defense. America's goal, they argued, should be protection of South Vietnamese people, not the destruction of communist forces in the country.[4]

Back in Washington, representatives of the Bermuda Group met with Secretary of State Dean Rusk, who listened politely but remained unconvinced by the group's "insistence on the importance of taking action designed to 'cool' the situation." Nonetheless, Secretary Rusk was "impressed," and perhaps daunted, that "such a group of responsible citizens had reached the substantial consensus" reflected in the Bermuda Group's memorandum. The Group's representatives also briefly saw White House aide W. W. Rostow and handed him a letter addressed to the president that encompassed the Group's suggestions. After Johnson declined to meet with the group, this letter was released to the press.[5]

The coolness of the administration to proposals for negotiation changed radically when Ridgway's old friend Clark Clifford replaced Robert S. McNamara as Secretary of Defense in 1967. By the time of the January–February 1968 Tet Offensive, Clifford initiated a complete reevaluation of the war and came to the conclusion that he had to persuade the president to open negotiations. Johnson, challenged by antiwar candidate Eugene J. McCarthy, meanwhile had suffered severe reversals in his reelection campaign and a massive loss of support for the war after the Tet Offensive.

On March 22, 1968, Clifford called Ridgway and invited him to join a special advisory group, "to examine the present posture of affairs in Vietnam." This was the group that some authors have referred to as the "wise men," experienced Cold War Warriors summoned to advise the president on how to extricate the United States from Vietnam. After a day and a half of consultations, the group met with the president on March 26, 1968. At the end of this meeting, President Johnson was heard to have said that "the establishment bastards have bailed out."[6]

The majority of the wise men favored deescalation; nonreinforcement of U.S. forces in Vietnam, except for those necessary for the training of ARVN (the American-supported South Vietnamese Army) and essential security of forces, and a halt in the bombing of Vietnam. Most of the sitting officials did not take a position; but of the eighteen members of the group, only General Bradley, Justice Fortas, Ambassador Robert Murphy, and General Maxwell Taylor said they opposed deescalation and a bombing halt.[7]

Ridgway favored such measures. His private advice to the president, though more detailed, followed the lines of his public proposals. He called for a program similar to that later dubbed "Vietnamization," including increased support for pro-American armed forces, a program to unite all anticommunist groups in Vietnam (though Ridgway conceded the difficulties might be insurmountable), withdrawal to a long-term occupation of defensive enclaves, accompanied by negotiations. After the meeting, Ridgway met with General William Westmoreland, the Army chief of staff, to discuss production levels for rifles destined for the ARVN, many of which would be manufactured by Colt Industries, of which Ridgway was a director.[8]

A few days after the meeting of the "wise men," on March 31, 1968, President Johnson stunned the country by announcing a reversal of his policy of escalation and adopting the recommendations of the "wise men." He also announced he would not run for reelection.[9]

Ridgway continued to study the problems of Vietnam, though he declined an invitation by Clifford, now in the opposition, to join Senators Hatfield, McGovern, and Ribicoff on a TV protest of Nixon's 1970 bombing of Cambodia. He did not want to go on TV and "did not have confidence in the Senators," he told Clifford, though Ridgway continued to criticize the war in other ways. In 1971, in the prestigious journal *Foreign Affairs*, Ridgway called for withdrawal once the ARVN was properly trained and for a reassessment in another six to nine months if it appeared that the South Vietnamese would never be properly trained. According to Ridgway, U.S. objectives had narrowed to repatriation of prisoners of war and strengthening the South Vietnamese government so it "would have a reasonable chance to survive without our armed support."[10]

He also examined the rationale for the Vietnam War, noting the phrases that he had used in his 1966 *Look* article to explain and justify U.S. objectives, such as to "halt aggression" and to enforce "the right of a people to choose their own government." "When these wore thin, as they did, we turned to broader generalities: our vital interests were at stake—just what interests and how was not spelled out." If we were indeed defenders of democracy, Ridgway asked, "would we have not have taken up arms for the Hungarian people in 1956? And for the Czechoslovaks in 1968?"[11]

Ridgway placed a surprising trust in the American people at this point, which does not appear earlier in his writing, which had usually been more concerned with the behavior of elites. "If our national security was indeed threatened and a vital interest was at stake, would not our people have whole-heartedly supported this war as they did when the designs of Imperial Germany became clear in 1917, and as they did even more resoundingly when Hitler, Mussolini and the Japanese militarists made their bid for world conquest?"[12]

In other words, Ridgway finally conceded that a popular consensus was necessary for the type of social harmony and cooperation that he believed fundamentally necessary for America to fight a major war. A society based on such consensus had always been Ridgway's ideal, and he still believed that in a real emergency the American people would cooperate as they had in World War II. Nonetheless, after all the mistakes of Vietnam, he still believed that a technically skilled elite should coordinate foreign policy and the social forces necessary to sustain it. "It should be clear now that neither partisan political influences nor chauvinistic clamor, to which segments of our society not infrequently give voice, should be allowed to sway those responsible for major decisions in the field of foreign policy, above all those decisions which involve resort to the use of armed force."[13]

RIDGWAY AND REAGANISM

By the early 1970s, Ridgway, who had easy access to the opinion-editorial page of the *New York Times*, had become concerned by the profound cultural changes occurring throughout the country. The United States was in a profound "spiritual malaise . . . pervading all levels of our people and for the first time to my knowledge, all armed forces ranks." Never before in American history, had the Army's reputation fallen so low, he wrote in a *New York Times* article entitled "The Ordeal of the Army." For Ridgway, this was a serious situation, as he considered that such martial, spiritual, and moral values were paramount; they were the unchangeable and inviolable principles that made a society worth living in and that enabled it to defend itself.[14]

The year 1971 also brought personal tragedy—the death of his only son, Matthew Jr., who was killed at the age of twenty-two by a train while he was working as a wilderness guide near Lodge Keewajaden Camp, three hundred miles north of Toronto. Ridgway first took the crushing news with the quiet stoicism of a battle leader, but he was visibly shaken when asked about his son by a reporter: "He accomplished more in his twenty-two years than I ever did," said the man who was famed for the intensity of his extra-curricular activities at West Point and who had commanded a company at the age of 22.[15]

The next year, Democratic presidential nominee George McGovern called

Ridgway on the phone to consult with him on defense policy, though too late to affect the campaign's position, which in some ways resembled the New Look. Though Ridgway loathed Richard Nixon, he never endorsed McGovern, as did his more liberal protegé General James Gavin. Ridgway argued that the nuclear stalemate would allow the Soviets to build up their conventional weapons.[16]

Through the seventies, Ridgway still favored a society whose principal priority remained sacrifice for defense spending, insisting that even serious economic and social problems were of little consequence compared to the menace posed from abroad. Ridgway called for sacrifice for defense—one might cynically suggest that the sacrifices he believed necessary were inflation, poverty, drug abuse, and crime, though he claimed it could be done through "better control" of spending practices. But Ridgway believed that sacrifice would bring a moral regeneration, and he is honest enough to admit that he believed such regeneration would come through the agency of a morally superior governmental elite of disinterested technocrats (presumably like himself). In such a process of regeneration through elite control, democracy was a secondary concern. Of these wise, men Ridgway wrote: "The masses will never perceive their worth, nor willingly follow them initially. But a minority will, and with true leadership that minority will steadily grow, as will the strength of our nation, which in the final analysis rests on the character of its people."[17]

The core of Ridgway's social vision, then, remained a hierarchy, which would be coordinated by principled, and technically skilled, men like himself. His commonwealth could be disrupted by unprincipled leaders such as Richard Nixon, whom he believed had helped create the "malaise" into which he thought society had sunk. In private, he argued that social unity was necessary because the nation was likely to be at war with the Soviet Union in the next decade or two, and he feared that the United States would be hard-pressed with our alliances in disarray. He later cited "the grave menace to our domestic tranquillity and unity of purpose posed by the large number of communists and radicals in our society," and the election of Jimmy Carter did not reassure him.[18]

At first, Ridgway retained good relations with the Carter administration, though he had been contributing money to the Republican Party since 1975. He wrote his old friend Averell Harriman that he was pleased that the president-elect was consulting Harriman, and he was delighted that Cyrus Vance had been appointed secretary of state. As a former Caribbean commander, Ridgway later gave valuable support to the Panama Canal Treaty, which was bitterly opposed by Republican conservatives.[19]

He soon became disillusioned, however, with the Carter administration's reductions in defense spending and in what he believed was the administration's apparent indifference to the threat of communism. Ridgway was also disenchanted with some of the egalitarian changes wrought by the civil rights and women's movements of the seventies. He wrote Senators Mike Mansfield and Goldwater and the *New York Times* protesting the admission of women to West Point and other service academies; he felt that the assertion of individual rights had been carried too far.[20]

If he had recalled one earlier incident, it might have put him in mind of some of the justice of some of these liberation movements. In October 1955, just after Ridgway's retirement, his long-time orderly, a man who had accompanied him through many battles in World War II and Korea, was separated from the service because of allegations that he was gay. Ridgway intervened to make certain that his discharge, evidently impossible to avoid, would be honorable, and Ridgway agreed to give him employment references after separation.[21]

Shortly after Carter's election, Ridgway helped form the Committee on the Present Danger, an organization of over two hundred men "of national stature" dedicated to increasing American military spending in the face of Carter administration cuts. Convinced of the imminence of a conventional conflict with the U.S.S.R., Ridgway compared the committee to the patriots of the American Revolution. His participation in the campaign for rearmament illustrates the close cooperation between army and industry in which Ridgway so deeply believed.[22]

By October 1978, information had begun to filter to Ridgway from Army sources about alleged deficiencies in the Army's readiness. Operation Nifty Nugget, a mobilization and readiness test, demonstrated, according to Ridgway, a shortage of hundreds of thousands of people in the ready reserve and the deterioration of the mobilization base, which, Ridgway claimed, in the event of a general conflict, would cause the Army in Europe to run out of weapons and ammunition a month after mobilization day.[23]

Alarmed by the military situation, Ridgway turned to his friend George A. Strichman, chairman of the board of Colt Industries, of which Ridgway was then a director, urged him to join the Committee on the Present Danger, and solicited him to get Colt to make a corporate contribution. Instead, Strichman organized a lobbying effort for rearmament that touched Congress, industry, the Army, and the news media. Ridgway provided Strichman with access to senior Army officers. By July, Strichman had contacted Representative R. Beard (R-Tenn.), a member of the House Armed Services Committee, who was eager to increase preparedness. Strichman and Beard had decided to form a group of twelve to fifteen corporate executives who were knowledgeable about the mobilization base, and Ridgway agreed to meet with the Joint Chiefs to find out what they would do if Beard and Strichman publicized the information that they had acquired.[24]

Ridgway then set up meetings with Army Chief of Staff General E. C. Meyer on July 12, 1979. Ridgway briefed General Meyer on his findings regarding the mobilization base and told him that the Strichman Group had concluded that it could help the Army get support for more funding to improve its readiness. He urged Meyer to meet with Strichman. According to Ridgway, Meyer supported the Strichman Group's plan. If asked by a congressional committee, Meyer would testify to the facts as he saw them, but he did not want to be portrayed in the media as being at odds with the president.[25]

A few days later, he met with General Alexander Haig, who had retired as commander of NATO two weeks earlier. Haig confirmed the allegations of unpreparedness. Ridgway relayed this information to Strichman, who called his contacts in the media. Strichman was able to stir up considerable media coverage—a long cover story in *Time*, October 29, 1979, entitled "What Price Power? Expanding America's Arsenal," written by *Time* Associate Editor Burton Pines, a mainstay of the conservative movement who later became vice president of the conservative Heritage Foundation. Commenting on the "heightened sense of urgency" about defense raised during the Senate hearings on the SALT II treaty, in which witnesses "armed with volumes of facts and statistics . . . have convinced a growing number of citizens that the U.S. can no longer afford to postpone tough and costly defense decisions if it intends to remain a superpower. As a result, a consensus has been emerging that favors a stronger U.S. military establishment, something that would have seemed impossible only a few years ago." The *Washington Star* also ran a three-article series from November 2 to 4, 1979.

In the Nifty Nugget controversy, Ridgway played an important role in making contacts between military, business, and media figures who were critical of the Carter administration defense policy. While far less important than the Iranian hostage crisis and the invasion of Afghanistan by the Soviet Union, the actions of Ridgway and his acquaintances clearly contributed to forging a public perception that President Jimmy Carter was weak on defense. Ridgway and other advocates of increased military spending already had considerable popular support. By June 1979, when Ridgway began to work to publicize the alleged low level of readiness, a CBS/*New York Times* poll showed that 43 percent of the American people believed the Soviet Union was militarily stronger than the United States, 30 percent believed the two sides were equal, and only 11 percent thought the United States was stronger. While ideology is not always opposed to truth, Cold War ideology prevented Ridgway and other proponents of military buildup from anticipating the surprising collapse of the Soviet Union thirteen years later.[26]

The election of Ronald Reagan, with his promise to strengthen the military establishment, was greeted with warmth by Ridgway. Reagan embarked on an unprecedented peacetime expansion of military spending. Reagan, Ridgway later wrote, had "halted and reversed the downward trend towards disaster." Upon the announcement of the retirement of Secretary of Defense Caspar Weinberger, Ridgway wrote that "the thoughtful knowledgeable U.S. citizen can sleep better these days, thanks to your conspicuously superior service to the Nation throughout your years as Secretary of Defense."[27]

At the age of ninety, Ridgway, in his last major political act, accepted a last-minute invitation to accompany President Ronald Reagan on a much-criticized trip to Germany. The old World War II general stood by and helped staunch the criticism when Reagan, in the company of German Chancellor Helmut Kohl, visited the German Army cemetery, at Bitburg, which also contained the bodies of forty-nine Waffen SS men, at least one of whom was known to have committed atrocities against American prisoners of war. Many of the soldiers in the cemetery had been killed in the Battle of the Bulge, in which Ridgway served as a commander. The theme of the visit, which took place just before the anniversary of VE-Day, was reconciliation between the United States and Germany. Despite efforts to assuage the furor in the United States with a Reagan-Kohl visit to the concentration camp at Bergen-Belsen, thousands of demonstrators in Boston, Miami, Atlanta, Milwaukee, Philadelphia, Newark, New Haven, and Bitburg itself protested the appearance.[28]

Nancy Reagan had opposed the trip. She feared that Reagan would lose his ability to speak, as sometimes happened when he got depressed, which she knew was bound to happen while visiting the cemetery and concentration camp. Reagan's handlers thought that pictures of President Reagan standing by General Ridgway—thus associating Reagan with one of the last living senior officers of World War II—which appeared on the front page of the *New York Times*, might staunch the criticism that the president was unpatriotically honoring dead Nazis. This did not happen. But according to a Reagan biographer, Ridgway's presence "made the ceremony easier for Reagan to endure." Ridgway went out of loyalty to Reagan, who had finally initiated part of the expanded military program that Ridgway had long favored. Reagan rewarded Ridgway the next year with a Presidential Medal of Freedom. Moreover, Ridgway had long been willing to appeal to the German Right to strengthen America's position in Europe, as when, while NATO commander, he urged clemency for certain war criminals. To promote the theme of reconciliation, Ridgway shook hands with World War II Luftwaffe ace General Johannes Steinhoff. According to Secretary of State George P. Shultz, who was present, the gesture by Ridgway "made history."[29]

Perhaps, but given the outcry over the event and the bizarre choice of setting for such a truce, Shultz's comment about Ridgway sounds forced. The same puritanical rectitude and hard-nosed warrior pragmatism that had come off so impressively in *Life* in 1952 did not play well in Bitburg. Ridgway's action could be seen as consistent with Christian forgiveness, but his main aim was political: to help the president and to strengthen the NATO alliance. Indeed, the Bitburg affair showed how the ideology of an unconditional and absolute Soviet threat to civilization and morality, which to Ridgway ethically justified the arms race, could lead him to symbolic actions that were politically expedient yet anathema to principles he had once claimed to fight for.

Matthew Ridgway died on July 26, 1993, and was buried at Arlington Cemetery, eulogized by Chairman of the Joint Chiefs of Staff General Colin Powell, who had visited him in 1991, accompanied by Senator Strom Thurmond (R–SC) and Senator Sam Nunn (D–Ga.) to present the general with a Congressional gold medal.[30] Ridgway left the Army a record as a great leader on the battlefield and as a manager in the increasingly industrialized milieu of modern war. In his eulogy General Powell remarked that "every American soldier owes a debt to this man. Men and women of the profession of arms in far away places around the world, some of whom may never have heard his name spoken or read of his exploits in the history books, have been touched by the legacy of this great fighting soldier."[31] He was less successful as his roles became more diplomatic and political. In diplomacy, the bluntness that became him as a commander, and his Progressive-era faith in the neutrality of technical solutions, made him too resistant to compromise. In the Joint Chiefs and at NATO, his military judgment was excellent, but his corporatist social vision of society sometimes brought him into conflict with civilian political leadership.

At Bitburg, the general who had famously exhorted his troops to save civilization from the barbarians, and who said he desired no other honorific than "soldier," grimly saluted the graves of Nazi officers who had massacred American GI prisoners. The crusader for preparedness stood beside Ronald Reagan, the man who had finally given the American military the budgetary carte blanche that Ridgway had sought since the end of World War II. Stiffly vigilant, he was still waiting for the barbarians; but in the words of poet C. P. Cavafy, "the barbarians never came."

NOTES

1. Some of the others were Lt. Gen. James M. Gavin; former Marine Commandant David Shoup; and Air Force General Lauris Norstad (see Bob Buzzanco, "The American Military's Rationale Against the Vietnam War," *Political Science Quarterly* 101, no. 4 (1986):559–577.

2. "Pull Out, All Out or Stand Fast," *Look*, April 5,1966. Fulbright to Ridgway, September 21, 1966; Ridgway to Fulbright, September 25, 1966; Fulbright to Ridgway October 5, 1966; Ridgway to Fulbright, October 7, 1966; Fulbright MSS University of Arkansas Library, Fayettville, Arkansas (My thanks to Gary Stone of Columbia University for providing me with copies of these correspondences).

3. Joseph E. Johnston to Ridgway, December 5, 1967, Ridgway MSS, Box 34. The Bermuda Conference, held December 1–3, 1967, included an influential group of academics, publishers, journalists, and former officials. In addition to Ridgway, the

conference was attended by Harding Bancroft, Prof. Lincoln Bloomfield, Charles D. Bolté Jr., John Cowles, Hedley Donovan, Daniel Ellsberg, Frances FitzGerald, Ernest A. Gross, Roger Hilsman, Joseph E. Johnson, Milton Katz, George Kistiakowsky, Franklin A. Lindsay, Richard Neustadt, Ithiel de Sola Pool, Marshall D. Shulman, Donald B. Straus, Kenneth W. Thompson, James C. Thomson, Stephen J. Wright, Adam Yarmolinsky, Charles Yost, and Kenneth Young.

4. Ibid.

5. Joseph E. Johnson to participants in Vietnam discussion, December 21, 1967 and January 17, 1968, Ridgway MSS, Box 34.

6. George C. Herring, *America's Longest War* (New York: Knopf, 1986), 206. In addition to Ridgway, the group included George Ball, General Omar N. Bradley, C. Douglas Dillon, Henry Cabot Lodge, Arthur Dean, Justice Abe Fortas, Dean Acheson, John McCloy, Robert Murphy, Cyrus Vance, General Maxwell D. Taylor, and MacGeorge Bundy, as well as officials at the highest level, including Secretary of State Dean Rusk, Secretary of Defense Clark Clifford, Ambassador-at-Large Averell Harriman, CIA Director Richard Helms, UN Ambassador Arthur Goldberg, and White House advisor Walt W. Rostow. There was also, in the course of the meetings, a briefing team consisting of General William DePuy, a former division commander in Vietnam, George Carver of the CIA, and Philip Habib (list from meeting with president, March 22, 1968, from annotation by Ridgway and attached memos, Ridgway MSS, Box 34F; see also Buzzanco, *Masters of War*, 334 n. 47).

7. List from meeting with president, March 22, 1968, from annotation by Ridgway and attached memos, Ridgway MSS, Box 34F.

8. Ibid.

9. Herring, *America's Longest War*, 206.

10. Memo of conversation with Clark Clifford, June 19, 1970, Ridgway MSS, Box 34f; Matthew B. Ridgway, "Indochina: Disengaging," *Foreign Affairs* (July 1971):583–592.

11. Ibid.

12. Ibid.

13. Ibid.

14. *New York Times*, April 2, 1971.

15. "Spit and Polish General Still Commands Respect," *Pittsburgh Sunday Tribune-Review*, "Focus Magazine," August 26, 1979.

16. Ridgway to McGovern, October 18, 1972, Ridgway MSS, Box 34; Matthew B. Ridgway, "Leadership," *New York Times*, September 14, 1972.

17. Ibid.

18. Draft for *New York Times* article, February 22, 1974. In the article, published April 4, 1974 as "Detente: Some Qualms and Hard Questions," direct criticism of Nixon was eliminated (Ridgway to General Lyman L. Lemnitzer, October 25, 1975 Ridgway MSS, Box 34D).

19. Ridgway to W. Averell Harriman, December 4, 1976, Ridgway MSS, Box 34c and Ridgway to Harriman, December 2, 1977, Ridgway MSS, Box 34c. On Panama, see Chapter 3.

20. "Spit and Polish General Still Commands Respect," *Pittsburgh Sunday Tribune-Review*, "Focus," August 26, 1979. Ridgway to Senator Barry Goldwater, September 22, 1975 and Ridgway to Senator Mike Mansfield May 28, 1975, Ridgway

MSS, Box 34f. Letter published in *New York Times*, June 4, 1975. Bob Considine "Female Cadets? General Ridgway Says No," *Boston Herald*, August 31, 1975.

21. Ridgway to Warrant Officer October 18, 1955, Ridgway MSS, Box 31.

22. *Pittsburgh Herald*, January 10, 1979. Ridgway to Eugene V. Rostow, April 16, 1978, Ridgway MSS, Box 31.

23. Ridgway to Averell Harriman, April 28, 1979 Ridgway MSS Box 34C.

24. Ridgway to Strichman, March 7, 1979 and Ridgway, "Records of Phone Conversations, July 5–6, 1979," Ridgway MSS, Box 34J.

25. Ridgway draft of proposed remarks to Army chief of staff, July 12, 1979, Ridgway MSS, Box 34J.

26. Ridgway handwritten notation on typescript entitled "Records of Phone Conversations July 5–6, 1979" and Ridgway to Strichman, January 21, 1980, Ridgway MSS, Box 34J.

27. Ridgway to General John A. Wickham, Chief of Staff, U.S. Army, March 10, 1986 and Ridgway to Weinberger, November 18, 1986, Ridgway MSS, Box 34J.

28. *New York Times*, May 6, 1985.

29. Ibid. Shultz to Ridgway, May 5, 1985, Ridgway MSS, Box 34 G. Lou Cannon, *President Reagan: Role of a Lifetime* (New York: Simon & Schuster, 1991), 587–588.

30. "General Matthew B. Ridgway to Chairman, Board of Trustees, Mellon Institute," press release, May 14, 1960. The Mellon Institute, which performed a wide variety of research and development projects under contract to private corporations, merged with the Carnegie Institute of Technology in 1967 to become Carnegie-Mellon University (Mellon Institute MSS, Carnegie-Mellon University Archives). See also obituary *New York Times*, July 27, 1993.

31. "Remarks by General Colin L. Powell, Chairman of the Joint Chiefs of Staff, at the Funeral Ceremony for General Matthew B. Ridgway, USA (Ret), At Arlington National Cemetery, July 30, 1993," typescript, in author's possession.

Selected Bibliography

MANUSCRIPTS

Archives Nationales, Paris
  Clippings Collection on Ridgway Riots F__7__15.374

Carnegie-Mellon University Archives, Pittsburgh, Pennsylvania.
  Mellon Institute MSS

Eisenhower Library, Abilene, Kansas
  Dwight D. Eisenhower MSS
    U.S. Army Chief of Staff MSS
    Presidential MSS
      White House Central Files
      Ann Whitman Files
      Ann Whitman Administration Files
  J. Lawton Collins MSS
  Alfred M. Gruenther MSS
  Lauris Norstad MSS

Library of Congress Manuscript Division, Washington, D.C.
  Frank R. McCoy MSS
  Francis LeJ. Parker MSS

George C. Marshall Foundation, Lexington, Virginia
  George C. Marshall MSS
  James A. Van Fleet MSS

Minnesota Historical Society, St. Paul, Minnesota
  Hubert H. Humphrey MSS

Center of Military History, Washington, D.C.
  Ridgway Files

Harry S. Truman Presidential Library, Independence, Missouri
  Harry S. Truman Presidential MSS
    White House Central Files
National Archives, Washington, D.C.
  RG 59, Department of State
  RG 84 U.S. Mission to the U.N.
  RG 218 Records of the Joint Chiefs of Staff
  RG 319 Records of the Army Staff
  RG 330 Records of the Department of Defense Executive Office

University of Vermont, Burlington, Vermont
  Warren Austin MSS

U.S. Army Military History Institute, Carlisle Barracks, Pennsylvania
  Clay Blair Collection
  Charles Bolté MSS
  Bruce Clarke MSS
  Willis D. Crittenburger MSS
  James M. Gavin MSS
  Barkesdale Hammlett MSS
  John Hull MSS
  Floyd Parks MSS
  Matthew B. Ridgway MSS

Western Historical Manuscripts Collection, University of Missouri, Columbia
  Stewart Symington MSS

ORAL HISTORIES

Interviews with Matthew B. Ridgway:

Interview by Maurice Matloff, April 18, 1984, U.S. Army Military History Institute, Carlisle Barracks, Pennsylvania.

Interview by Major Matthew Caulfield and Lieutenant Colonel Robert Elton, August 29, 1969, U.S. Army Military History Institute, Carlisle Barracks, Pennsylvania.

Interviews by John Blair, Senior Officers Debriefing Program, November 24, 1971 and March 24, 1972, U.S. Army Military History Institute, Carlisle Barracks, Pennsylvania.

Interview by John Child, May 10, 1977, Ridgway MSS, U.S. Army Military History Institute, Carlisle Barracks, Pennsylvania.

Interview by Harold L. Hitchens and Harold L. Hetzel, University of Pittsburgh, March 5, 1982, Columbia University, Oral History Research Office, New York.

Interview by Forrest Pogue, February 26, 1959, Marshall MSS, George C. Marshall Foundation, Lexington, Virginia.

Others:

James M. Gavin, interviewed by Lieutenant Colonel Donald G. Andrews and Lieutenant Colonel Charles H. Ferguson, May 29, 1975, Senior Officers Debriefing Program, U.S. Army Military History Institute, Carlisle Barracks, Pennsylvania.

Colonel John Trussell, interview by author, March 14, 1990

General Andrew J. Goodpaster, interview by author, June 24, 1994

Brigadier General Walter F. Winton, interview by author, May 19, 1990.

PUBLISHED WORKS BY MATTHEW B. RIDGWAY

"How Europe's Defenses Look to Me." *Saturday Evening Post*, October 10, 1953.
Soldier. New York: Harper, 1956.
"Pull-out, All-out, or Stand Fast in Vietnam?" *Look*, April 5, 1966.
The Korean War. Garden City, N.Y.: Doubleday, 1967.
"Troop Leadership at the Operational Level," with Walter F. Winton Jr. Excerpts from transcript of a seminar at the U.S. Army Command and General Staff School, Ft. Leavenworth, Kansas, May 9, 1984. Reprinted in *Military Review* 70, no. 4 (April 1990): 57–67.

PERIODICALS

Atlanta Constitution
Baltimore Sun
Ce Soir
Chicago Defender
Chicago Sun-Times
Chicago Tribune
Indianapolis Star
L'Aurore
Leader (Eau Claire, Wisconsin)
Le Figaro
L'Humanité
Life
Le Monde
News-Messenger (Marshall, Texas)
Newsweek
New York Herald-Tribune
New York Sunday News
Pittsburgh Press
Saturday Evening Post

St. Louis Post-Dispatch
Time
Tribune (South Bend, Indiana)
United Nations Weekly Bulletin
U.S. News and World Report
Washington Post
Washington Star

AUTOBIOGRAPHIES AND PUBLISHED PRIMARY SOURCES

Acheson, Dean. *Present at the Creation*. New York: Norton, 1969.

Auriol, Vincent. *Journal du Septennat*. Edited by Dominique Boché. Vol. 7. Paris: Armand Colin, 1978.

Bland, Larry I. ed. *The Papers of George C. Marshall*. 4 vols. Baltimore: Johns Hopkins University Press, 1991.

Blumenson, Martin, ed. *The Patton Papers, 1940–1945*. 2 vols. Boston: Houghton Mifflin, 1996.

Braden, Spruille. *Diplomats and Demagogues*. New York: Arlington House, 1971.

Bradley, Omar N. *A Soldier's Story*. New York: Henry Holt, 1951.

Bradley, Omar N., and Clay Blair. *A General's Life*. New York: Simon & Schuster, 1983.

Brereton, Lewis H. *The Brereton Diaries*. New York: Morrow, 1946.

Chandler, Alfred D., Jr., et al., eds. *The Papers of Dwight D. Eisenhower*. 17 vols. Baltimore: Johns Hopkins University Press, 1970.

Collins, J. Lawton. *Lightning Joe: An Autobiography*. Baton Rouge: Louisiana State University Press, 1979.

Eisenhower, Dwight D. *Crusade in Europe*. New York: Doubleday, 1948.

———. *Mandate for Change, 1953–56*. Garden City, N.Y.: Doubleday, 1963.

———. *Waging Peace, 1956–61*. Garden City, N.Y.: Doubleday, 1965.

Ferrell, Robert, ed. *The Diary of James Hagerty*. Bloomington: Indiana University Press, 1983.

———. *Eisenhower Diaries*. New York: Norton, 1981.

Finger, Seymour Maxwell. *American Ambassadors at the UN: People, Politics and Bureaucracy in Making Foreign Policy*. 2d ed. New York: Holmes & Meier, 1988.

Gavin, James M. *On to Berlin: Battles of an Airborne Commander, 1943–1946*. New York: Viking, 1978.

Goodman, Allen E., ed. *Negotiating While Fighting: The Diary of Admiral C. Turner Joy at the Korean Armistice Conference*. Stanford, Calif.: Hoover Institution Press, 1978.

Groves, Leslie L. *Now It Can Be Told*. New York: Harper, 1962.

James, D. Clayton. *The Years of MacArthur*. 3 vols. Boston: Houghton Mifflin, 1985.

Juin, Maréchal Alphonse. *Memoires*. Vol. 2. Paris: Fayard, 1960.

Langenhove, Fernand van. *La crise du système de securité collective des Nations Unies, 1946–1957*. Brussels, 1958.

Lie, Trygve. *In the Cause of Peace: Seven Years with the United Nations*. New York: Macmillan, 1954.

Lilienthal, David E. *The Journals of David E. Lilienthal.* Vol. 2, *The Atomic Energy Years, 1945–1950.* New York: Harper and Row, 1964.

MacArthur, Douglas. *Reminiscences.* New York: McGraw-Hill, 1964.

Radford, Admiral Arthur. *From Pearl Harbor to Vietnam.* Stanford, Calif.: Hoover Institution Press, 1980.

Roosevelt, Eleanor. *On My Own.* New York: Harper, 1958.

Taylor, General Maxwell D. *The Uncertain Trumpet.* New York: Harper, 1960.

———. *Swords and Plowshares.* New York: Norton, 1972.

Twining, Nathan F. *Neither Liberty Nor Safety: A Hard Look at U.S. Military Policy and Strategy.* New York: Holt, Rinehart & Winston, 1966.

Walters, Vernon A. *Silent Missions.* Garden City, N.Y., Doubleday, 1978.

White, Theodore H. *In Search of History.* New York: Warner, 1978.

PUBLIC DOCUMENTS

United Nations. Department of Public Information. *Yearbook of the United Nations, 1947–1948.* 1949.

United Nations Security Council. *Security Council Official Reports* (S.C.O.R.). 1946, 1947.

U.S. Congress. House. Committee on Foreign Affairs. *Hearings on H. R. 3836, Inter-American Military Cooperation Act.* 80th Cong., 1st sess., 1947.

U.S. Congress. Senate. Committee on Appropriations. *Inter-American Military Affairs Executive Sessions of the Senate Foreign Relations Committee.* 82d Cong., 1st sess., 1976. vol. 1, Historical Series 6.

U.S. Congress. House. Appropriations Committee. *Department of the Army Appropriations for FY 1955.* 83d Cong., 2d sess., 1954.

U.S. Congress. House. Appropriations Committee. *Department of the Army Appropriations for FY 1956.* 84th Cong., 1st sess., 1955.

U.S. Congress. House. Appropriations Committee. *Defense Subcommittee Department of Defense Appropriations for 1957.* 84th Cong., 2d sess., 1956.

U.S. Department of State. "The United States and the United Nations: Report by the President to the Congress for the Year 1947." *Foreign Relations of the United States, 1939–1956.* Department of State Publication 3024 (Wash. 1048).

UNPUBLISHED DISSERTATIONS AND THESES

Cassata, John Anthony. "The Eisenhower Indochina Policy: 1954 and Military Intervention." Ph.D. diss., New York University, 1986.

Curtin, Mary Therese. "Hubert Horatio Humphery and the Politics of the Cold War, 1943–1954." Ph.D. diss., Columbia University, 1986.

Duchin, Brian R. "The New Look: President Eisenhower and the Political Economy of National Security." Ph.D. diss., University of Texas, Austin, 1987.

Gray, Chris Hables. "Post-Modern War: Computers as Weapons and Metaphors." Ph.D. diss., University of California, Santa Cruz, 1991.

McCarley, J. Britt. "General Nathan Farragut Twining: The Making of a Disciple of American Strategic Air Power, 1897–1953." Ph.D. diss., Temple University, 1989.

Pach, Chester J. "Arming the Free World: The Origins of the United States Military Assistance Program, 1945–1949." Ph.D. diss., Northwestern University, 1981.

Pelletier, George Eugene. "The Ridgway Regime at SHAPE." Masters thesis, Georgetown University, 1955.

Stamey, Roderick A., Jr., "The Origin of the U.S. Military Assistance Program." Ph.D. diss., University of North Carolina, Chapel Hill, 1972.

BOOKS

Aliano, Richard. *American Defense Policy from Eisenhower to Kennedy*. Athens: Ohio University Press, 1975.

Allen, Craig. *Eisenhower and the Mass Media: Peace, Prosperity, and Prime-Time T.V.* Chapel Hill: University of North Carolina Press, 1993.

Althusser, Louis. *For Marx*. Translated by B. R. Brewster. London: Verso, 1977.

Ambrose, Stephen. *Eisenhower: Soldier, General of the Army, President-Elect, 1890–1952*. New York: Simon & Schuster, 1983.

———. *Eisenhower: President and Elder Statesman, 1952–1969*. New York: Simon & Schuster, 1984.

———. *Rise to Globalism: American Foreign Policy Since 1938*. New York: Penguin, 1987.

Ambrose, Stephen, and J. A. Barber. *The Military and American Society*. New York: Free Press, 1972.

Anderson, David L. *Trapped by Success: The Eisenhower Administration and the Vietnam War, 1953–61*. New York: Columbia University Press, 1991.

Appleman, Roy E. *South to the Naktong, North to the Yalu*. Washington, D.C.: Department of the Army, 1961.

———. *Ridgway Duels for Korea*. College Station: Texas A & M University Press, 1990.

Bacevich, A. J. *The Pentomic Era: The U.S. Army Between Korea and Vietnam*. Washington: National Defense University Press, 1986.

———. *Diplomat in Khaki: Major General Frank Ross McCoy and American Foreign Policy, 1898–1949*. Lawrence: University Press of Kansas, 1989.

Bechhoefer, B. G. *Postwar Negotiations for Arms Control*. Washington, D.C.: Brookings Institution, 1961.

Becker, Jean Jacques. *Histoire politique de la France depuis 1945*. Paris: A. Colin, 1988.

Bentley, Eric. *A Century of Hero Worship: A Study of the Idea of Heroism in Carlyle and Nietzsche*. Boston: Beacon, 1957.

Bernstein, Barton J., ed. *Politics and Policies of the Truman Administration*. New York: Harper, 1966.

Betts, Richard K. *Soldiers, Statesmen and Cold War Crises*. Cambridge: Harvard University Press, 1977.

Biggs, Bradley. *Gavin*. New York: Archon, 1980.

Billings-Yun, Melanie. *Decision Against War: Eisenhower and Dienbienphu*. New York: Columbia University Press, 1988.

Blackett, P. M. S. *Fear, War, and the Bomb: Military and Political Consequences of Atomic Energy*. New York, 1949.

Blair, Clay. *Ridgway's Paratroopers*. Dial Press: Garden City, New York: 1985.

———. *The Forgotten War*. New York: Times Books, 1987.

Bloomfield, Lincoln Palmer. *The United Nations and American Foreign Policy: A New Look at the National Interest*. Rev. ed. Boston: Little, Brown, 1967.

Boorstin, Daniel J. *The Image: A Guide to Pseudo-Events in America*. New York: Atheneum, 1978.

Booth, T. Michael and Duncan Spencer. *Paratrooper: The Life of James M. Gavin*. New York: Simon & Schuster, 1994.

Breuer, William B. *Shadow Warriors: The Covert War in Korea*. New York: John B. Wiley & Sons, 1996.

Brown, Anthony Cave, ed. *Dropshot: The United States Plan for War with the Soviet Union in 1957*. New York: Dial Press, 1978.

Bundy, McGeorge. *Danger and Survival: Choices About the Bomb in the First Fifty Years*. New York: Random House, 1988.

Buscher, Frank M. *The U.S. War Crimes Trials in Germany, 1946–1955*. New York: Greenwood Press, 1989.

Buzzanco, Robert. *Masters of War: Military Dissent and Politics in the Vietnam Era*. New York: Cambridge University Press, 1996.

Cameron, Craig. *American Samurai: Myth Imagination and the Conduct of Battle in the First Marine Division, 1941–1951*. Cambridge: Cambridge University Press, 1994.

Caraley, Demetrios. *The Politics of Military Unification*. New York: Columbia University Press, 1966.

Child, John. *Unequal Alliance: The Inter-American Military System, 1938–1978*. Boulder, Colo.: Westview Press, 1980.

Childs, Marquis. *Eisenhower: Captive Hero. A Critical Study of the General and the President*. New York: Harcourt, Brace, Jovanovich, 1958.

Cohen, Warren I., and Akira Iriye, eds. *The Great Powers in East Asia, 1953–60*. New York: Columbia University Press, 1990.

Cole, Hugh M. *United States Army in World War II: The European Theater of Operations. The Ardennes: Battle of the Bulge*. Washington, D.C.: Department of the Army, 1965.

Condit, Kenneth W. *The Joint Chiefs of Staff and National Policy, 1947–1949*. Vol. 2. Washington, D.C.: Joint Chiefs of Staff, 1976.

Conil Paz, Alberto, and Ferrari, G. *Argentina's Foreign Policy, 1930–1962*. South Bend, Ind.: University of Notre Dame Press, 1966.

Conn, Stetson, and Byron Fairchild. *The Framework of Hemispheric Defense*. Washington, D.C.: Office of the Chief of Military History, 1960.

Cook, Blanche Wiesen. *The Declassified Eisenhower: A Divided Legacy*. Garden City, N.Y.: Doubleday, 1981.

Cumings, Bruce. *The Origins of the Korean War: Liberations and the Emergence of Separate Regimes, 1945–1947*. Princeton: Princeton University Press, 1981.

Dalfiume, Richard M. *Desegregation of the Armed Forces*. Columbia: University of Missouri Press, 1969.

Dennett, R., and J. E. Johnson, eds. *Negotiation with the Russians*. Boston, 1951.

Dockrill, Saki. *Eisenhower's New Look National Security Policy, 1953–61*. New York: St. Martin's Press, 1996.

Donovan, Robert J. *Conflict and Crisis: The Presidency of Harry S. Truman, 1945–1948*. New York: Norton, 1977.

———. *Tumultuous Years: The Presidency of Harry S. Truman, 1949–53*. New York: Norton, 1982.

Dozer, Donald Marquand. *Are We Good Neighbors?* New York: Johnson Reprint, 1972.

Duggan, L. *The Americas: The Search for Hemispheric Security*. New York: Henry Holt, 1949.

Eagleton, Terry. *Ideology: An Introduction*. New York: Verso, 1991.

Edwards, Paul M. *General Matthew B. Ridgway: A Bibliography*. Westport, Conn.: Greenwood, 1993.

Eisenhower, John S. D. *The Bitter Woods*. Nashville, Tenn.: Battery Press, 1969.

Foner, Jack. *Blacks and the Military in American History*. New York: Praeger, 1974.

Foot, Rosemary. *The Wrong War*. Ithaca, N.Y.: Cornell University Press, 1985.

———. *A Substitute For Victory: The Politics of Peacemaking at the Korea Armistice Talks*. Ithaca, New York: Cornell University Press, 1990.

Fox, Richard Wightman, and T. J. Jackson Lears, eds. *The Power of Culture: Critical Essays in American History*. Chicago: University of Chicago Press.

Frank, Gary. *Juan Perón v. Spruille Braden: The Story Behind the Blue Book*. Lanham, Maryland: University Press of America, 1980.

Gaddis, John Lewis. *Strategies of Containment*. New York: Oxford University Press, 1982.

Gardner, Lloyd C. *Architects of Illusion: Men and Ideas in American Foreign Policy, 1941–1949*. Chicago, 1970.

———. *Approaching Vietnam: From World War II Through Dienbienphu, 1941–1954*. New York: Norton, 1988.

Geelhoed, Bruce. *Charles E. Wilson and the Controversy at the Pentagon, 1953–1957*. Detroit: Wayne State University, 1979.

Gibson, James. *The Perfect War: The War We Couldn't Lose and How We Did*. New York: Vintage, 1988.

Goldhamer, Herbert. *The 1951 Korean Armistice Conference: A Personal Memoir*. Santa Monica, Calif.: RAND, 1994.

Goodrich, L. M., E. Hambro, and A. P. Simons. *Charter of the United Nations Commentary and Documents*. 3d ed. rev. New York: Columbia University Press, 1969.

Goulden, Joseph C. *Korea: The Untold Story of the War*. New York: Times Books, 1982.

Gray, Colin S. *The Geopolitics of Superpower*. Lexington: University Press of Kentucky, 1984.

Green, David L. *The Containment of Latin America*. Chicago: Quadrangle, 1971.

Grele, Ronald J. *Envelopes of Sound: The Art of Oral History*. Chicago: Precedent, 1985.

Gromyko, Andrei. *Memoirs*. Translated by Harold Shukman New York: Doubleday, 1989.

Guhin, Michael. *John Foster Dulles: A Statesman and His Times*. New York: Columbia University Press, 1972.

Hagan, Kenneth J., and William R. Roberts, eds. *Against All Enemies: Interpretations of American Military History from Colonial Times to the Present*. Westport, Conn.: Greenwood, 1986.

Halberstam, David. *The Best and the Brightest*. Greenwich, Conn.: Fawcett, 1972.

Hamby, Alonzo L. *Beyond the New Deal: Harry S. Truman and American Liberalism*. New York: Columbia University Press, 1973.

Hammond, Paul Y. *The Reluctant Supplier: U.S. Decision Making for Arms Sales*. Cambridge: Harvard University Press, 1983.

Harrelson, Max. *Fires All Around the Horizon: The UN's Battle to Preserve the Peace*. New York: Praeger, 1989.

Haynes, Richard. *The Awesome Power: Harry S. Truman as Commander in Chief*. Baton Rouge: Louisiana State University, 1973.

Herken, Gregg. *The Winning Weapon: The Atomic Bomb in the Cold War, 1945–1950*. New York: Knopf, 1980.

Hermes, Walter. *Truce Tent and Fighting Front: United States in the Korean War*. Washington, D.C.: Center of Military History, 1966; reprint 1992.

Hersh, Burton. *The Mellon Family: A Fortune in History*. New York: Morrow, 1978.

Hogan, J. Michael. *The Panama Canal in American Politics*. Carbondale: Southern Illinois University Press, 1986.

Horowitz, Daniel. *The Morality of Spending: Attitudes Toward the Consumer Society in America, 1875–1940*. Chicago: Ivan R. Dee, 1992.

Hunt, Michael. *Ideology in American Foreign Policy*. New Haven: Yale University Press, 1987.

Huntington, Samuel. *The Soldier and the State: The Theory and Politics of Civil-Military Relations*. Cambridge: Harvard University, 1957.

———. *The Common Defense*. New York: Columbia University Press, 1961.

Isaacson, Walther, and Evan Thomas. *The Wise Men: Six Friends and the World They Made: Acheson, Bohlen, Harriman, Kennan, Lovett, McCloy*. New York: Simon & Schuster, 1986.

Ismay, Lord. *NATO: The First Five Years, 1949–1954*. Paris: NATO, n.d.

James, D. Clayton. *The Years of MacArthur: Triumph and Disaster, 1945–1964*. Vol. 3. Boston: Houghton-Mifflin, 1985.

Jameson, Frederic. *Fables of Aggression. Wyndham Lewis: The Modernist as Fascist*. Berkeley: University of California Press, 1979.

Janowitz, Morris. *The Professional Soldier: A Social and Political Portrait*. Glencoe: Free Press, 1960.

Jordan, Robert, ed. *Political Leadership in NATO: A Study in Multinational Diplomacy*. Boulder, Colo.: Westview Press, 1979.

———. *Generals in International Politics: NATO's Supreme Allied Commander, Europe*. Lexington: University Press of Kentucky, 1987.

Kaplan, Lawrence S. *The United States and NATO: The Formative Years*. Lexington: University Press of Kentucky, 1984.

Kinnard, Douglas. *President Eisenhower and Strategy Management*. Lexington: University Press of Kentucky, 1977.

Kirkendall, Richard S., ed. *The Truman Period as a Research Field*. Columbia: University of Missouri Press, 1967 and 1974.

Kolko, Gabriel. *The Roots of American Foreign Policy: An Analysis of Power and Purpose*. Boston: Beacon, 1969.

Kolko, Gabriel, and Joyce Kolko. *The Limits of Power: The World and United States Foreign Policy, 1945–1954*. New York: Harper, 1972.

Korb, Lawrence. *The Joint Chiefs of Staff*. Bloomington: University of Indiana Press, 1976.

Langley, Lester D. *The U.S. and the Caribbean in the Twentieth Century*. 4th ed. Athens, Ga.: University of Georgia Press, 1989.

LeFeber, Walter. *The Panama Canal: The Crisis in Historical Perspective*. 2d ed. New York: Oxford University Press, 1989.

Leffler, Melvyn. *A Preponderance of Power*. Stanford, Calif.: Stanford University Press, 1992.

Lichterman, Martin. "To the Yalu and Back." In *American Civil-Military Decisions*, edited by Harold Stein. Tuscaloosa, AL: University of Alabama Press, 1963.

Lieberman, Joseph I. *The Scorpion and the Tarantula: The Struggle to Control Atomic Weapons, 1945–49*. Boston, 1970.

Lyon, Peter. *Eisenhower: Portrait of a Hero*. Boston: Little, Brown, 1974.

Macaulay, Neil. *The Sandino Affair*. Durham: Duke University Press, 1985.

MacDonald, Callum. *Korea: The War Before Vietnam*. New York: Free Press, 1992.

MacGregor, Morris J. *Integration of the Armed Forces, 1940–1965*. Washington, D.C.: U.S. Army Center of Military History, 1981.

Marshall, S. L. A. *Night Drop: The American Airborne Invasion of Normandy*. Boston: Little, Brown, 1962.

May, Elaine Tyler. *Homeward Bound: The Family in the Cold War*. New York: Basic Books, 1988.

Mazuzan, George. *Warren R. Austin at the U.N., 1946–1953*. Kent, Ohio: Kent State University Press, 1977.

McCann, Frank. *The Brazilian-American Alliance*. Princeton: Princeton University Press, 1973.

McNeil, William H. *America, Britain and Russia: Their Cooperation and Conflict, 1941–1946*. London: Oxford University, 1953.

Mélandri, Pierre. *L'alliance Atlantique*. Paris: Gallimard/Juillard, 1979.

Messer. Robert L. *The End of an Alliance: James F. Byrnes, Roosevelt, Truman and the Origins of the Cold War*. Chapel Hill: University of North Carolina, 1982.

Miller, Merle. *Plain Speaking: An Oral Biography of Harry S. Truman*. New York: Barkely-Putnam, 1973.

Millis, Walter. *Arms and Men: A Study in American Military History*. New York: Capricorn, 1956.

Morelock, J. D. *Generals of the Ardennes: American Leadership in the Battle of the Bulge*. Washington, D.C.: National Defense University Press, 1994.

Morgan, Iwan W. *Eisenhower v. the Spenders*. New York: St. Martin's Press, 1990.

———. *Deficit Government: Taxing and Spending in Modern America*. Chicago: Ivan R. Dee, 1995.

Mossman, Billy C. *Ebb and Flow, November 1950–July 1951: United States in the Korean War*. Washington, D.C.: Center of Military History, 1990.

Nogee, Joseph L. *Soviet Policy Towards Control of Atomic Energy*. South Bend, Ind.: Notre Dame University Press, 1961.

Oshinsky, David. *A Conspiracy So Immense: The World of Joe McCarthy*. New York: Free Press, 1983.

Pach, Chester J. *Arming the Free World: The Origins of the United States Military Assistance Program 1945–1950*. Chapel Hill: University of North Carolina Press, 1991.

Parmet, Herbert S. *Eisenhower and the American Crusades*. New York: Macmillan, 1972.

Pignet, Michel. *Au Coeur de l'activism communist des annees de Guerre Froide: La manifestation Ridgway*. Paris: L'Harmattan, 1992.

Pogue, Forrest C. *George C. Marshall*. 4 vols. New York: Viking, 1963–1987.

Potash, Robert I. *The Army and Politics in Argentina, 1945–1962*. Vols. 1 and 2. Stanford, Calif.: Stanford University Press, 1980.

Pruessen, Ronald W. *John Foster Dulles: The Road to Power*. New York: The Free Press, 1985.

Rabe, Stephen G. *Eisenhower and Latin America: The Foreign Policy of Anti-Communism*. Chapel Hill: University of North Carolina Press, 1988.

Rioux, Jean-Pierre. *France de la IVe République*. 2 vols. Paris: Seuil, 1980–1983.

Russell, Ruth B. *United Nations Experience with Military Forces: Political and Legal Aspects*. Brookings Staff Paper. Washington, D.C.: Brookings Institute, 1964.

Ryan, Mark A. *Chinese Attitudes Towards Nuclear Weapons: China and the United States During the Korean War*. Armonk, N.Y.: M. E. Sharpe, 1989.

Schaller, Michael. *Douglas MacArthur: The Far Eastern General*. New York: Oxford University Press, 1989.

Schilling, Werner, ed. *Strategy, Politics and Defense Budgets*. New York: Columbia University Press, 1962.

Schnabel, James F. *Policy and Direction: The First Year*. Washington, D.C.: Department of the Army, 1972.

Schnabel, James F., and Robert J. Watson. *The Korean War*. Washington, D.C.: Joint Chiefs of Staff, 1978.

———. *The History of the Joint Chiefs of Staff: The Joint Chiefs of Staff and National Policy Part II*, reprint. Wilmington, DE: Michael Glazier, n.d.

———. *The Story of the Joint Chiefs of Staff and National Policy, 1945–1947*. Vol 1. Washington, D.C.: Historical Department, Joint Chiefs of Staff, 1979.

Schonberger, Howard B. *Aftermath of War: America and the Remaking of Japan, 1945–1952*. Kent, Ohio: Kent State University Press, 1989.

Schwartz, Jordan A. *The Speculator: Bernard M. Baruch in Washington, 1917–1965*. Chapel Hill: University of North Carolina Press, 1981.

Selser, Gregorio. *Sandino*. Translated by Cedric Belfrage. New York: Monthly Review Press, 1981.

Sherry, Michael S. *Preparing for the Next War*. New Haven: Yale University Press, 1977.

———. *The Rise of American Air Power: The Creation of Armageddon*. New Haven: Yale University Press, 1987.

———. *In the Shadow of War: The United States Since the 1930s*. New Haven: Yale University Press, 1995.

Sherwin, Martin. *A World Destroyed: The Atomic Bomb and the Grand Alliance*. New York: Knopf, 1975.

Slotkin, Richard. *The Fatal Environment*. New York: Atheneum, 1985.

———. *Gunfighter Nation: The Myth of the Frontier in Twentieth-Century America*. New York: HarperPerennial, 1993.

Spanier, John. *The Truman-MacArthur Controversy and the Korean War*. Cambridge, Mass.: Belknap, 1959.

Spanier, John W., and Joseph L. Nogee. *The Politics of Disarmament: A Study in Soviet-American Gamesmanship*. New York, 1962.

Spykmann, N. J. *America's Strategy in World Politics*. New York: Harcourt, Brace, 1942.

Stephanson, Anders. *Kennan and the Art of Foreign Policy*. Cambridge: Harvard University Press, 1989.

Steuck, William. *The Korean War: An International History*. Princeton: Princeton University Press, 1995.

Stiller, Jesse H. *George S. Messersmith: Diplomat of Democracy*. Chapel Hill: University of North Carolina Press, 1987.

Stimson, Henry L. *American Policy in Nicaragua*. New York: Scribners, 1927.

Stone, I. F. *The Hidden History of the Korean War*. Boston: Little, Brown, 1952.

Toland, John. *In Mortal Combat: Korea, 1950–1953*. New York: Morrow, 1991.

Vagts, Alfred. *A History of Militarism, Civilian and Military*. Rev. ed. New York: Free Press, 1959.

Virilio, Paul, and Sylvère Lotringer. *Pure War*. Translated by Mark Polizotti. New York: Semiotexte, 1983.

Walzer, Michael. *Obligations*. Cambridge: Harvard University Press, 1970.

———. *History of the U.S. Army*. Bloomington: Indiana University Press, 1984.

Weigley, Russell. *Eisenhower's Lieutenants*. Bloomington: Indiana University Press, 1981.

Weiler, Laurence D., and Anne Patricia Simons. *The United States and the United Nations: The Search for International Peace and Security*. New York: Manhattan, 1949.

Williams, Phil, Donald M. Goldstein, and Henry L. Andrews. *Security in Korea*. Boulder, Colo.: Westview Press, 1994.

Young, Marilyn B. *The Vietnam Wars, 1945–1990*. New York: HarperPerennial, 1991.

ARTICLES

Albert, Robert C. "Profile of a Soldier: Matthew B. Ridgway." *American Heritage* 27, no. 2 (February 1976): 4–7, 73–82.

Bernstein, Barton J. "The Quest for Security: American Foreign Policy and the International Control of Atomic Energy, 1942–1946." *Journal of American History* 60 (March 1974).

Blaisdell, Donald C. "Arming the United Nations: Special Agreements under Article 43 of the Charter." *U.S. Department of State Bulletin* 17, no. 422A (August 3, 1947): 239–246.

Block, Fred, Lloyd Gardner, and William O. Walker III. "Symposium on Empire and Domestic Reform." *Radical History Review* 45 (1989): 98–123.

Brands, H. W. "The Age of Vulnerability." *American Historical Review* 94, no. 4 (October 1989): 963–989.

Buzzanco, Bob. "The American Military's Rationale Against the Vietnam War." *Political Science Quarterly* 101, no. 4. (1986): 559–577.

Cumings, Bruce. " 'Revising Postrevisionism,' or The Poverty of Theory in American Diplomatic History." *Diplomatic History* 17 (Fall 1993): 539–569.

Erskine, Helen Worden. "Pretty Penny Ridgway." *Collier's*, May 16, 1953.

Furniss, Edgar S. "The United States, The Inter-American System and the United Nations." *Political Science Quarterly* 65, no. 3 (September 1950): 415–430.

Gerber, Larry G. "The Baruch Plan and the Origins of the Cold War." *Diplomatic History* 6 (1982): 69–95.

Griffith, Robert. "Dwight D. Eisenhower and the Corporate Commonwealth." *American Historical Review* 87 (February 1982): 87–122.

Hawley, Ellis W. "The Discovery and Study of a 'Corporate Liberalism.' " *Business History Review* 52 (Autumn 1978): 309–320.

Hogan, Michael J. "Corporatism." *Journal of American History* 77 (June 1990): 153–168.

Immerman, Richard H. "Confessions of an Eisenhower Revisionist." *Diplomatic History* 14, no. 3 (Summer 1990): 319–342.

Johnson, Joseph E. "The Soviet Union, The United States and International Security." *International Organization* 3 (1949): 9–12.

Koistinen, P. A. C. "Mobilizing the World War II Economy." *Pacific Historical Review* 42 (1973): 443–478.

Lee, R. Alton. "The Army Mutiny of 1946." *Journal of American History* 53, no. 3 (December 1966): 555–571.

Leffler, Melvyn "The American Conception of National Security and the Beginnings of the Cold War, 1945–1948." *American Historical Review* 89 (April 1984): 346–400.

Lempke, Duane A. "Ridgway's Leadership Legacy." *Military Review* 68, no. 11 (1988): 69–75.

MacGregor, Greg. "Front Line General." *New York Times Magazine*, March 4, 1951.

McCormick, Thomas J. "Drift or Mastery? A Corporatist Synthesis for American Diplomatic History." *Reviews in American History* 10 (December 1982): 318–330.

Michener, James. "A Tough Man for a Tough Job." *Life*, September 12, 1952.

Milza, Pierre. "La guerre froide à Paris—'Ridgway la peste,' " *L'Histoire* 25 (Juillet–Août 1980): 38–47.

Nelson, Anna Kasten. "The 'Top of Policy Hill': President Eisenhower and the National Security Council." *Diplomatic History* 7 (Fall 1983): 307–326.

Pach, Chester J., Jr., "The Containment of U.S. Military Aid to Latin America, 1944–1949." *Diplomatic History* 6 no. 3 (Summer 1990): 226–243.

Panitch, Leo. "Recent Theorizations of Corporatism: Reflections on a Growth Industry." *British Journal of Sociology* 31 (June 1980): 159–186.

Petreus, David H. "Korea, the Never-Again Club, and Indochina." *Parameters* 17, no. 4 (1987): 59–70.

Rabe, Stephen G. "Inter-American Military Cooperation, 1944–1951" *World Affairs* 137, no. 2 (Fall 1974): 132–142.

Samuels, Gertrude. "Ridgway—Three Views of a Soldier." *New York Times Magazine*, April 22, 1951.

Schnabel, Lt. Col. James F. "Ridgway in Korea." *Military Review* (March 1964): 2–14.

Schumach, Murray. "The Education of Matthew Ridgway." *New York Times Magazine*, May 4, 1952.

Soapes, Thomas F. "A Cold Warrior Seeks Peace: Eisenhower's Strategy for Nuclear Disarmament." *Diplomatic History* 4 (Winter 1980): 57–71.

Soffer, Jonathan. "Oral History and the History of American Foreign Relations." *Journal of American History* 82 (September 1995): 607–616.

———. "All for All or One for One: The U.N. Military Staff Committee Negotiations." *Diplomatic History* 21 (Winter 1997): 45–69.

Westbrook, Robert B. " 'I Want a Girl, Just Like the Girl, That Married Harry James': American Women and the Problem of Political Obligation in World War II." *American Quarterly* 42, no. 4 (December 1990): 587–603.

Weathersby, Kathryn. "Soviet Arms in Korea and the Origins of the Korean War, 1945–1950: New Evidence from the Russian Archives." Cold War International History Project Working Paper No. 8, November 1995.

Index

About the Author

JONATHAN M. SOFFER is Assistant Professor of Humanities and Social Sciences at Polytechnic University in Brooklyn, New York.

ISBN 0-275-95074-3

90000>

EAN

9 780275 950743

HARDCOVER BAR CODE